The
LEIGHTON BUZZARD
LIGHT RAILWAY

Second Edition

by
Sydney A. Leleux

THE OAKWOOD PRESS

© Sydney A. Leleux and Oakwood Press 1996

First Edition 1969
Second Enlarged Edition 1996

ISBN 0 85361 460 1

Typeset by Oakwood Graphics.
Repro by Ford Graphics Limited, Ringwood
Printed by The Witney Press, Witney, Oxon.

Arnold - Chamberlain's Barn: No. 6 MR 7403 at the lorry tip on 8th January, 1960. Note the assistance given to dislodge wet sand!   *Author*

Front Endpaper: Guests mill about the two locomotives at Billington Road on opening day, 20th November, 1919.   *Joseph Arnold & Sons*

Rear Endpaper: An illustration from a Motor Rail brochure, showing prototype 5 ton 50 hp 3-cylinder diesel locomotive MR 11001 on a train of Arnold's wagons near Leedon in September 1955.
Author's Collection

Published by
The Oakwood Press
P.O. Box 122, Headington, Oxford OX3 8LU

Contents

Arnold - Billington Road: A loaded train descends from Page's Park loop to the washing plant, headed by No. 41. It had been brought in by No. 43 which has already run round, ready to return with the empties, and is now providing braking on the descent. Note that the front of the train is already curving round to run parallel to Billington Road, 4th January, 1961.   *Author*

Introduction & Acknowledgements
to Second Edition

When I approached the Oakwood Press to publish the first edition there was some doubt as to the amount of interest in a rail network which has been almost exlusively non-steam. Events proved that this fear was not justified and eventually the tables were turned when Oakwood asked me to revise the text for a new edition.

Revision has been an enjoyable process, even though other demands on my time have made it take a very long time. My hope is that the result is worth the wait.

I must thank members of the Leighton Buzzard Narrow Gauge Railway Society for their support and encouragement, especially Rod Dingwall who also made available his collection of LBLR and quarry photographs and Graham Stroud. Two great grandsons of Joseph Arnold, Peter R. Arnold and David A. White, kindly supplied information about their family business, which played such an important role in the formation of the railway in the first place. Other information was provided by H. Dagnall, F. North, W. Smith, G. Webb, plus others whose names I did not record but whose contribution was valuable none the less.

The Narrow Gauge Railway Society, Industrial Locomotive Society, Industrial Railway Society, Bedfordshire Records Office, and British Geological Survey records have been very useful. I am particularly indebted to Ian Jolly for his painstaking notes about the Motor Rail Locomotives used in the area. Several other railway enthusiasts have been of direct assistance, including C. Daniels and the late E.S. Tonks..

The text was typed by Mrs P. Turgott, who created pages ready for the publisher from the original text, with annotations and new pages added in my poor writing. She brought order into an amazing collection of paper. The maps were drawn by David Gould who did a wonderful job of interpreting the outlines, sketches and notes I provided.

Finally I must thank my wife for her tolerance and patience during the time revision has been in progress.

Sydney A. Leleux
Stanton-by-Dale
Ilkeston
Derbyshire
May 1995

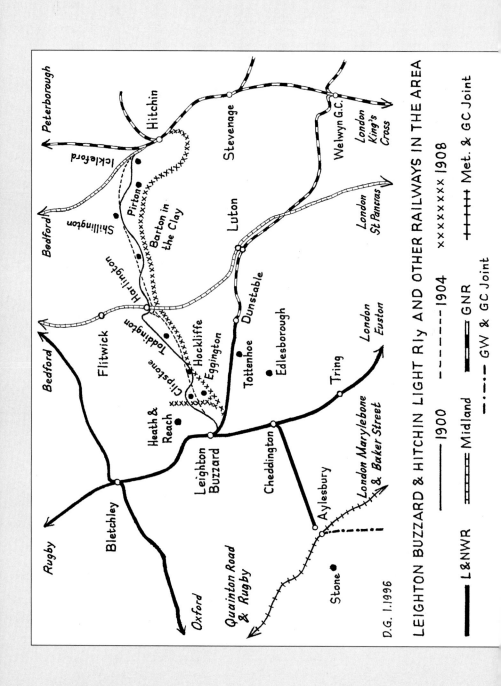

LEIGHTON BUZZARD & HITCHIN LIGHT Rly AND OTHER RAILWAYS IN THE AREA

D.G. 1.1996

——— 1900   – – – 1904   ×××××× 1908

▬▬▬ L&NWR   ▭▭▭ Midland   ▬▬▬ GNR

▬▬▬ GW & GC Joint   ┼┼┼┼ Met. & GC Joint

Peterborough

Hitchin

Ickleford

Bedford

Shillington

Pirton

Barton in the Clay

Stevenage

Harlington

Welwyn G.C.

London King's Cross

Luton

Flitwick

Toddington

London St Pancras

Bedford

Clipstone

Hockliffe

Eggington

Dunstable

Tottenhoe

Edlesborough

Heath & Reach

Tring

London Euston

Rugby

Bletchley

Leighton Buzzard

Cheddington

Aylesbury

London Marylebone & Baker Street

Oxford

Quainton Road & Rugby

Stone

Introduction & Acknowledgements to First Edition

In 1957 I visited Leighton Buzzard and made my first acquaintance with the local sand pit railways. Unfortunately I did not appreciate the historic interest of the locomotives then in use and made no notes. Later, it was suggested by a leading member of the Narrow Gauge Railway Society that I should write a history of the Leighton Buzzard Light Railway. This has taken about ten years intermittent work, during which time there have been great changes in the sand pit railways. Despite the slow progress of this history, I have found the research very rewarding.

Directors of the two major sand companies, J.E. Arnold of Joseph Arnold & Sons Ltd, and J.G. Delafield of George Garside (Sand) Ltd, have been very helpful, as has P.Cooke, Manager of Bedford Silica Sand Ltd. Manufacturers of railway equipment used, Robert Hudson (Raletrux) Ltd, Hudswell, Clarke & Co. Ltd, and especially Motor Rail Ltd have kindly given information as far as their records allow.

Documentary sources used are the *Leighton Buzzard Observer*, the Memorandum and Articles of Association together with a few balance sheets of the LBLR, Ministry of Transport returns, Ordnance Survey, especially the 1926 and 1937 editions of 25 in. maps (which account for the frequency of these dates in the text), the *Victoria County History of Bedfordshire*, *Light Railways of the First World War* by W.J.K. Davies, *The New Era Illustrated* of June 1930, and records at Shire Hall, Bedford.

Many railway and quarry employees have patiently answered my questions, amongst whom I would particularly like to mention A. Eggleton, C. Gaskin, G. Guess, S. Higgs, Mr Jackson, T. Lambourne, H.G. and P.G. Lathwell, W. Major, C. Nash, F.G. North, F.C. Rickard, W. 'Old Bill' Smith, A. Tearle, and F.W. Turney. I am most grateful too, to those others whose names I do not know.

The publications and records of the Industrial Railway Society and Narrow Gauge Railway Society have been of great use especially with regard to the locomotive stock. Members of these two Societies, P.R. Arnold, F.H. Eyles, F. Jux, A. Keef, R. Leleux, R. Peaman, P. Roberts, D. Semmens, G.H. Starmer, M. Swift, E.S. Tonks, B. Webb, and A.G. Wells have lent me their notes, observations and photographs.

At Leighton Buzzard I have been assisted by C. Daniels who has also done much fieldwork in response to my queries from Yorkshire. Without his help the final stages of preparation of this book would have been much more prolonged. He has been a very able and enthusiastic assistant.

My aunt Mrs R. Higgs has always been generous in her hospitality on my visits to Leighton Buzzard.

Lastly I am greatly indebted to my wife who first had to endure piles of paper while I wrote, and then typed my untidy draft.

Sydney A. Leleux
Keighley
Yorkshire
July 1969

Abbreviations Used

AB	Andrew Barclay, Kilmarnock
Arnold	Joseph Arnold & Sons Ltd (and predecessors) - sand quarry company
Bg	Baguley Cars, Burton-on-Trent
DeW	De Winton, Caernarvon
ECC	English China Clays
FH	F.C. Hibberd, London
FOB	Free on Board
FOT	Free on Train, i.e. loaded in works siding
Freud	Freudenstein, Berlin
Garside	George Garside (Sand) Ltd (and predecessor) - sand quarry company
GNR	Great Northern Railway (London terminal - King's Cross)
HC	Hudswell, Clarke, Leeds
HE	Hunslet Engine Co., Leeds
HU	Robert Hudson, Leeds
IHRR	Iron Horse Rail Road (later LBNGRS)
KS	Kerr, Stuart, Stoke-on-Trent
L	Lister, Dursley
LB&HR	Leighton Buzzard & Hitchen Railway
LBLR	Leighton Buzzard Light Railway
LBNGRS	Leighton Buzzard Narrow Gauge Railway Society
LBO	*Leighton Buzzard Observer* (published on Tuesdays)
LNWR	London & North Western Railway (London terminal - Euston)
MR	Motor Rail Ltd - Previously MRTC, Bedford
MRTC	Motor Rail & Tramcar Co., Bedford (MR on and after 1-5-31) 'Simplex'
MW	Manning, Wardle, Leeds
OK	Orenstein & Koppel, Drewitz near Berlin
OS	Ordnance Survey
RH	Ruston Hornsby, Lincoln
ROF	Royal Ordnance Factory
TVO	Tractor Vaporising Oil (paraffin)
UDC	Urban District Council
VCH	Victoria County History
WDLR	War Department Light Railway (World War I)
0-4-0DM	4 wheel diesel locomotive, wheels coupled by side rods, no carrying wheels, mechanical transmission
4wDM	4 wheel diesel locomotive, wheels coupled by chains, mechanical transmission
4wPM	4 wheel petrol locomotive, wheels coupled by chains, mechanical transmission
F	Flameproof locomotive (for use in explosive atmospheres)
ST	saddle tank - water tank around top part of boiler.
T	side tank - water tank either side of boiler
WT	well tank - water tank between frames
VB	vertical boiler
IC	inside cylinders
OC	outside cylinders
VC	vertical cylinders

Chapter One

A Visit to Leighton Buzzard

(*Note*: The following description is an amalgam of several visits I made in 1960/61. It is not intended to be an accurate picture at any one date, but rather to give an overall impression of the period.)

In your imagination, come with me to Leighton Buzzard on a day in 1960. I will meet you at the station. Make sure that you bring a bicycle for travelling between the quarries.

We cycle from the station to the main Aylesbury road, cross the canal and River Ouzel and enter Leighton Buzzard itself. Up the broad main street, past the market stalls, and then turn right down Lake Street. Crossing over the Clipstone Brook we see straight ahead a gentle climb to Pages Park. We stop at the brow of the hill as the scene suddenly changes from the ordinary townscape hitherto.

On the right a large open area, obviously an old sand pit, is visible through the roadside trees, with the gas works in the distance. The floor of the pit is covered with a mixture of trees, water and railway lines. Beside the right hand side of the road, apparently as far as the white gates of Billington Crossing (just discernible in the distance ¼ mile away), is a long row of wood and corrugated iron buildings from which come the sounds of rotating machinery and flowing water. On the left are some old corrugated iron sheds half hidden in the bushes, a white painted office and a long building made of concrete blocks. Behind all this is a sand pit.

As we take in the view there is the steady pulsating noise of a slow-running diesel engine and the rumble of wagons. A flagman appears just in front of us and a small green locomotive comes gingerly down the bank on our left, emerges on to the road and crosses into the buildings on the right. It is followed by wagon after wagon of golden sand and then at the rear comes a second, larger, locomotive. It is the same basic design as the first, very boxlike with a radiator mounted prominently fore-and-aft at the front, but distinguished by high iron weights which envelope the cab and front end. This locomotive stops just after crossing the road. Investigating we find the sand is being emptied into hoppers for washing.

Just as we begin to walk towards the crossing, having left our bikes in the hedge, another flagman appears a hundred yards ahead of us. A train of empty wagons comes from our right and across the road, again hauled by a large boxlike locomotive. The trucks clatter and squeal on a sharp curve while the driver opens up his engine as he hits a gradient on our left. The noise gradually fades into the distance. Looking in at the gate from which the train emerged we see the foreman, who grants permission to come and look around.

A small locomotive called *Devon Loch* with no cab chugs towards us from the buildings, hauling a couple of bogie flat wagons loaded with sacks. We follow it along the track bordered by trees until we come to a transhipment dock. The sacks are slid down a plank into waiting BR wagons. Returning from the transhipment dock we look briefly at an unusual caterpillar tracked excavator. The body is fixed rigidly to the tracks, only the jib can pivot. The railway divides here, and we follow the left hand track which drops down from the one that came from the road.

This track swings round to the left and goes under the screens and washing plant. Another locomotive is parked here. The track continues to swing round and disappears into some bushes - willows probably. Our attention is held as the bushes seem to have grown up round a locomotive grave yard. Here there are a dozen or more identical locomotives, cabless but more or less complete. Identifying them is difficult. There is not a works plate to be seen. Names and numbers are painted on the bonnet covers, but what do you do if the name on either side is different, or if the paint has weathered and flaked, exposing a second name beside the first? Scrapping has begun as fragments of other locomotives lie around and an unusual rail-mounted hand crane has been used to load a tipping wagon with other bits . . . . We retrace our steps to the road, arriving in time to see a short train at yet another level crossing ahead of us.

Passing a derelict industrial site we hurry towards the crossing, to find no less than three tracks across the road. Two emerge from the sand pit we saw earlier, cross the road and climb a gantry where the wagons of the short train are being tipped into BR wagons. The third track enters the derelict industrial site and is lost in the weeds. The train comes down the gantry and goes down into the sand pit. In its place comes another short train from the yard between the road and the sand pit. All this activity! We turn into the yard.

The yard has several long loops, one with a long rake of empty tippers. Looking towards Page's Park we can see a train there as it comes creeping along, on the far side of the sand pit, and watch as it comes down into the yard, stopping in the loop. It is only a short train with a small locomotive. The concrete block building on our left turns out to the locomotive shed with workshops at the end, where a locomotive has been stripped down to its bare frame. By the shed entrance is a wooden shed housing the fuelling pumps. Behind it is a dump of old cabs and bonnet covers.

It is time to move on if we want to see more of this busy railway, so we return to our bikes and look at the map. If we go back into town and then straight up the road to Heath and Reach we will come to a sand pit, which the map shows is connected to the railway system. We pedal off.

The foreman at Chamberlain's Barn sand pit is agreeable to us looking round. Near the gate a lorry is being loaded from an elevated tip. Going into the quarry area we find the washing plant. A row of wagons full of washed sand stand dripping. Holes have been drilled in the base of the bodies to let the water out. We watch, and hear, a man hitting the bottom of a tipped wagon with a sledgehammer in an attempt to dislodge the wet sand still stuck inside. Several locomotives, each with half a dozen tipping wagons, are moving about. Round a corner from the washer is the locomotive shed, which houses some spare locomotives and a trailer air compressor. This is mounted on a skip chassis so it can be taken into the quarry itself.

Going back to our bikes we retrace our steps towards town before cutting through some side streets to reach Vandyke Road. An ungated crossing sign soon comes into sight. The railway comes up the side of a field on our right, across the road and turns on an amazing curve to take up position beside the road. We can hear a train coming up the grade so we wait for it. It is only a short train, and to our surprise it does not go along the road where we could have raced it. Instead the driver stops, throws a point near the exit of the curve, and the train disappears behind an estate of modern houses. The map shows this is the connection to the quarries we have just left.

We ride along the road, catching glimpses of rails through the hedge. A throbbing noise heralds the approach of a train, which clatters past with the loaded skips swaying. We have noticed occasional piles of sand beside the rails which showed where a skip swayed once too often!

As we approach Stonehenge Brickworks with its piles of pure white bricks we see a train approaching us. It turns off into the works yard. We can see the wagons being tipped into the brickworks building (what do they want sand for; bricks are made from clay, surely?) but do not investigate. We cycle up the hill past Miletree Farm in time to see a train come out of quarries on our left. Riding abreast of the train, it passes the triangular junction to a plant visible in the distance and then crosses the road to enter an industrial complex. We watch it bear round to the right and disappear.

Parking our bikes in the hedge again we walk back a few yards along the main line to a shed we saw from the road. Outside it is a small locomotive with a heavy vice bolted to its frame. Nearby an unusual small steel open wagon stands derailed. A couple of men working in the shed explain that they are fitters who repair the excavators in the quarries. The locomotive is their runabout and workbench.

We return to the road and enter the left hand yard, belonging to Joseph Arnold & Sons. There is no difficulty getting permission to walk round. Close to the road are some brick buildings, with wooden awnings covering sidings alongside, occupied by three or four wooden bogie open wagons. Down in the yard there are dozens of tracks and hundreds of tipping wagons, around the washers and other plant. Several locomotives are moving about. In a lull we hear another locomotive but can see nothing; the sound is coming from beyond the hedge. Obviously the plant next door, where we saw the quarry train go, has a number of locomotives too. At the bottom of the yard is the large shed with a few spare locomotives in it. We follow the tracks past the shed and down a cutting into the quarry.

The quarry is a large open space with the face in the distance. Parts are flooded and a pair of swans float gracefully over the surface of the water. Rusty lines branch off at intervals but the polished tracks head towards the face. We step aside to let a train of empties pass us and see it stop by the distant excavator at the face. The driver gets into the excavator and proceeds to load sand into the train. When he has finished he returns to the locomotive and chugs back past us, the skips swaying on the rough track.

Beyond the excavator is a low ridge of sand, about waist high. Looking over we see another quarry, with rusty rails coming towards us. We scramble up and over, and follow the tracks. Eventually we come to a washing plant, where a train is being shunted. We get into conversation with the driver who offers us a lift back to the road, which we gladly accept. The afternoon is well advanced, tramping through loose sand is tiring, and we must have walked miles!

We ride on the front of the locomotive grasping a handrail attached to the top of the radiator. At our feet are an assortment of spare coupling chains, shovels and rerailing ramps. Almost immediately the train goes over a bridge, then enters a length of double track. This continues almost the whole way back to the works yard.

Once in the yard the driver stops and we alight. He uncouples from his train and the locomotive disappears into a small leanto at the end of the building ahead. We follow a track to the right and re-enter Arnold's yard, close to the level crossing, and retrieve our bikes for the ride back to Leighton (two miles according to the sign post at the road junction). It has been a good day.

* * * * * * * * * * * *

In your imagination, come with me to Leighton Buzzard on a Sunday in 1992. I will pick you up at the recently rebuilt BR station.

We drive from the station to the main road, cross the River Ouzel and the canal, then take a bypass round the northern and eastern sides of the town centre. At intervals brown signs with a symbolic steam locomotive point in the direction of the Light Railway. They lead us to a car park in Billington Road (the A4146 to Hemel Hempstead). Good, there's a space!

Before us is a green, single storey building. A canopy over the front door proclaims that this is Page's Park station. The place is full of excited children and adults, buying tickets, souvenirs, guide books, drinks and snacks.

A loud whistle causes many people, ourselves included, to go out on to the platform behind the building. A large, dirty-brown steam locomotive with a strange chimney is entering the station, hauling a train of red painted carriages, some open, some closed. The train stops and disgorges its load of smiling people. Some stop to have their photograph taken beside the locomotive, *Elf*, which has been uncoupled from its train and is preparing to run round it.

After coupling on the front of the train we watch *Elf* taking water, and notice to our surprise that the fireman is feeding the fire with wood, not coal. The chimney contains a spark arrester, just like the ones in the American West.

The train is filling up fast, so we take our seats, before the guard comes along clipping tickets. Departure time and a green flag is waved. The guard blows his whistle, the driver replies with a toot on the engine's hooter, and we are off!

As we gather speed we pass a long shed at the end of the platform, and beyond it is a yard with a number of locomotives, steam and diesel, waiting their call to duty or shunting. After the shed we can see the golden cliffs of a large sand quarry, which the guide book we bought reminds us was the reason for building the railway back in 1919.

The train passes along the back of hedges and gardens. After a while the exhaust of the locomotive ceases and the train slows, so that flagmen can jump off and hurry ahead to hold up the traffic at the approaching level crossing. They rejoin the train and the driver continues very cautiously through factory buildings. The guide book gives the reason for this caution. We are descending Marley's Bank, 1 in 24 with a sharp curve at the foot.

Safely down the bank the driver opens up, the train picks up speed, and soon rattles into a loop where another train is waiting. It is headed by a large blue locomotive called *Doll*. Passengers wave to each other as the trains cross. We see the blockman controlling the loop exchange train staffs with our driver and we continue.

Shortly afterwards we slow for Hockliffe Road level crossing. Our passage holds up quite a lot of cars. Over the road, the train runs right through a housing estate, crosses a river and then the locomotive has to work hard - the crisp exhaust is a joy to hear - as we climb up a long gradient. At the top is a school, yet another ungated level crossing over a road, and an amazing sharp right-hand curve. Sitting in the front carriage of the three coach train we feel we could shake hands with people in the last one.

The scenery is now rural, with fields of cattle or crops on both sides of the train. On our right we catch frequent glimpses of the road through the lineside hedge. The train slows and whistles vigorously for another level crossing. We seem to have arrived at a tile works, but there is a station here as well. The journey has taken half an hour. We alight and look around, while the locomotive takes water.

In sidings beside the station and in the factory yard are lots of locomotives, steam and diesel. Some are obviously usable, others in various stages of repair. Volunteer railway staff in their boiler suits are busy on several of them, but not so busy that they ignore our questions. In addition to the locomotives there are wagons of all shapes and sizes. Many of them are stored on two long sidings near the road. This was once a double track section of the old main line and takes us about half an hour to explore. Just look at some of those rail joints!

We heard *Elf* depart as we explored the site and examined everything, but soon *Doll* reappears with the next train. Clambering aboard we take our seats for the return journey to Page's Park and the promise of a cup of tea at the buffet. We must come again as there was lots to see, and we noticed posters for a special Steam Gala in September.

Chapter Two

Leighton Buzzard Sand

Leighton Buzzard is a market town at the western end of Bedfordshire, 40 miles north of London. The market of Leighton was mentioned in the Survey of 1086. It has always been held on a Tuesday and stalls are still erected every week along the High Street. The ancient parish of Leighton Buzzard included the hamlets of Billington, Eggington, Heath, Reach and Stanbridge. These were made into civil parishes in the last quarter of the 19th century. The parish of Heath and Reach 'is studded with sandpits, many of which are in use, the most extensive being in the south east corner at Shenley Hill. From one of these pits the sand used in the composition of the Crystal Palace was dug, owing doubtless to the influence of Sir Joseph Paxton, a native of this part of Bedfordshire and architect of the Crystal Palace (VCH Bedfordshire Vol.III, 1912).

The Lower Greensand (Lower Cretaceous period) crosses Bedfordshire from south-west to the north-east near Potton, and forms a prominent escarpment. Four main layers can be identified in the Woburn Sands: from base upwards they have been given the desciptive terms 'brown sands', 'silver sands', 'silty beds' and 'red sands'.

The 'brown sands', exposed in pits to the north of Leighton Buzzard, comprise up to 45 m (150 ft) of ferruginous, fine-to-medium-grained, cross-bedded quartz sands with glauconite and other dark grains. The brown colour is due to an abundance of hydrated iron oxide associated with clay partings and trace fossil burrows. Irregular sheets of 'iron pan' and burrows in ferruginous preservation are conspicuous on weathered quarry faces. A bed of sandy, pebbly (quartz and chert), ferruginous clay separates the 'brown sands' from the overlying 'silver sands' and forms a prominent marker bed in several of the sand pits. The clay bed represents a nonsequence, and was followed by a transgressive episode.

The 'silver sands', from 6 m to 15 m (20-50 ft) thick, consist of white, pebbly, well-sorted and well rounded, medium-to-coarse-grained, almost pure quartz sands with a little fine-grained material. the pebbles include chert, 'lydite' and quartz and are up to 7 mm (¼ in.) in diameter. In places, 'carstone reefs' occur within the 'silver sands'. There are sandstones with a ferruginous cement and form linear features; they may be 10 to 25 m (33-83 ft) in width and 2 to 3 m (6-10 ft) in height. Abundant fossil wood fragments occur within the sands; strong planar cross-bedding, commonly showing reversal of direction, is indicative of deposition in tidal conditions.

The 'silty beds', up to 4.5 m (15 ft) thick, are present locally. These comprise mottled silt, silty sand and subordinate clay; all are characterised by carbonaceous and ferruginous streaks and bands, and sporadic coarse pebbly (mainly quartz) lenses. (British Geological Survey: *Geology of the Country around Leighton Buzzard*, HMSO 1994, pages 34 & 35.)

		Current Geological Data for selected Quarries			
Quarry	Overburden		Sand Type		
		Red	Silting Beds	Silver	Brown
	m	m	m	m	m
Chamberlain's Barn*	11	5		2	
Groovebury		15 †			
Munday's Hill	16	4	4.5	4-10m	5 compo.
New Trees	4			6	3
Nine Acre				in past	10 compo
Pratts		10			
Reach Lane	20		2	15	25
Stone Lane	16			6	12

* Output almost entirely to adjacent concrete tile works.
† Dredged; exposed 10-12 m high, plus 5 m under water.
(*ibid* pages 46-49.)

In view of Joseph Arnold's early involvement with peat as well it is worth quoting the relevant section.

Extensive areas of peat have been mapped along the flood plain of the River Flit between Flitton and Clophill. The deposit comprises a dark brown to almost black silt, very rich in peaty organic matter . . . The thickness varies up to several metres. Its formation . . . could be linked to high water levels in the underlying Woburn sands giving rise to fairly permanent water-logged conditions in the past. (*ibid* page 92)

Economic Geology: The facies variation within the area, and indeed within certain pits, is such as to yield products ranging from building and asphalting sand, and fine aggregate for concrete to foundry sand and filtration media. In 1988, 15 sizeable pits were extracting material from the Woburn Sands around Leighton Buzzard. A number of former pits have been back filled, levelled or built over. In the past, a large number of small sand pits provided material for local use but these have generally been back filled or ploughed over. Large scale exploitation commenced about a century ago when rail and canal links made the products available to wider markets. (*ibid* page 100)

In 1984 the output for all Bedfordshire quarries was almost 1¼ million tons: building sand 470,000 tons, concrete and fill 475,00 tons and industrial sand 280,000 tons.
     Modern treatment plants operated by several major companies within the area are capable of washing, grading and blending sands to produce specified products. In general most high quality silica sand products are derived from the Silver sands division of the formation while the building sands and concreting sands come from 'brown sands' and the 'red sands'. These latter divisions are characterised by sands with considerable variation in grain size and degree of roundness, which contain much ferric oxide . . .

Most of the constuctional sands are used for building purposes. The screening out of the finer grades produces raw material suitable for the making of asphalt and mortar. Minor quantities are used for concrete roofing tiles and other applications such as horticulture . . .
     The silica (industrial) sands are derived from the 'Silver sands' which lie near to the top of the Woburn Sands succession and can reach up to 15 m (50 ft) in thickness. These sands are restricted to a relatively small area centred on Shenley Hill, adjacent to the village of Heath and Reach, north east of Leighton Buzzard. They have a silica content which exceeds 98 per cent and a ferric oxide content which is less than 1 per cent, except in and near sporadic carstone 'reefs'. Narrow ranges of particle size distribution are typical. Some of the silica sands are marketed as foundry sands which need to have a closely defined grain-size distribution, to be clean and consistent in quality. Bands and lenses of coarse-grained, particularly well-rounded and well-sorted quartz sands are washed and screened to produce material which is ideal for filtration purposes in water treatment.
     The sands were formerly used for glass making, but are not of the quality currently acceptable for coloured glass manufacture. (*Ibid* page 101)

An advertisement dated March 1894 for Joseph Arnold's sand from pits at Heath and Reach lists various grades of sand and their cost per ton.

Best white glass sand	2s. 6d. to 6s.	(12½p to 30p)
Foundry sand	10s.	(50p)
Red sand	3s. 6d.	(17½p)
Yellow sand	3s. 6d.	(17½p)
Building sand	1s. 6d.	(7½p)

A letterhead of the same period shows that he was also supplying '"Special Sand" for Water and Sewage Filtration'.

However, Leighton sand has not always been in a very competitive position. Before World War I there was only a small profit in the sand trade due to foreign competition, especially from Belgian sand used as ship's ballast and then dumped in this country. The Leighton sand merchants sought to increase their profitability by reducing operating costs, particularly the cost of transport. Even in 1930 foreign sand could be obtained in the north of England for less than the cost of rail carriage from Leighton Buzzard.

The sand is found under fairly shallow cover, beneath a layer of blue clay of variable thickness, and iron sandstone which often needs to be blasted. This hard, dark brown ferruginous sandstone has a limited use as building stone. It also occurs in isolated masses called 'doggers' by quarry men.

In the 1960s Garside said that the economic importance of the sand arose from the range of colours - white, through cream and rust to dark brown - and the range of grain sizes, mainly 8 to 50 mesh, which made it suitable for processing into dry graded sand for which there was a large demand, at home and abroad.

In the 19th century sand had to be carried in carts from the pits to market, railhead or canal, but the continuous heavy traffic damaged the roads and resulted in claims for compensation by the Bedfordshire County Council. Steam wagons offered some advantages, but they also damaged the macadamed surface. Around 1900 there had been plans for a railway to take the traffic off the roads, but nothing had materialised. Before 1914 the sand merchants' difficulties were acute.

The German invasion of Belgium in August 1914 cut off, almost overnight, supplies of Belgian foundry sand. At the same time the demand for such sand by the English munition factories was increasing rapidly. To alleviate the impending crisis, English sources of supply were sought and Leighton sand was found to be ideal. Production was increased and 'enormous quantities' were sent daily by rail and canal to the munition centres.

Once peace had been restored the quarry companies were informed that they would again be liable for damage caused to the roads by their steam tractors. They were forced to return to the sand carter, and in the meantime pressed on with plans for a 2 ft gauge private railway to link the major quarries with the main line railway. This, the Leighton Buzzard Light Railway, was formally opened on Thursday 20th November, 1919.

For over 40 years it carried sand from quarries to the main line, although some sand continued to be delivered by road direct from the quarries. After World War II, and in particular after a major rail strike in 1953, the proportion delivered by road increased. Modernisation of the quarries and the construction of new sand processing plant in the Double Arches area, away from the cramped locations at Billington Road, Leighton Buzzard, further reduced sand traffic on the railway. By the mid-1960s only Arnold's traffic used the line south of Vandyke Road, although the section thence to Double Arches remained in use for internal traffic.

Arnold's sand was no longer carried to Billington Road in 1969, and in 1971 trains ceased running to New Trees quarry, so there was no sand traffic west of Stonehenge. Stonehenge sand trains stopped running early in 1977 with the result that the only sand trains on the LBLR were from Munday's Hill quarry to Double Arches. These ceased in June 1981 and with them the last of the internal quarry railway systems which had been progressively replaced by rubber tyred dumpers from the mid-1970s.

However, the decline of the sand traffic left a railway about 2½ miles long idle, ripe for redevelopment. Narrow gauge railway enthusiasts obtained control of the line and public passenger services began on Sunday 3rd March, 1968. This present line has subsequently grown into a major attraction, with a large mixed fleet of locomotives, English and Foreign, steam and diesel.

Before the sand can be quarried the clay overburden must be removed. Originally this was done by gangs of four men, who removed it in strips 18 ft wide, running perpendicular to the face. A few inches of the underlying sand was dug out to a depth of 4 ft into the face, leaving three 18 in. square pillars of sand at the front to support the clay and top soil, one each end and one in the middle. One man would then begin to chop these legs while another kept watch for cracks. As soon as the section began to fall, and it was not always necessary to remove all the legs, the digger ran. Sometimes there were casualties. The loosened soil was removed by wheelbarrow or a ½ cu. yd truck running on very light gauge tracks to the spoil tip in a worked-out part of the pit. The barrow runs were carried across the face to the tip on tall wooden trestles. If trucks were used the track would be laid as a 'Y'. The pair of men on one arm had a side-tipping wagon and the other pair on the other arm had an end-tipping wagon so that together they could lengthen and widen the spoil embankment. The wagons would be pushed by the men, or sometimes a horse was used.

Steam excavators on caterpillar tracks with wide wooden shoes were introduced for overburden removal in the 1930s. They burnt a tipping wagon (one ton) of coal a day and used three tank wagons of water (about 690 gallons). In 1934 a ¾ cu. yd Ruston-Bucyrus steam navvy on caterpillar tracks was used to strip overburden at Double Arches quarry, while a 1 cu. yd Ruston-Bucyrus steam shovel on road wheels was used at Twenty One Acre quarry to remove 20 to 30 ft of stiff gault clay overburden. Mechanical stripping had a number of advantages, including less chance of overburden mixing with the sand if there were a fall, and having large quantities of uncovered sand available for rush periods. The first diesel excavators came around 1935.

Horses, and later locomotives, were used to haul the spoil away to be tipped in old workings. Traces of these overburden lines remained, heavily overgrown, in 1960. From the 1950s contractors have been employed to remove up to 60 ft of overburden, using bulldozers and scrapers or, later, self-propelled scrapers. In the mid-1980s Arnold dug overburden with a 30RB excavator and carried it by Hanlamatic dumper to the tip in a worked out quarry. The clay banks are now sloped back at 45 degrees to ensure stability. If ironstone is uncovered rock drills are used to bore shot holes and then it is blasted away.

For years the sand was dug by hand. Garside last used men (prisoners of war) around 1945 but Arnold did not cease hand loading until the mid-1960s, although excavators had been introduced years before. Hand loading facilitated the selection of different grades of sand, hence probably its continued use for so long. Men were paid piece-work, and on average a man could load 24 wagons (30 tons) daily at 1s.0d.(5p) each, giving a weekly wage of £2 12s. 0d. (£2.60). (*Note*: These figures do not tally! Either the typical man only worked half-time or the wagon rate was 6d. (2½p), later increased to 1s. 0d.)

The quarrymen used picks to cut a horizontal groove two or three feet (60 to 90 cm) deep, across the base of the face so that a whole section would slide down. When the face fell the diggers did not turn and run, as the advancing sand would knock them onto their faces and bury them. Instead, they faced the avalanche, and then fell to lie on top of the sand. The finer the sand the harder it was to make it fall. The sand was screened as it was loaded by throwing it through an inclined metal sieve (like those builders still use) mounted on top of the wagon or cart. Washing the sand was introduced during World War I.

Sometimes carts were taken to the face along sleeper roads. In other cases light tramways were laid and the sand tipped by the road for reloading into carts. The horses used would haul four or five wagons on the level, but only one wagon if there was a steep climb out of the pits. If, as was often the case, the wagons were not braked they were stopped by jamming a stout wooden pole, six or seven feet long, under the wheels. An alternative to horses was to have a a winch to haul wagons out of the pit, supplied with steam from a vertical boiler.

Excavators, either face shovels or draglines, were later used to dig the sand and load the wagons. Face shovels have the bucket, a cube, attached to the end of an arm pivoted about half way along the sturdy jib. Wire ropes from the top of the jib pull the bucket up into the sand. (Many face shovels also have a mechanism to rack the bucket arm out while digging.) The load is emptied when the arm is horizontal through a hinged door in the back of the bucket. Draglines have a long shallow bucket suspended by two ropes from a long lattice jib. One rope is attached to each end of the bucket, usually by heavy chains. The rear rope is used to lift the bucket and drop it well away from the excavator. The front rope then pulls it in, scooping up material. Altering the tension in the ropes tilts the bucket, emptying the contents through the open end.

In the mid-1970s a few hydraulic drag shovels were used. The bucket which faced inwards was pivoted to the end of an arm about as long as the jib and pivoted to the end of the jib. Instead of wire ropes, operation was by means of hydraulic rams which controlled the jib, bucket arm and bucket. However, the real breakthrough came when rubber tyred front loading shovels were introduced. The outward facing bucket on hydraulically operated arms could dig the sand, carry it within the quarry and load either the hopper for the screens or direct into a lorry. A John Deere JD 544 articulated wheel loading shovel was introduced with Arnold's Pratts Pit in 1976. Powered by a 105 hp turbo charged diesel engine and fitted with a 1.75 cu. yd bucket, it loaded 15 ton lorries from the stockpile, dug at the face, carried sand to the screen hopper and cleared the quarry floor. Within the year two more followed, at New Trees and Stone Lane quarries.

The screens for the sand were of two main types. The shaker had a vibrating screen of ½ in. mesh which was made of taut piano wire, sufficient for building sand. Sand for filter beds, foundries etc needed to be washed to remove gravel and very find sand or silt. A conveyor took the sand from the tipping hopper to a sloping trough where it was washed by a stream of water onto a vibrating screen with ⅛ in. holes called the 'Niagara'. The sand fell through the holes (if it were dry ½ in. mesh could be the smallest that could be used) while the gravel slid off the screen and down a chute into a wagon. The sand was washed into a tank where it was stirred and the silt washed out to be pumped away to old workings. A bucket conveyor lifted the sand out of the washing tank to a chute which fed the wagons. Perforations in the buckets allowed water to drain off, and the wagons had a row of holes in their bottoms as well. Barrel washers, comprising a horizontal rotating drum made of sieves of gradually increasing coarseness, used to be used. These worked on much the same principles.

At some quarries, particularly in the Grovebury area south of Leighton Buzzard, much of the sand lies below the water table so the quarries are naturally flooded. Sand used to be dug by a steam grab crane mounted on a barge. When the barge was loaded it was moved to a landing stage where the sand was dumped for reloading into wagons or carts. Later a suction dredger mounted on a pontoon was used, pumping a sand/water mixture to the shore through a 9 in. pipe. This pipe was supported at intervals by small pontoons made of a pair of oil drums in a simple wooden frame. On the edge of the lake the pipe discharged the sand into hoppers where the water drained off. Further washing was unnecessary but sand still had to be screened to remove gravel and grit. A disadvantage of dredging is that it is not possible to grade the sand but it does give a mixture of uniform composition.

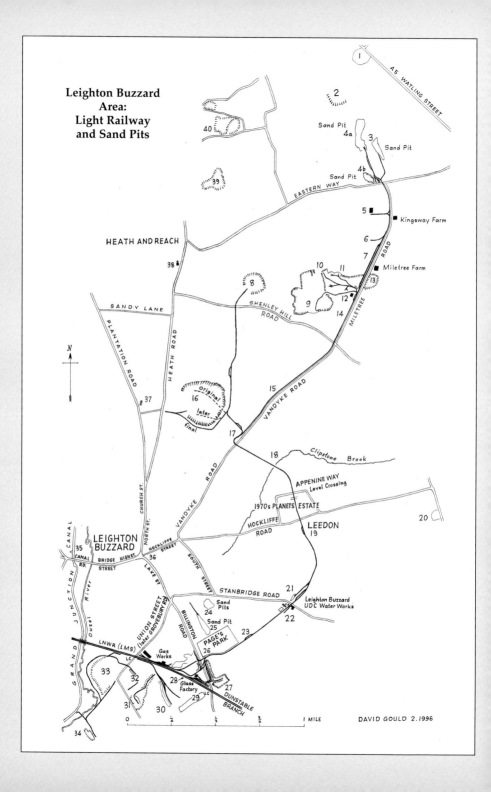

Leighton Buzzard
Area:
Light Railway
and Sand Pits

A5 WATLING STREET

2

40

Sand Pit
4a

3

Sand Pit

4b

Sand Pit

EASTERN WAY

39

5

Kingsway Farm

6

7

Miletree Farm

HEATH AND REACH

38

10

11

8

9

12

13

14

ROAD

MILETREE

SANDY LANE

SHENLEY HILL
ROAD

N

PLANTATION ROAD

HEATH ROAD

37

Original

16

later

final

15

17

VANDYKE ROAD

18

Clipstone Brook

APPENINE WAY
Level Crossing

1970s PLANETS ESTATE

HOCKLIFFE
ROAD

LEEDON
19

20

CHURCH ST.

VANDYKE ROAD

NORTH ST.

CANAL

LEIGHTON
BUZZARD

35

CANAL
RD.

BRIDGE HIGHST.

STREET

HOCKLIFFE

STREET

36

LAKE ST

SOUTH STREET

GRAND JUNCTION CANAL

Ouzel River

STANBRIDGE ROAD

21

Sand
Pits

24

Sand Pit

25

23

22

Leighton Buzzard
UDC Water Works

UNION STREET
(later GROVEBURY RD.)

BILLINGTON ROAD

PAGE'S
PARK

26

LNWR (LMS)

Gas
Works

33

32

28

Glass
Factory

27

DUNSTABLE
BRANCH

29

31

30

34

0   ¼   ½   ¾   1 MILE

DAVID GOULD 2.1996

Map Key

1. Potsgrove (Leighton Buzzard Brick Co. Ltd)
2. Churchways Quarry - Double Arches (Garside) (Original Double Arches quarry)
3. Long Stretch Quarry - Double Arches (Garside)
4. Double Arches Quarries (Arnold)
5. Eastern Way Plant (Garside)
6. Munday's Hill Quarry (Garside)
7. Double track
8. New Trees Quarry (Arnold)
9. Parrot & Jones Quarry
10. 9 Acre (Chance's) Quarry (Arnold)
11. 21 Acre Quarry (Arnold)
12. Stonehenge Brickworks
13. Shenley Hill (Garside)
14. Driroof tileworks
15. Bryan's Loop
16. Chamberlain's Barn Quarry (Arnold)
17. Co-op Loop
18. Swing Swang Bridge over Clipstone Brook
19. Leedon Loop and 'dud loop'
20. Harry Sear's Pit
21. Marley Tiles Ltd, loop and siding
22. Leighton Buzzard Concrete Co. Ltd siding
23. Red Barn Loop
24. H.G. Brown's Pit
25. H. Paul breeze block plant
26. Page's Park Loops, LBNGRS Depot
27. Pratt's Pit (Arnold)
28. Billington Road Depots (Arnold, Garside, LBLR)
29. Spinney Pool (Arnold)
30. Firbank Pits (Leighton Buzzard Sand Co. Ltd)
31. Brickyard Pits (Garside)
32. Eastwoods Ltd
33. Rackley Hill (Arnold, Garside)
34. Grovebury Quarries (Garside)
35. Linslade, Leighton Buzzard Wharf
36. White House (Garside)
37. Sandymount (Arnold)
38. St Leonard's Church, Heath
39. Bedford Silica Sand Mines Ltd, Reach Lane
40. Stone Lane Quarry (Arnold)

Arnold's house 'Sandymount' in Plantation Road, Leighton Buzzard, in 1992.   *R. Dingwall*

Garside's house 'The White House', Hockliffe Street, Leighton Buzzard in 1992.   *R. Dingwall*

Chapter Three

The Sand Companies

Two firms dominated the Leighton Buzzard sand trade, Joseph Arnold & Sons Ltd and George Garside (Sand) Ltd.

Joseph Arnold & Sons Ltd
The earliest known record of the Arnold family is the marriage of William Arnold at Soulbury, three miles north-west of Leighton Buzzard, in 1774. His third child Thomas was married in 1808 in Leighton Buzzard Methodist Church, and he had two sons, John and William. The 1841 Census lists Thomas, John and William as carpenters. John married in 1835 and his third child, Joseph, was born at Heath in 1841.

Although Joseph Arnold seems to have regarded Heath as his home (in the mid-19th century several members of the Arnold family lived in Birds Hill, Heath) he operated a builders' merchant business based at 32 St Pauls Road (now Agar Grove), Camden Town, London. This was situated close to where the North London Railway crossed the Midland Railway as it approached St Pancras. His father, John appears to have travelled a lot, probably in connection with the business. Joseph opened his first sand pit at Stone Lane, Heath, in about 1860. Most of the sand was carted to the canal wharf at Old Linslade for transport. John died in 1880 and, with his wife Ann (died 1886), is buried at St Leonard's Church, Heath.

Joseph was living in Somers Town at the time of his marriage in 1873, and was probably the manager of the Camden Town premises while his father travelled. For a time in the 1870s John's youngest son George was also in the business, which traded as J.J. & G. Arnold, but later he left to work on his own account leaving Joseph in control of the family firm. John's other son, John Alfred, was a Baptist Minister and worked for 49 years with the London City Mission. He took no part in the sand trade. Joseph was a keen organist and gave a recital at the opening of the Wesleyan Church in Leighton Buzzard. *Gardening World* published an article about Joseph Arnold's sand pits in 1896, and in 1901 the company had a stand at the Building Trades Exhibition, Agricultural Hall, Islington.

Joseph developed the sand business, opening further quarries at Shenley Hill and Grovebury. He also supplied peat and loam from the Stockgrove Estate about a mile from Heath, as well as from other sources in the UK. He was strong and could bend a coin between the fingers of one hand! In 1907 he moved to a new house, 'Sandymount', which he had had built in Plantation Road, Leighton Buzzard (SP922265), and died there in 1911. On 9th April, 1909 control of the business had passed to his sons Albert and Ernest (born in 1875 and 1879), although they did not change the name to Joseph Arnold & Sons until 1918, when the London office moved to 124 Tottenham Court Road, W1. St Pauls Road was then closed.

Joseph had opened a sand quarry at Flitwick, nine miles north-east of Leighton Buzzard, in 1902, but the sand seems to have been of inferior quality and it was short lived. The land was sold in 1922. He was also an important witness at the public hearings of the proposed Leighton Buzzard and Hitchin Railway in 1900 and 1904. Albert and Ernest bought the quarry at Stone from Mr C. Castle, proprietor of the Aylesbury Sand Co., in 1908. This quarry produced fine white sand, and was closed in 1973.

Albert married around the turn of the century and lived in north London, moving to 32 St Pauls Road around 1907. On his father's death he moved to 'Sandymount'. He had four daughters and died in 1939.

Ernest married Mary Morgan of 25 St Pauls Road and lived at Tuffnell Park. By 1907 he had moved to Linslade (which an outsider might describe as that part of Leighton

Buzzard, west of the River Ouzel, which lay in Buckinghamshire), where his sons Joseph and Frederick were born.

In 1911 the company had eight quarries in operation, presumably Stone Lane, Shenley Hill, Nine Acre, Grovebury, Spinney Pool, Billington Road (all in or near Leighton Buzzard), Stone (Aylesbury) and Flitwick.

Ernest and Albert continued to develop the sand business. World War I gave an enormous impetus to home producers, as previously much foundry sand had been imported from Belgium. The German invasion in August 1914 cut off this supply almost overnight and alternative sources were sought as a matter of national urgency. Leighton Buzzard sand was found to be ideal and production was increased. The Arnolds opened new quarries in 1916 at Double Arches, between Heath and the Watling Street, to meet the demand. The local roads took a terrible punishment, and on the restoration of peace the sand merchants became responsible for the damage they caused. It is hardly surprising then that much of the correspondence in 1919 concerning the proposed narrow gauge railway from Leighton Buzzard to the sand quarries emanated from Arnold's Tottenham Court Road Office. The company also guaranteed about three-quarters of the sand traffic when the light railway opened.

Joseph Arnold & Sons moved their Leighton offices from Union Street to Billington Road in the second half of 1919, probably at the time the LBLR opened in November. The Union Street site was sold in February 1926, part being purchased by the Leighton Buzzard Gas Co.

Between 1905 and 1924 the company owned at least five horse drawn narrow boats which took sand by canal to the London area. Their names were; *Albert*, *Felix*, *John*, *Joseph*, and *Why Not*.

A pair of Joseph Arnold & Sons narrow boats, *John* and *Joseph*, returning empty to Leighton Buzzard leave lock 55 at Berkhampstead hauled by a single horse, in 1910. The boats are 'breasted up' by ropes at each end. Note the lighter ropes connecting the two tillers and rudders so that one person can steer both.   *Joseph Arnold & Sons*

During the 1920s and 1930s the company steadily improved its position, introducing new types of rotary sand driers and improved screens. Various official parties visited the quarries. The Ballast, Sand & Allied Trades Association, under the Chairmanship of Albert Arnold, devised the cubic capacity system for measuring loads in 1936, which was incorporated into the Weights and Measures Regulations of 1938.

Albert and Ernest became the two Directors when Joseph Arnold & Sons Ltd was formed on 1st January, 1937. Albert died early in 1939, so Ernest's sons Joseph (2) and Frederick joined their father as Directors. When Ernest died in 1949 they became Joint Managing Directors. Joseph managed the quarries from Billington Road while Frederick was based at the London office (until it closed in 1967), handling customer liaison and financial matters.

In the post-war period restrictions on road transport were steadily eased so that increasingly customers collected their own sand. The development of bulk carrying vehicles encouraged the switch from rail to road delivery. Starting in the 1960s roads were laid into quarries and weighbridges were installed to facilitate direct loading of road vehicles. Hydraulic excavators and dump trucks replaced the remaining internal railways. The railways were inflexible, requiring constant movement to follow the working face, and modern loading shovels could not economically load trains as one bucketful would fill three rail skips. In 1990 three Terex 2366 type dumpers were available, moved from quarry to quarry as required. Alongside this, the fixed plant (screens, washers, graders and driers) was steadily modernised. A radio control system between the quarries and head office was introduced in 1982. A new drying and grading plant at Double Arches costing £3 million was commissioned in 1985, capable of producing 38 different grades depending on grain size and shape.

Joseph (2) Arnold retired as Managing Director in 1977 and his son Peter (who was born in 1945 and joined the company in 1962) became Assistant Managing Director. Frederick retired in 1980, although retaining a seat on the Board, and Peter became Managing Director with Joseph as Chairman. Frederick Arnold died in November 1991.

There were further changes in February 1988. The descendants of Ernest Arnold, including the then Managing Director Peter, resigned from the Board, leaving control in the hands of descendants of Albert Arnold, Joseph (1) Arnold's first son. Albert's grandson Colin White became Chairman and his brother David a Director and Company Secretary. (The Managing Director, Ron Bradley, was formerly with British Industrial Sand and is not a descendant of Joseph.) Despite the changes, however, the business continues to be owned and controlled by the great grandsons of the founder.

The company had a distinctive nameboard at its quarries. It was rectangular, divided diagonally, with the top left half white and the lower right half black. The name, Joseph Arnold & Sons Ltd, was painted horizontally in black and white, depending on the background at that point. The new management's logo is also distinctive, a vertical orange rectangle with a white 'A' (without the horizontal bar) at the lower end. While the company name remains the same it now trades as Arnold Sands, (incorporated May 1992) to emhasise its line of business. It is part of the Arnold White Group plc, registered office 40 West Street, Dunstable.

Developments continued following the 1988 management changes. More sophisticated products such as dried sands and close graded sands are increasingly important. Annual production is currently (1992) about 300,000 tonnes, of which 80 per cent goes to the building and construction industry. In 1994 Pratt's and Stone Lane quarries were in continuous operation, while Chamberlain's Barn, Double Arches and New Trees were operated in rotation depending on production requirements. Contractors were used to take sand in 8-wheel trucks to Double Arches for cleaning and grading.

The firm remains market leaders in industrial sands, with the output being used for purposes as diverse as a filler in plastic pipes and for filling golf bunkers (the ball just sits on the sand without sinking). It obtained BS5750 quality assurance certification in September 1993.

George Garside (Sand) Ltd

George Garside opened his first sand quarry at Billington Road in 1885. The 1910 Bedfordshire Trade Directory described him as 'silver and building sand pit owner, gravel and peat merchant, brickmaker, 28 Lake Street'. By 1914 he had moved to White House, Hockliffe Street (SP925252). Around 1960 the stables at the White House were given to Leighton Buzzard Urban District Council for use as offices. Later the firm exchanged the White House itself for the stables (by then occupied by the South Bedfordshire District Council and called 39 Hockliffe Street).

He had no children but was assisted by a nephew, Hugh F. Delafield. After World War I Hugh returned to his uncle's business, although in 1920 he was given a separate entry in the Trade Directory. When George Garside died in 1926 he managed the firm for Mrs Garside until she died in 1931. Complete control then passed to him until he died in 1957. Then the business passed to his sons J.G. & W.H. Delafield, who entered on a period of expansion and modernisation. One of the first results of this was the formation of a limited company, George Garside (Sand) Ltd, on 1st January, 1960.

As Garside's first pit in Billington Road was becoming worked out during World War I he began to quarry at Grovebury, on the other side of the LNWR Dunstable branch. He already had a small quarry at Rackley Hill, operational by 1898, and around 1918 purchased the adjoining quarry from Joseph Arnold & Sons, and, in addition, opened two new pits in a field nearby (behind the present Redland Tile Works).

Rackley Hill became flooded as the quarry deepened. As the pit was nearing the end of its life another one, the present Grovebury quarry, half a mile to the south was expanded in the mid-1920s. An extensive 2 ft gauge railway system developed here. The trade recession of the late 1920s brought the need to economise. Production was then concentrated at Grovebury pit and towards the Watling Street, and Rackley Hill was closed.

The wartime demand for sand made transport problems of secondary importance (all his existing pits were close to the LNWR) and so quarries were opened at Shenley Hill and Double Arches, although the sand had to be carted several miles to the railway or canal. These quarries were served by the LBLR when it opened in 1919. Another quarry connected to the LBLR was opened nearby in 1925 at Munday's Hill, opposite Miletree Farm. This quarry probably replaced Garside's Shenley Hill pit. There were also small quarries at Heath and Reach but they did not have railways.

A washing plant, screens, and a drying plant with coal fired ovens, was build in the old Billington Road quarry soon after the LBLR opened. This lasted until 1964 when a large new drying plant was opened at Eastern Way, where Garside already owned land near the quarries.

Until about 1946 the company owned barges on the Grand Union Canal, but canal traffic dropped in favour of rail, or especially road, and the barges were sold.

The company became part of the English China Clays (ECC) Group in December 1978, but continues to trade as George Garside. Following the demise of the quarry railways the company was using Volvo BM 6x6 articulated dumpers in 1990.

Chapter Four

Grovebury Area Sand Quarries

Although Arnold's first sand quarries were at Heath and Shenley Hill, the main centre of sand quarrying was originally about half a mile south of Leighton Buzzard, on either side of the LNWR Dunstable branch (opened 1st June, 1848, extended to Luton 3rd May, 1858). Grovebury sidings beside Grove Crossing formed a convenient railhead. The Grand Junction Canal (Grand Union Canal from 1st January, 1929) was also nearby, although the nearest wharfs were in the town, over a mile by road from Grove Crossing. There were four main quarrying areas:

a) the triangle bounded by Union Street (now Grovebury Road), Billington Road and the LNWR
b) the area between the LNWR and Grovebury Farm (Firbank and Brickyard Pits, Spinney Pool, Rackley Hill)
c) the triangle between the LNWR, the canal and Grovebury Road
d) the area south west of Grovebury Farm (Grovebury Quarry)

The last area remains in operation but the others have long since been worked out.

Union Street (Grovebury Road)/Billington Road
Arnold - Union St.   (SP924244)
Harris   (SP926243)
Garside   (SP928241)
Arnold - Billington Siding   (SP928240)

Arnold had a quarry in Union Street, north of the gas works, by 1898. When this was exhausted the site was retained for a depot and the Leighton Buzzard offices. Sand was carted down the street past the Poor Law Institution to the LNWR goods yard. Later Arnold appears to have worked an additional area, between the gas works and Billington Road, up to the northern boundary of Gregory Harris sand pit, which had opened in 1879. Although the frontage on Billington Road was only 85 yards long, the quarry stretched some 320 yards to the LNWR. Harris had a siding from the LNWR at Grovebury goods yard (agreement dated 27th March, 1899). In October 1906 he signed an agreement allowing Arnold to load sand at it, Harris in return having the right to dump rubbish (overburden) in Arnold's worked out pit. However, this agreement terminated in January 1908. South again was George Garside's pit, opened in 1885, with a tramway to take sand to the main line sidings. This was 50 cm (1 ft 7½ in.) gauge and may have been the 20 in. gauge equipment advertised for sale in December 1919. Quarry returns show that 17 men were employed in 1909, falling to five in 1918 but rising to 24 in 1920. Perhaps this represented an all-out effort to work out the quarry before concentrating production elsewhere.

In the south-eastern corner of the site was Arnold's Billington Siding which Arnold had had constructed in 1903 (agreement dated 19th March, 1903). The LNWR extended Harris' siding and charged Joseph £360 6s. 6d. (£360.32½). The common link to Grovebury yard was over LNWR land, and was maintained by the LNWR at the traders' expense: 65 yards by Harris and 276 yards by Arnold. Arnold's letterhead of the period states 'New Private Siding and Building Sand Pits. Billington Crossing L. & N. W. RY and Grand Junction Canal'. As the ground here (the site of Arnold's main tipping dock

Illustrations from an undated guide to Leighton Buzzard. *Above*: Firbank Pit. Note the standard gauge wagons at the face and the planks on trestles for the men barrowing overburden. The gas works is in the distance. *Below*: Grovebury area quarry, with a steam grab crane mounted on a barge. Note the two holds, one full and one empty, and the waiting horses and carts at the landing stage. *Author's Collection*

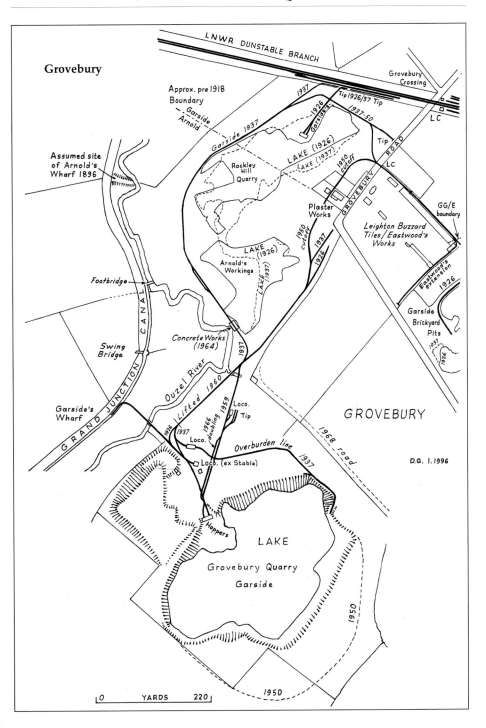

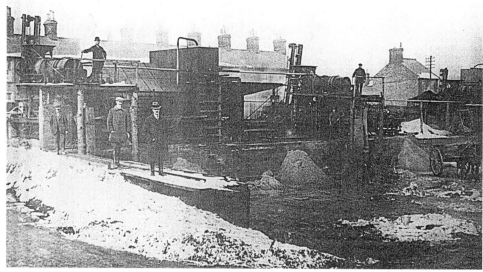

Arnold's Union Street yard. *Joseph Arnold & Sons*

Firbank: The standard gauge Manning, Wardle & Co. locomotive *Avon* used for a short time around 1920. The boy on the footplate is the owner's son, H. Dagnall *H. Dagnall*

in LBLR days) shows no sign of quarrying, and Pratt's Pit across Billington Road was not then open, it is probable that the siding was built to serve Spinney Pool pit, south of the LNWR a few yards beyond Billington Crossing.

Firbank Pit
Leighton Buzzard Sand Co. (SP924240)

The Leighton Buzzard Sand Co. operated Firbank Pit on the south side of the LNWR. The quarry was served by a long siding (agreement dated 4th March, 1897) which ran from a junction opposite Grovebury sidings about quarter of a mile south-east towards Billington Road. The 1925 map shows a long loop in the quarry, which by 1937 has been partly lifted to leave a pair of sidings spanned by a building. This was probably a hopper for sand pumped from a dredger in the now flooded pit, although early photographs show conventional hand loading took place, and later a barge-mounted crane was used. Shunting was by a horse or main line locomotive, except for a short period in the early 1920s when No. 19 *Avon*, a Manning, Wardle 0-6-0ST with 12 in. diameter inside cylinders was used. It was very similar to *Sir Berkeley* preserved on the Keighley & Worth Vally Railway.

Details of *Avon* were published in the *Industrial Railway Record*, issues 123 and 129. *Avon* had been built in 1881 and had been owned by the contractor L.P. Nott. It may have been used during World War II by the Ministry of Munitions, and appears to be the lcoomotive advertised by Wm Muirhead, MacDonald, Wilson & Co. Ltd of Fulham in *Machinery Mart* on 8th August, 1919. Some time later, Dagnalls Ltd of Cricklewood advertised in *Machinery Mart* (14th May, 1920) for a locomotive to hire for a period of 12 months or more, and obtained *Avon* for use at their sand pit at Leighton Buzzard. Firbank Pit is assumed as no other had a standard gauge system and another informant told me this quarry had hired a black locomotive with six wheels 'from Dagenham'. However, *Avon* did not stay long. Other records suggest it was returned to Wm Muirhead in 1921, and was subsequently used by Charles Brand & Son Ltd on the construction of the London Transport Northern Line extension from Golders Green to Hendon in 1922/23.

Radford Arthur Dagnall, always known as Rad, was well established as a haulage contractor in Willesden Green (part of the Cricklewood district of north west London) by the time of his marriage in 1913. Trading as Dagnalls Ltd he had a depot behind Willesden Green station. While the site of Dagnall's wharf, which included a siding from the Metropolitan Railway, has disappeared under building, the office (5 Station Road, Willesden Green) still stood in 1992, backing onto platform 4. He specialised in hauling fairground and agricultural equipment between showgrounds, and for a time between 1915 and 1919 was a showman himself. Also during the war he did haulage work for the War Office.

Hower, Rad had to sell his 'complete roundabout travelling set' (Savage roundabout, Foster compound steam tractor) and about ten other road locomotives (plus trailers etc.) in July 1918. There was another sale at Dagnall's Wharf in March 1920. Despite this he continued in business. In 1919 Rad transported the new flagpole for Kew Gardens, a Douglas Fir over 200 ft high and 2 ft 9 in. diameter at the base, from Brentford, where it was unloaded from a barge, to the nearby gardens. He then assisted with its erection. Rad was working on the Upper Welsh Harp land reclamation project in Hendon in 1921, in which rubbish and soil from all over north London was dumped into this old reservoir to form building land. Around this time too, he started the London Mortar

Mills at Hendon to supply material to the many home-building projects in the area. This was perhaps the reason for operating Firbank Pit. Although *Avon* was the only railway locomotive Dagnall owned it was numbered in the same series as the firm's road vehicles, hence the number 19 it carried. As stated above, *Avon* appears to have left Leighton in 1921, and Rad's involvement with the local sand trade seems to have finished about the same time. He began building houses in 1922 in Rickmansworth and Amersham, and also founded a bus company in Rickmansworth in late 1922.

The 1929 Railway Clearing House *Handbook of Stations and Sidings* listed the Bedfordshire Tile Co. as using part of the Leighton Buzzard Sand Company's siding.

By the late 1950s the pit was long out of use and had become a tip for BR. Engineer's wagons were stored there. The sidings had then been relaid almost to the crossing.

Dagnalls Ltd Locomotive (standard gauge)
19 Avon   0-6-0ST IC MW 738   1881   Hired from Wm Muirhead mid-1920-1921

Spinney Pool
Arnold (SP927237)

South-east of Firbank Pit, at right angles to Billington Road, was Spinney Pool pit, opened by Arnold in the 1880s. The new siding laid in 1903 (*see above*) was probably built to serve this pit, as it reduced the distance by road to the railhead from about a mile to a few yards. At one time this old quarry was used as a bathing pool (marked Spinney Pool (Bathing Pond) on 1926 OS map). The quarry seems to have closed towards the end of World War I. In May 1918 a crane on a float (partly sunk) was advertised for sale at Billington Crossing.

Brickyard Pit
Garside (SP923237)

Behind Firbank Pit was the small Brickyard Pit, opened by Garside during around 1912, presumably to replace Billington Road then approaching exhaustion. Sand was dug by a steam grab crane mounted on a barge and unloaded on to a staging at the water's edge. At the sand dump two gangs of men loaded it into 2 ft tipping wagons, which were hauled, one at a time, by horse to a tipping dock spanning a siding in Firbank Pit approximately 300 yards away. At the dump there were two sidings, one for each gang. Around 1922 an air-cooled Austro-Daimler locomotive was introduced, hauling two wagons at a time. The tip was then rearranged to be parallel to the standard gauge. There were three wagons, two in use and one spare. The quarries closed about 1925, probably when Grovebury opened. The locomotive probably went there.

Grovebury/Rackley Hill Quarry
Arnold, and Garside (SP920241)

It seems that Arnold and Garside both had workings here in the 1890s, Arnolds at the south-west end of the site and Garside at the northern end. Around 1918 Arnold sold their part to Garside.

Joseph Arnold had an important quarry 'on a low hill on a 20 acre site' at Grovebury in 1896. The quarry was low lying and the 30 feet of sand was dug by a barge mounted grab crane. In 1896 the output was 100 tons per day. The article in *Gardening World* said 'Mr Arnold has constructed a bridge over the River Ouzel, and laid down a light railway, connecting the pits with a new wharf on the banks of the canal, at a cost of over £1000'. This railway was 2 ft gauge, horse operated. The bridge was probably about 180 yards north of the footbridge marked at SP917239. The 'numerous carts' sent to the sidings were probably emptied at Grovebury yard. The quarry mainly produced building sand although there was a washing and screening plant. It was sold to Garside, who already had workings nearby, probably in mid-1918 as Arnold advertised 2 ft gauge wagons and turntables for sale at Rackley Hill in May 1918. The sale was probably a consequence of Arnold's development at Double Arches.

Garside was operating at Rackley Hill by 1898. After purchasing Arnold's part a round 1918, Rackley Hill became Garside's main quarry during the 1920s and was worked out in the early 1930s, when production was transferred to the quarry near Grovebury Farm. A short line ran from hoppers at the northern end of the pit 100 yards to an elevated wooden tipping dock beside a standard gauge siding at (map reference) SP920242. The quarry tramway ran for 27 yards on LNWR land at the tipping dock, the siding agreement with Mr Garside being dated 25th October, 1898 according to LNWR diagrams of private sidings, published in January 1909 (diagram 996). The pit was flooded and sand was dug by a steam grab mounted on a pontoon. When full the ensemble moved across to the hoppers and the sand was transferred. The level fell considerably when the water table was lowered following the construction of new water boreholes in the neighbourhood in the late 1950s.

Horses were used initially. The first locomotives came second-hand in the early 1920s. They were both made by Austro-Daimler. In one the driver sat side-ways in the middle, and in the other a wagon was incorporated as part of the locomotive. Later it was de-engined and used as a 'Bogie'.

Grovebury Quarry
Garside (SP919234)
Leighton Buzzard Tiles (SP921240)

Grovebury quarry was opened in the 1900s, and being remote from roads probably had a railway from the beginning. A railway is shown on the 1926 map, the line running from the pit north-westwards to the River Ouzel where it divided. One branch crossed the river by a sleeper bridge and then continued on a low embankment for about 100 yards to the Grand Union Canal, turning sharp left on to a private wharf where the track was set in concrete. Sand was sent by boat to London, and while in the late 1950s traffic dropped to about a boat a fortnight, the last boat was not loaded until October 1965. The other branch curved sharply through a right angle and ran straight for about 400 yards to a tip near the site entrance. From the absence of any structure by the water's edge it is likely the floating crane unloaded directly into the wagons.

Leighton Buzzard Tiles Ltd opened its works in 1930/31 close to Grovebury Crossing. The firm seem to have taken over and expanded the Bedfordshire Tile Co. Ltd who were listed at Grovebury in 1928. A long extension was built to supply the works with sand from Grovebury quarry. About 250 yards from the quarry entrance the tileworks branch curved sharply left from the route to the lorry tip to run round the western and northern sides of Rackley Hill quarry where it made connection with the older line to the LNWR tipping dock. Leaving the ramp to this dock the track continued towards Grovebury

Grovebury: Garside's wharf beside the Grand Union Canal, looking north. The railway curved through a gate in the boundary hedge, crossed the River Ouzel and then entered the quarry area, 22nd October, 1973. *Author*

Grovebury: Sand hoppers at the edge of the lake, showing the 9 in. pipe bringing sand and water from the dredger, 26th October, 1965. *Author*

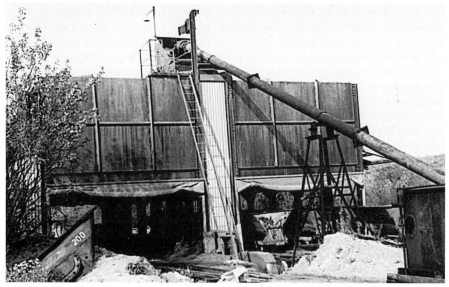

Garside - Grovebury: Hoppers for loading sand pumped in suspension from the dredger on the lake, 10th August, 1968. *C. Daniels*

Road, which it crossed by an ungated level crossing and ran along the side of the tileworks for 50 yards. Here sand was tipped. The distance from the sand hoppers, which had been built at the edge of the lake in the pit in 1926 (when a sand pump was installed), to the level crossing was about 1200 yards. (The direct distance from the sand hoppers to the level crossing was about 800 yards, so the extent of the deviation round the old pit can be seen.)

By 1937 a corrugated iron locomotive shed had been built beside the old wooden stables at the canal branch junction, and later the stables were used for locomotives as well. Also, a branch had been built continuing from the original line beside the quarry approach road to a tipping dock just inside the quarry entrance. The dock had a wooden floor supported by steel girders resting on brick piers. The overburden was removed by rail at this time, the 1937 map showing a line running from near the locomotive shed round the eastern lip of the quarry.

After World War II the system was progressively modified. The first alteration was the construction of a short line from near the tipping dock entrance to join the tileworks line by the level crossing, so avoiding the long journey around the old pit. This was brought into use in about 1950 and the route round the old pit fell into disuse, as little sand was sent away by rail. The railway tip was last used in April 1965. However, the first few yards of this line had received a new lease of life in June 1964 when Readymix Transite Ltd built a concrete mixing plant beside it, near the site of a loop shown on the 1937 map but gone by 1958. Sand was tipped into a sunken hopper feeding a conveyor which took it up into the top of the mixing plant.

At the quarry, trains from the sand hopper had to travel round two sides of a triangle to reach either the lorry bay or the tile works. A deviation was built along the hypotenuse and opened in December 1958. This part of the line was laid in a wooded cutting and was very picturesque, as also was the line to the west of the old pit which ran through a wood.

The section alongside the river from the new line to the old locomotive sheds was no longer needed and was lifted in 1960. However, the sheds remained in use and the rest of the old line from the pit was retained to give access to them and to the wharf. After closure of the wharf in October 1965 this section became very overgrown.

A spur was laid off the new line to a hopper sunk in the ground near the junction with the old route. A conveyor took the sand from this hopper to an elevated hopper from which lorries were loaded. A small screen was incorporated and grit fell off into a wagon on a short siding. With the introduction of this hopper the lorry tip by the gate lost its importance, but was used to hold a stockpile in slack periods as a reserve against breakdown. In mid-1965 a second line was laid beside the hopper. At both positions a corrugated iron shelter was provided for the man tipping the wagons.

With the deviation in use the locomotive sheds became remote; they were also small and inconvenient. Accordingly, in the latter part of 1962, a new wooden shed, 46 ft by 18 ft 9 in., with a single road to take four locomotives, was built beside the new tipping hopper. The floor of the new shed was still only sand, with no pit. The old sheds remained in the wilderness for some years until the 1970s, the locomotive shed still in faded maroon paint.

In 1934 Eastwoods Ltd took over Leighton Buzzard Tiles (1934) Ltd as a subsidiary. Sometime after 1937 the tileworks line was extended to serve more tipping positions at the back of the factory. The line beside the works remained Garside's as it was a potential source of access to Garside's old quarries (Brickyard Pit) behind the works if they should ever be reopened. It also gave access to land south of the farm purchased by Garside since 1945. Eastwood's extension was about 150 yards long and terminated

Grovebury: The new locomotive shed and tipping point. Note the shelters. The line on the far left served the tile works and the concrete plant, 26th October, 1965. *Author*

Grovebury: 6-wheel wagons built to carry a new sand dredger to the lake, 12th April, 1961. *Author*

on a gantry about 7 ft high across a brick sandstore. Sand was kept here in case the supply from Garside should ever be interrupted. Following a period when Garside had a number of locomotives out of action, the company acquired about a dozen wagons and an Orenstein & Koppel diesel locomotive in 1957 so that the firm could collect its own sand. One informant said that a locomotive was borrowed from Eastwood's Barrington Cement Works for a year before the Orenstein & Koppel came.

Further emergencies rarely arose. The locomotive was used but once and stood idle at the end of the gantry. Birds nested in its radiator. Redland Tiles Ltd took control on 1st April,1963, and the new owners reorganised the works. It was found more convenient to have sand delivered by lorry and the railway became redundant from May 1964. The track was soon lifted (apart from the rails in the level crossing) and by late 1965 a factory yard was being extended over the old track bed. The locomotive disappeared, presumably for scrap, in 1964.

The track from the sand hoppers to the tips was doubled in 1966 and the connection at the pit to the old sheds and wharf was taken out. This was the last modification. The existing plant involved double handling and so new equipment which loaded direct to the lorries was installed on the eastern edge of the pit. This came into use at the end of May 1968. The stocks of sand in the old hoppers were sufficient to supply Readymix for the first week of June and then the railway closed. The equipment subsequently had painted on it 'Keep' (to be sent to Double Arches later) or 'Scrap'.

Horses were used initially. The first Motor Rail locomotive, supplied in March 1926, probably marked the beginning of major expansion. The two Austro-Daimler locomotives from Rackley Hill may have ended their days here. A Motor Rail locomotive was supplied in July 1931 (for the tileworks traffic) and two more in December 1936. There were three locomotives in 1945. In the 1950s and 1960s the stock was usually four locomotives, with occasional transfers to and from Double Arches for heavy repairs.

Garside's locomotives had the standard green livery with white uppers to the cab. They all ran with the bonnet facing the pit. Eastwood's diesel had black bonnet and frames, and its well constructed home made cab was painted cream with 'Eastwood's Limited' in black on the closed side. This locomotive faced the other way.

The first horse drawn wagons had been combined side and end tippers, later Hudson side tipping skips holding 1 cu. yd, (25 cwt) of sand were used. In the 1960s there were about 50 to 60 wagons on the site although only about 36 were in use. At the closure 35 wagons were marked 'keep' and the rest 'scrap'. Eastwood had 12 similar wagons, up to four stored near the locomotive and the remainder scattered beside the track at the back of the works as sand was normally brought in Garside's wagons.

In addition to the skips there were four other wagons. One was a skip frame carrying a rectangular oil tank. It was kept behind the sand hoppers. Two wagons were robust home-made 6-wheel flats, each with a centrally pivoted bolster. The frame was channel steel (6 ft 1 in. long over buffers, 3 ft 1 in. wide, 3 ft 8 in. bufferbeam, 1 ft 2½ in. to the top of the frame from the rail, 2 ft 3 in. wheel base, 10 ft by 1 ft bolster). It was well braced, and had buffers from a Motor Rail petrol locomotive at each end. The wheels and bearings were standard Hudson products. The centre pair of wheels was flangeless. These two wagons were made to carry a new pontoon weighing 21 tons down to the lake. It arrived on 12th March, 1959. A siding was laid down into the water by the sand hoppers and the loaded wagons, coupled by a long steel bar, pushed down it into the water. When the pontoon had floated clear the wagons were recovered and dumped on the old line close to the original terminus. These wagons were used in late 1968 to carry the dismantled hoppers up to the new locomotive shed. The fourth wagon was a bogie flat which came from Billington Road around 1965 and was used for carrying stores etc. The 6-wheel and bogie wagons, and the locomotives, were transferred to Double Arches in the early months of 1969.

Three locomotives were normally in daily use. All trains were hauled from the pit and the empties pushed back. Trains were of 6 wagons, making a load of about 7½ tons of sand. The normal weekly quarry output was about 3,500 tons. The tileworks took normally 16 train loads a day and the Readymix plant up to 12 a day. Trains passed either at the sand hopper, one leaving as soon as one arrived, or at the tip junction. For winter operation a small buffer beam snowplough was kept by the old locomotive shed, but this had gone to Double Arches by the 1960s, presumably in the hard winter of 1962/63.

By 1960 the clay overburden was being removed by scraper and dumped in old workings behind the face. After leaving the soil to settle for three to five years the made ground was covered with top soil and returned to agriculture. Under the clay was a 50 ft bed of sand containing several well defined bands, but the dredging process produced a uniform material suitable for concrete tile manufacture, concrete, general building purposes, and for moulding in iron and steel foundries.

In 1990 the quarry was still operational, but little remained of the railway. There were still rails on the wharf but the bridge across the river had been dismantled. Girders of the lorry tip by the entrance remained, and there were sleepers round the back of Rackley Hill quarry. An embankment beneath a large bramble was all that remained of the railway tip, but the brick wall at the end of Eastwood's line still stood. The north end of the quarry area had been landscaped and was under crops, as also was the meadow between the river and the canal.

Garside (Sand) Ltd Locomotives
For details of Garside's locomotives used on this system see Chapter 15.

Eastwood's Ltd Locomotives
4 wDM on loan from Barrington Cement Works *c*. 1956/57.
4 wDM OK 4105 ex-Eastwood's Bobbing ClayPits, Kent *c*. 1957 scrapped 1964.

Grovebury - Leighton Buzzard Tiles: OK 4105 out of use at the sand store behind the works, April 1961. The brick wall was still standing in 1993.   *Author*

South Eastern Leighton Buzzard

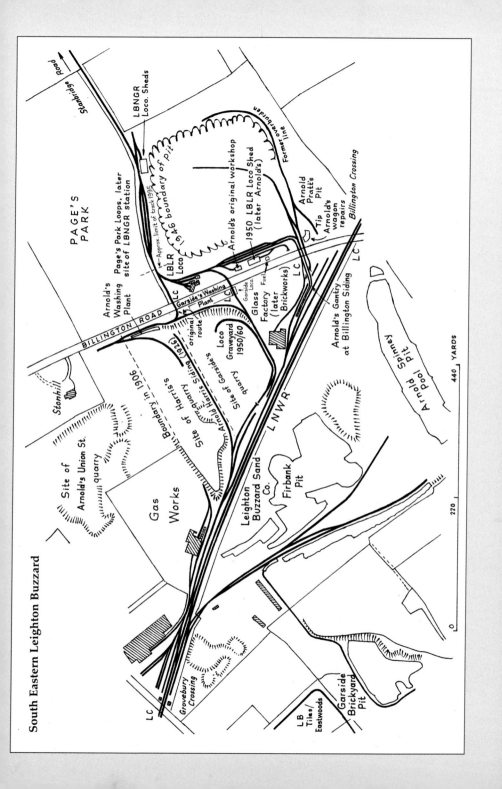

PAGE'S PARK

Stanbridge Road

LBNGR Loco. Sheds

Page's Park Loops, later site of LBNGR station

Approx. limit of track 1995

1946 boundary of pit

LBLR Loco

Arnold's original workshop

overburden

Formerline

1950 LBLR Loco Shed (later Arnold's)

Arnold Pratt's Pit

Tip

Arnold's wagon repairs

Billington Crossing

Arnold's Washing Plant

BILLINGTON ROAD

LC

LC

Garside's Washing Plant

Garside Loco Fuel

Glass Factory (later Brickworks)

LC

LC

Stonhill

Site of Arnold's Union St. quarry

Boundary in 1906

Site of Harris's quarry

Arnold Harris's original route

Site of Garside's quarry

Loco Graveyard 1950/60

Arnold's Gantry at Billington Siding

LNWR

Gas Works

Leighton Buzzard Sand Co.

Firbank Pit

Arnold Spinney Pit

Arnold Pool Pit

440 YARDS

220

0

LC

Grovebury Crossing

LB Tiles/ Eastwoods

Garside Brickyard Pit

Chapter Five

Leighton Buzzard & Hitchin Light Railway

The LNWR was approached around 1892 to build a railway north-eastwards from Leighton Buzzard, but it was not interested. Accordingly the promoters turned to the Midland Railway, and in May 1899 the Leighton Buzzard & Hitchin Light Railway applied to the Board of Trade for a Light Railway Order. The Engineer was Arthur C. Pain and solicitors were Baxter & Co., Westminster. The Board of Trade considered the application and appointed the Earl of Jersey and Colonel Boughley Commissioners 'as to enquire into the expediency of granting the application made by W.S. Cooper (Esquire, of Toddington Manor), John Waugh (Surgeon, of Toddington) and John Henry Green (Maltster, of Leighton Buzzard)'. The powers were sought under the Light Railways Act 1896.

The public enquiry was held on 9th November, 1899 in the Assembly Room, Corn Exchange, Leighton Buzzard, and was duly reported in the *Leighton Buzzard Observer* (14th November, 1899).

One of the barristers appearing for the promoters, H.C. Richards MP, said that there were a number of sand pits in the locality, and it was intended to connect them to the line, to convey the valuable material to either the LNWR or Midland Railway. The brick trade could also expect to be developed as there was clay as well as sand in the pits.

Joseph Arnold, of Camden Town, said he was engaged in the sand trade in the neighbourhood. The line would save him 1s. (5p) per ton cartage . . . . he carted 50,000 tons in a year. It would also enable him to compete more successfully with other markets . . . . George Garside, also interested in the sand trade, gave evidence to a similar effect.

The Light Railway Order was granted early in 1900 and allowed three years to take up powers of compulsory purchase and five years for completion of the works. The single track standard gauge line would be 19 miles 7 furlong 0.5 chains long and the estimated cost was £98,631 (£1,908 per mile), out of an authorised capital of £110,000.

The proposed railway would have had stations near Leighton Buzzard, Hockliffe, Toddington, Harlington, Barton in the Clay, Shillington, and Ickleford if required. It joined the LNWR Dunstable branch near Grove Crossing, and the Midland Railway Hitchin branch near its junction with the GNR main line at Hitchin. On leaving Leighton Buzzard the line swung to the north, away from the Clipstone Brook, presumably to take it closer to the sand quarries. At Harlington the line made an S-bend, to run southwards past the Midland Railway station before turning east under the main line by a bridge capable of carrying six tracks. The line continued north-eastwards and then turned east to run through Barton in the Clay, after which it turned north-east again to serve Shillington. Here the direction became south of east to join the Midland Bedford to Hitchin branch at Ickleford, half a mile short of the junction with the GNR main line north of Hitchin.

Rails would have been at least 56 lb. per yard, to take an axle load of 14 tons. A speed limit of 25 mph would have been imposed, reduced to 15 mph for tender locomotives running in reverse, and to 10 mph at level crossings and at curves of less than 9 chains radius. The maximum gradient would have been 1.75 miles of 1 in 50, against trains from Hitchin, with a summit near the Toddington to Milton Bryant road. Some earthworks were begun, and cuttings could still be seen south of Barton in the Clay, near the A6, in 1977. However, lack of money seems to have killed the project.

A new application was made in May 1902 by John Cumberland (a local auctioneer and valuer), John Waugh and J.H. Green. The public enquiry was again in the Corn Exchange before the Earl of Jersey and Colonel Boughley. It was held on 24th September, 1902 and the *Leighton Buzzard Observer* reported that 'there was a large company in the room'. Solicitors were Fowler & Co., Westminster, and the Engineer G.W. Usill, who unfortunately died soon after attending a site meeting on 17th September, a week before the enquiry.

The route was generally similar to the 1900 scheme, but mainly south of it between Leighton Buzzard and Harlington and then north of it to the junction near Hitchin which was at the same place as before. The main differences were the provision of stations at Eggington and Pirton, and a triangular junction at Harlington. Approaching Harlington from the south-west the main line curved east, under the Midland Railway and on towards Barton in the Clay. At the entrance to the curve a spur led north-eastwards to a junction at the Midland station, and a north to east curve completed the triangle.

The provision of Eggington station, besides benefiting the travelling public (268 inhabitants at Eggington) 'would have a considerable commercial influence having regard to the facilities for transferring sand, which is plentiful in the neighbourhood'.

There were also proposals for a branch line from Eggington station (situated half a mile from village, in the hamlet of Clipstone) north-westwards to Shenley Hill, then following the route of the later LBLR to Double Arches (where the quarries had not yet opened but where Joseph Arnold had already purchased land in anticipation). A map suggests that this line went diagonally across Shenley Hill crossroads, which would have been an unusual level crossing to say the least!

Surviving correspondence on rates and revenue between Arnold, Garside, Fowler and Cumberland during the period June to October 1904 refers to this quarry branch as a siding, worked by the LB&HR and thus standard gauge. For example, one letter proposed;

> . . . that the sand pit owners should pay 3*d.* per ton from Clipstone to Leighton Buzzard, plus 8*d.* to 1*s.* 2*d.* (depending on distance) per ton over the siding from Clipstone. Thus they would pay 11*d.* to 1*s.* 5*d.* per ton, as against 1*s.* 4*d.* to 1*s.* 9*d.* by cartage, a saving of 5*d.* per ton (31% to 23%) on transport to Leighton Buzzard.

It was also proposed that the rate to London from any of the three mainline junctions should be 2*s.* 6*d.* per ton.

Arnold had reservations about the proposal, not least:

a)   the need for any fresh competitor to be bound by the same rates
b)   the need to realign the route closer to Mile Tree [*sic*] crossroads, thus shortening the siding (and presumably reducing the charge for its use without a corresponding increase on the Clipston-Leighton component)
c)   would the LB&HR promoters pay for the siding
d)   rebates for large tonnages

On 18th or 19th September Arnold and the solicitor Fowler met to agree Arnold's evidence, which had to be given to Counsel before Monday 22nd September, the public enquiry being on the 24th. The agreed 'Proof of Mr Joseph Arnold' was:

> That he is engaged in the sand trade near Leighton and carries on an extensive business therein.
> That the building of the proposed line would tend to considerably increase the sand trade in the neighbourhood, especially if the suggested tramways were made to connect the pits with the railway.

Witness carts or loads in the aggregate about 50,000 tons of sand a year and with better facilities he could considerably increase this.

The construction of the proposed railway would save him 1s. ton in cartage to Leighton and would also by its connection with the Midland and Great Northern Railways open new markets. Witness is very much in favour of the line.

There was no opposition from the three main line railways concerned (LNWR, Midland Railway, GNR) and very little from the owners or occupiers of land affected (14 dissentions of 362 people affected).

The Chairman of the enquiry recommended that the scheme be approved and the BoT gave its approval on 6th April, 1903. Once again nothing happened. Probably Arnold's reservations and Unsill's death killed the project.

Brief details survive of a scheme dated 1908 and signed by J. Wilmer Ransome, Engineer, of Cheapside, London. This was a yet more southerly route, from a junction at Billington Road, Leighton Buzzard to Pirton, where the line turned south-eastwards to run round Hitchin to a junction with the GNR main line a mile south of Hitchin station. A triangular junction was again provided at Harlington. A second, larger, triangular junction at Eggington connected a branch that ran due north to the quarry area at Double Arches. This crossed Mile Tree Road close to Mile Tree Farm and, surprisingly, had no connection to the quarries at Shenley Hill. Perhaps it was just an outline map. Certainly nothing was done and the project lapsed.

A view of Arnold's Foden steam wagon 'Big Lizzie'.   *Courtesy Bedfordshire Education Service*

Chapter Six

Origins and Birth of the LBLR

Following the failure of the LB&HR schemes the quarry owners continued to cart their sand along local roads, either to the railhead at Grove Sidings or to a canal wharf. The outbreak of World War I exposed the deficiencies in the local transport arrangements. Pre-war, a major source of British foundry sand was Belgium, but the German invasion cut off supplies almost overnight. At the same time demand for such sand from munition factories was increasing rapidly.

Then the British Government had to turn to English sands. After experimenting Leighton Buzzard Silica Sand was adopted with great success. (Joseph Arnold had advertised foundry sand from Heath & Reach pits in 1894.) Messrs Arnold were then approached by the Ministry [of Munitions] - they, the Ministry would have put the Light Railway in force themselves but owing to the shortage of labour and secondly that all rails were being shipped to the various bases in France etc. they substituted Road Traction (*LBO* report of meeting on 3rd June, 1919).

It is interesting to speculate what the LBLR would have looked like had the Ministry of Munitions built it. I suspect that it would have been remarkably similar to the line that eventually materialised, which was equipped with standard War Department steam and petrol locomotives.

In fact the existing fleet of carts, assisted by a couple of steam tractors, was augmented by 10 more tractors, each hauling five or ten tons of sand, seven days a week. The roads began to take fearful punishment and the Roads Board was compelled to take charge of the affected routes. Union Street (site of Arnold's depot) and the route to Grovebury Sidings cost as much in upkeep as Bedford High Street.

The state of the roads gave such cause for concern that Bedfordshire County Council instructed Mr H. Percy Boulnois MInstCE (of Victoria Street, London SW1) to report on certain roads in and near Leighton Buzzard. In the company of Mr Marks, clerk to Bedfordshire County Council, and of Mr Wakelam, County Surveyor of Middlesex, he inspected the roads on Saturday 17th March, 1917. Below is a summary of his report.

1. Billington Road - Stonhill to Billington Crossing: carriageway about 18 ft wide deep ruts and the surface practically destroyed due to extensive traffic to the siding at Billington Crossing. Beyond the crossing the road was quite suitable for the traffic that used it.
2. Stonhill to Union Street: recently resurfaced with broken metal (i.e. roadstone). Resurfacing was recommended, but really it required reconstruction including drainage of the sub crust.
3. Union Street to Heath Road: practically a town street, with recent patching, it really needed reconstruction.
4. Commencement of Heath Road to Messrs Arnold's Sand Pits [i.e. Chamberlain's Barn] : suburban character with footpaths either side and rough kerbs. Surface recently metalled but worn into ruts.
5. Mile Tree Road, from Kingsway Pit [Double Arches assumed] to Nine Acre Pit: considerably rutted, recently repaired with metal near Kingsway Farm, reconstructed about eight years ago but the work was not properly completed, so needs consolidation and a coating of hard metal.
6. Garside's Pit to Urban District Boundary of Leighton Buzzard [Nine Acre to Shenley Hill Crossroads assumed] : inspected 24th February, 1912 and rebuilt about 1913, it had withstood the heavy traffic well but was showing signs of starting to break up, so something harder and more durable than ordinary water bound macadam was required.
7. Shenley Hill Crossroads to Leighton Buzzard: surface was cut up by traction engines and patches were 'licked up' by their wheels. Reconstruction - or at least reforming and metalling - was required.

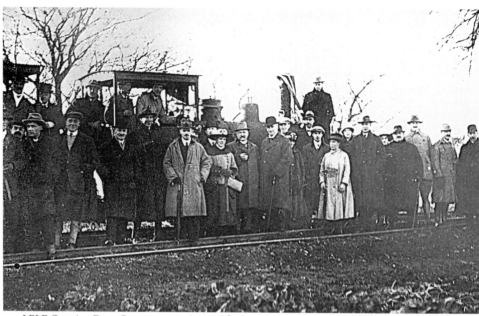

LBLR Opening Day: Guests pose in front of the two steam locomotives at Billington Road. Note that they face in opposite directions, 20th November, 1919.   *Joseph Arnold & Sons*

Guests prepare to travel to Double Arches in the specially constructed temporary train, 20th November, 1919.   *J. King*

Acknowledging that the roads could not be rebuilt in time of war, and as the munitions traffic had to be kept going, Boulnois recommended that the surfaces should be lightly scarified (broken up with spikes) and shaped to a proper contour, followed by laying broken metal, rolling, and consolidation to a depth of at least 3½ inches. Tar macadam was preferable to water-bound macadam, if available, as it withstood heavy wear better. In view of the report it is easy to understand why road repairs due to the sand traffic rose to £1,000 per month, and exceeded £25,000 during the war period.

Following the Armistice in November 1918 the Roads Board handed back the sand routes to the County Council. The Quarry Companies were informed that 'all the Tractors must be disposed of before the end of January (1919) otherwise they should be held liable for damage to the roads' caused by their extraordinary traffic (*LBO* 3rd June, 1919).

Accordingly, the tractors were sold by auction on Wednesday 5th February, 1919. It was held by Messrs Stafford Rogers & A.W. Merry Ltd and Cumberland & Hopkins at Arnold's Union Street depot. Heavy snow fell for most of the time but 'the 12 steamers, as they were lined up for sale, made an imposing show, each machine drawing up to the auctioneer's stand under full steam'. There was bidding for many items from the haulage contractors and others who had come to the sale from all over the Midlands. The ten 5-ton compound steam tractors, of various makes, with working pressures of 200 psi and upwards, fetched about £550 each. Two traction engines were included in the sale, as well as wagons, spring trailers and accessories.

The sand carter came back into his own, but his swan song was brief, until the sand companies built their own light railway to reduce costs. The railway opened in November 1919. The local paper carried his obituary:

He came into existence many many years ago when the sand trade began to develop from a purely local into a national trade .... As a type he was unmistakable. He was generally young and hefty; a knotted muffler his neck wear; he wore his cap at a 'don't care' angle, and a fag end gave him his final touch of freedom and independence. He might be met at any time of day between 7 am and 4 pm, singly or in strings, making one of his 4 journeys a day between Shenley Hill or Double Arches and Grovebury Crossing, and he had the reputation of beating all records in the twin arts of wearing out horses and roads .... Nothing disturbed him, nothing perturbed him. Old ladies might glare as he rode by, basking in the sun like some eastern potentate on a throne of golden sand. Little he cared ....

The war brought him to the height of his prosperity. While lesser fry such as shop assistants and the owners of one man businesses were called up he was protected even after (grade) A men from other businesses had been ruthlessly combed out. But the greater the eminence the greater the fall. Saturday (November 29th) saw the dismissal of a big batch of carters and this week will see the sale by auction of 36 of the horses and some 40 of the carts. The cheapening of the transport costs from the pits to the railway sidings will provide other and perhaps less congenial work in the pits, but the sand carter as a local institution is gone. Mr Marks (of Bedfordshire County Council Highways section) will not weep; the aforesaid old ladies will not weep, and those 36 horse, 'all out of hard work' as the auctioneer naively put it, will not shed crocodile tears. (*LBO* 2nd December, 1919)

The sand carter eventually faded out about 1922, and the light railway reigned supreme for the next 25 years. Before 1914 sand carting was one of the few jobs available to 15 to 18 year old boys.

Plans for a narrow gauge railway from the sand quarries around Shenley Hill to the main line railway appear to have been formulated in the early months of 1919. The tractor sale on 5th February had probably been the final spur to take effective action. Even allowing for the fact that the surviving correspondence came from Arnold's records one cannot help but feel they were the driving force behind the project. The first letter, dated 3rd April, 1919, was from Lamb & Co of 107 Clerkenwell Road, London EC who wrote to Messrs Arnold & Son [*sic*], Union Street, Leighton Buzzard:

Re our conversation as to the construction of a small railway to connect your pits with the Dunstable siding [presumably the name of Arnold's 1903 siding at Billington Road], we are prepared to at once make a survey of this line and submit you an estimate for the construction of same.

Arnold replied, from the Tottenham Court Road office, on 5th April, accepting Lamb's terms. The plan was made public at the Annual General Meeting of the Leighton Buzzard Urban District Council (UDC) on the evening of Thursday 17th April, 1919.

The scheme, briefly, is to construct a light tramway which will tap all of the sand pits at Two Arches [*sic*] and Shenley Hill and deliver sand into the railway trucks at Billington Road siding without bringing it through the town . . . . Though at first the line will be only a single line for horse drawn traffic with loops at intervals, enough land is being taken in to provide room for a double track. The rails are heavy enough to carry any locomotive made for 2 ft gauge; and it is contemplated that steam will eventually replace horses as motive power. All the gradients will be easy, and one horse will be able to draw three one ton trucks on each journey . . . . The object frankly is to retain for Leighton Buzzard the enormous sand traffic captured during the war by the cessation of foreign competition. (*LBO* 22nd April, 1919)

Arnold wrote to Lamb on 25th April:

As arranged with you verbally yesterday we beg to confirm quotation given you for 4 ft sleepers . . . . 2*s*. 6*d*. each (12½p) delivered on site of Light Railway. Timber to be used is fir and larch. Ballast from Billington Road and Rubble from Chamberlain's Barn and Shenley Hill quarries all at 1*s*. 6*d*. (7½p) per wagon consisting of one cubic yard. You to perform all labour.

A handwritten note, dated 'May 7/19' reads:

Mr Lambs figures	4¼ miles	=	7480 yards including Siding
@ 32s. (£1.60)yd	£11,968		i.e. 5 loops @ 75 yards
Mr Arnold said	3½ miles	=	6160 yards 32s. £9856
Main line	3m 54c (i.e. 3⅜ miles SAL)		
CB ext	24c (i.e. 528 yd) Sdgs to add.		

Here, perhaps, is the source the different lengths of the LBLR which have been quoted in the past.

The survey was complete by 14th May, 1919, and the cost for 'the building of a two foot gauge road laid with about 30lb. to the yard rail suitably ballasted and all necessary points, crossings, switches, culverts, drains, bridges, road crossings, field gates etc.' was 32*s*. 0*d*. per lineal yard. A postscript to Lamb's letter suggested that their contact should include the supply of 'two 6-wheeled locomotives at cost price, viz. £1225 each FOR (Free on Rail) Leeds plus cost of carriage' which they as contractors could hire from the company to assist construction. Nothing more is heard of this proposal in the surviving correspondence, and in due time Lamb bought a new 20 hp Simplex locomotive for this contract.

During the second half of May Arnold requested further details from Lamb. 'You will understand that we are ourselves familiar with the nature of the work proposed but other interested people wish naturally to have the full information before them before committing themselves to any contract' (16th May). Several letters ensued, one listing constructional details:

Rails	28 or 30lb. (allowance in price if only 28lb. used)
Sleepers	6 x 4 in. fir, 4 ft long
Ballast	Boxed up to top of sleepers and 1¼ ft wide from rails on each side, 6in. under sleepers
Bridge	Concrete with wings with 2 Rolled Steel Girders 6 in. x 5 in. with timber floor
Gates	Creosoted Oak 10 ft opening with spring catch
Posts	10 x 10 and 8 x 8 Oak Stop with self acting Iron Stop

Lamb and Co. also agreed to take £1,000 in shares in lieu of the final payment.

In May, Arnold, on behalf of himself, Garside and Harris, (all sand quarry owners at Leighton Buzzard), applied to the County Highways Committee for permission to construct nine level crossings as shown in the accompanying plans. The Leighton Buzzard UDC had already passed unanimously a resolution recommending that the Highways Committee approve the crossings, and 'the clerk of the Council was instructed to prepare an agreement with Messrs, Arnold & Sons for the construction of such level crossings as may be found necessary, and to enter into the agreement on behalf of the Council'.

The proposed level crossings were as follows:

A	Eastern Way	
B	Mile Tree Road into Garsides Quarry	- present triangular field
C	ditto	- next field west
D	Shenleyhill Road	
E	Vandyke Road	
F	Hockliffe Road (Leedon)	
G	Stanbridge Road (Water Tower)	
H	Billington Road	- north end, by Page's Park
I	ditto	- south end, close to LNWR Billington Crossing

The County Council imposed 18 conditions on the proposed level crossings, including:

1. They were of 24 in. gauge and 'special rails with outside square section shall be used'.
2. They were level across the roads.
3. The tracks shall be laid so that there was no fall towards the roads.
4. The rails would be flush with the road surface and flangeways as narrow as possible.
5. Space between the rails and 2 ft either side paved with well dressed granite setts approved by the Bedfordshire County Surveyor.
6. Roads not totally closed to traffic during construction.
14. They were only to be used during daylight hours except by BCC permission.
15. Pedestrians and traffic not to be delayed by trains more than 2 or 3 minutes at any one time.
16. Rolling stock was not to stand on the crossings.
18. Erect and maintain boards facing the road each way showing the times the crossing was in use.

The Agreement was signed by A.J. Arnold and G. Garside, Directors, and R.G. Walton, Secretary, of the Leighton Buzzard Light Railway.

The level crossings were protected by five bar gates normally closed across the railway. The boy who rode on the locomotive opened them and then held up the road traffic. The gates seem to have fallen out of use in the 1950s.

Meanwhile A. Arnold had been in correspondence with his friend W.B. Shaw of Babtie, Shaw & Morton, Civil Engineers of 17 Blythswood Square, Glasgow. Shaw knew a Mr Murray who could undercut Lamb's prices 'even allowing say 1s. 6d. per lineal yard for earthworks and say £250 for the bridge over the brook', and so save £2,500 to £3,500. What Arnold said to Lamb on 30th May is not recorded, but Shaw wrote to Arnold on 2nd June congratulating him on the reduction he had obtained. Lamb wrote to Arnold on 3rd June confirming a price of 30s. 0d. per lineal yard (with an allowance of ¼ invoiced cost of rails if they were only 28lb. and not 30lb.), and on the understanding that they would no longer have to take any payment in shares. Arnold accepted the terms on 4th June. The construction contract price was now £11,220, a saving of £748.

On 3rd June, 1919 a meeting was held at the Swan Hotel, Leighton Buzzard, to hear details of the proposed light railway to carry sand. J.H. Green was elected Chairman; 'he knew nothing about the railway, except it was in the air'(!) Also present and responsible for the scheme were Messrs A. & E. Arnold, H.W. Clough, H. Delafield, A.W. Merry, R.G. Walton; G. Garside was unavoidably absent. Mr A. Arnold explained the difficulties of the sand trade and said that the only solution lay in the construction of a railway which might also carry farm produce in special wagons. The railway might also carry stone or materials for use by Bedfordshire County Council on the Watling Street.

It was stated that the Ministry of Munitions 'would have put the Light Railway in force themselves but owing to shortage of labour and secondly that all rails were being shipped to the various bases in France etc. they substituted Road Traction'. However, the quarry companies had had to sell their road tractors in January to avoid liability for road repairs.

Mr Walton, who had been interested in the railway from the start gave details of the proposed company, the Leighton Buzzard Light Railway Limited. The nominal capital would be £20,000 in £1 shares and the estimated capital expenditure was £15,000. The sand merchants had guaranteed a minimum annual traffic of 70,000 cubic yards for 10 years, the rates for which were open to periodic revision. (Traffic Guarantees later caused some friction. For example, at the 1922 AGM (4th April, 1922) Arnold was asking for variation due to effects of the Coal Strike on trade, as the original agreement made no provision for the effects of 'strike, communism, riot, disaster or Act of God'.) With an estimated annual expenditure of £2,875 including sinking fund he thought that a 10 per cent dividend was probable. Wayleaves over most of the route had already been obtained for 30 years and few difficulties were expected in completing this part. The Directors of the proposed company were A. and E. Arnold, G. Garside, H. Delafield (sand merchants) R.G. Walton (Solicitor), T. Bromhead Bassett (backer). Most of the capital had been promised at the meeting and the remainder was soon subscribed, the sand merchants contributing about one third.

On 3rd June Robert Hudson of Leeds, suppliers of light railway equipment, who were already negotiating with Arnold for the supply of locomotives, quoted for the supply of all track material: rails, fishplates, bolts and nuts, dogspikes etc. at 10s. 3d. per yard (£902 per mile) FOR Bedford or Leighton Buzzard station. Lack of time prevented them quoting for the complete construction of the line.

Pettit Walton & Co. Solicitors of Leighton Buzzard, wrote to Lamb about a formal contract on 10th June. The letter, headed 'Leighton Buzzard Light Railway Limited' began 'We are acting for this proposed Company, which is about to be registered . . . .' Lamb was unsure what to make of this letter and wrote to Arnold on 14th June, who replied on 18th June saying 'We hereby confirm that the Contract is between yourselves and ourselves, and if we subsequently assign the Contract to a Company it will not alter the position as far as you are concerned'. Arnold also informed Lamb that an independent engineer would be appointed to represent their interests, and would be authorised to sign certificates for payment.

Lamb wrote on 20th June agreeing to make the Clipstone Brook bridge suitable for double track although they would not include the extra superstructure required. They also agreed to improve the gradient through Nash's field, reducing it from 1 in 28 to 1 in 40 or thereabouts, without extra charge.

Also on 20th June Shaw wrote to Arnold about independent engineers, suggesting a Mr W.J. Chapman, who might charge £300 to £500 for the job, (Chapman had been Engineer and Contractor's Agent with Topham Jones & Railton Ltd, on their recent contract constructing a railway 4½ miles long at Banbury for the Oxfordshire Ironstone Co., and was now wishing to start on his own) or to employ a consulting engineer such as himself. His fee, for inspecting the plans and subsequent fortnightly visits to see the works in progress, would be 2 per cent on the cost of the works (i.e. about £220) plus travelling expenses. Shaw was appointed. He sent a telegram to Arnold, at Sandbags Eusroad London, on Tuesday 24th June, 'Will see you London Thursday can visit Leighton Buzzard that afternoon please have plans ready for inspection. Shaw'. Lamb was informed of his appointment on 26th June. The opportunity was taken to tell Lamb of Shaw's suggestion that Lamb should guarantee the stability of the works for six months after completion. To this end it was proposed to withhold 5 per cent of the price for six months, when it would be paid with accrued interest assuming all was still in order. In particular it would test the ability of the Clipstone Brook bridge to withstand floods 'which we are rather afraid of'.

On 7th July Shaw wrote to Arnold and Lamb pointing out that the drawing of the Clipstone Brook bridge showed a double track with rails only 18 inches apart, totally insufficient for two trains to pass. He stipulated 3 ft 6 in. between the rails and brick pillars, and told Lamb to get the clearance between two sets of wagons from Arnold. Arnold wrote on 12th July to Shaw about loops in fields 448 and 457 (other loops were inferred). (Field 448 was combined with field 283 before 1926 and was immediately east of Page's Park. This was Red Barn Loop. Field 457 became the site for Billington Road yard and Pratt's Pit.) By now, construction seems to have begun.

The Company Secretary/Solicitor R.G. Walton wrote to the proposed shareholders of the Proposed Light Railway Company on 9th July. At a previous meeting (probably referring to the one on 3rd June) the sand merchants had been prepared to guarantee traffic of 70,000 cubic yards i.e. wagon loads per year for 10 years. It was now necessary to revise this to:

53,846 waggons [*sic*] per annum guaranteed for 10 years and the balance of 16,154 waggons was guaranteed 'only during the lifetime of the George Garside' [he died in 1926]. It must also be understood that if in any year the guaranteed quantity is exceeded, the amount of such excess will be carried forward to the credit of the Sand Merchants for the ensuring year'.

Walton's letter finished by giving the proposed shareholders the option of reconsidering their share allotment but 'I must say that some of the largest Shareholders have already said that the alteration does not in any way affect their decision'.

Except for an undated item which will be considered later this marks the end of the surviving correspondence, excluding that relating to locomotives (q.v.).

The company was 'incorporated the 26th day of July 1919', with its Registered Office at 20 Bridge Street, Leighton Buzzard. The objects for which the company was established were to construct, purchase, or lease light railways in Bedfordshire and Buckinghamshire and to fit out, maintain and operate the same with 'horse, or by electricity, steam or other mechanical power'. The company could provide road services for passenger and freight, could generate and supply electricity for any purpose, and could carry on practically any business except that of sand merchants.

The company was a 'Private Company' within the meaning of the Companies Act 1908 and 1913. This meant that it:

a)   restricted the right to transfer its shares
b)   limited the number of shareholders to 50
c)   prohibited any invitation to the public to subscribe for its shares and debentures.

In return for these restrictions the company gained a number of privileges, including the right to commence trading as soon as it was incorporated and (until the 1967 Companies Act) was freed from the necessity of sending a copy of each year's accounts to the Registrar of Companies, Bush House, London. The company, while having the advantages of limited liability, was thus enabled to maintain considerable privacy in its affairs. The LBLR has in fact deposited very few records with the Registrar.

Lamb and Phillips constructed the railway to the detailed scheme prepared by H.F. Firth (of Lamb and Phillips?). They appear to have skimped the work by laying 28lb. rail, and by springing rails for curves instead of bending them properly. Under traffic the rails straightened and had to be relaid.

The formal opening of the LBLR took place on the afternoon of Thursday 20th November, 1919, although the branch lines to the pits remained to be completed. The ceremony began with lunch at the Swan Hotel, at '1 o'clock sharp'. The meal, costing 3s. 6d. per head for about 20 people, included soup, joint (beef or mutton) and cheese. Other requirements included six bottles of Scotch whisky, 12 siphons of soda, and sufficient beer (sale or return) supplied by Mr Higgs of Bridge Street. It was attended by the Directors, some shareholders, and others including representatives of the sand merchants' customers (John Brown, steel, Sheffield; Chance, glass, Smethwick; Contractors of Birmingham Corporation, water) as well as Mr M.G. Townley MP, 'who had left the Commons in spite of a three line Government Whip because he felt his duty was with his constituents, especially in regard to such an undertaking'. Subsequently Mr Townley 'baptized the two locomotives in traditional manner' by cracking a bottle of wine on one of them.

The guests then traversed the line in a specially constructed temporary train, made of forms fastened to four trolleys, and drawn by a petrol engine (probably the contractor's) the steam locomotives being too smoky for passenger traffic. On some parts of the line a good speed was obtained - probably nearer 20 mph than 10, and some of the inexperienced passengers reflected uneasily of the 2 ft gauge beneath them. But all passed off well and when the wind made sport of hats the train obligingly stopped to permit their being recovered. Despite the absence of springs on the temporary train there was little jolting, a fact which testified eloquently to the solidity of the line . . . . At the far end of the line the party gathered in a building for refreshments and speeches of congratulations were made. Mr Townley said he had been approached by Mr Arnold and others as to their desirability of building a light railway and it reflected great credit . . . . that the work had been executed so quickly . . . . Mr Marks, Clerk of the Bedfordshire County Council promised to help and carried it out to the letter. The line was the first light railway constructed since the war. It would have been to the country's advantage if it had been built five years earlier . . . . Some of the land passed through looked like market gardening land, which would benefit, and the railway could bring in manure. He congratulated the directors, and the LNWR for bringing in material so promptly. He wished it every success. (*LBO*, 25th November, 1919)

Mr Walton said that there had been no obstruction to their endeavours, they had built 4¼ miles of railway on wayleaves 'without having to purchase a single piece of land or invoking the assistance of the Light Railway Commissioners.' Telegrams were read from the Refractories Association, 'who . . . . congratulate the directors on the object lesson they are giving the Ministry of Supply' and Mr Syme of the Ministry of Munitions who telegraphed good wishes and apologised for not attending. The meeting finished with a vote of thanks for Mr Townley proposed by Mr J.H. Green.

The opening train was an articulated unit, with three sections if the local paper accurately reported 'four trolleys'. The trolleys were probably skip frames. The carriage floor was timber about three inches thick attached to a cross timber of similar thickness at each end. The cross timbers rested on the trolleys, over the axles on the intermediate trolleys and probably centrally on the end ones, and were probably pivoted to a central longitudinal frame member. Each section had seating for about 16 people, back to back on a longitudinal seat. The official party thus numbered 40 to 50 people. A central pole at each end of each section supported the roof, a wooden framework covered with a striped awning. It must have made an impressive sight, and no wonder the wind 'made sport of hats'.

The railway, including the branch lines to the quarries, was soon completed. The majority of the sand carters were discharged as redundant on Saturday, 29th November and rail traffic presumably began the following Monday 1st December, 1919. It may be coincidence, or a reflection of the date of opening for traffic, that the LBLR financial year ended on 2nd December. Advertisements were published in the issues of 25th November and 2nd December of the *Leighton Buzzard Observer*, for an 'Important Sale of Contractors and Hauliers Stock', the Sale being due 'to completion of the new Light Railway'. The Sale, conducted by Cumberland & Hopkins, was to take place on Wednesday, 3rd December at Arnold's Union Street depot at 11 am.

This sale was on behalf of Messrs Joseph Arnold & Sons and George Garside. Included were: 36 horses, 'all out of hard work', 40 constructors carts, three large sand washers by 'Baxter' of Leeds (from Arnold's Union Street depot?) 'about 500 yards Jubilee track 20 in.', (from Garside's Billington Road quarry?) followed by '12 tip wagons, points and crossings' presumably from internal sand pit lanes now linked to the LBLR, or from old workings at Billington Road or Union Street, six contractors tip wagons 3 ft gauge, probably from Miletree Road sand pit, and a 3 ton Coles steam crane with steel gib [*sic*] and ¾ yd grab (by Stothert Pitt), probably from a Billington Road quarry.

One curious feature is the lack of any mention of the LBLR in the Ministry of Transport (previously Board of Trade) records. A normal light railway owned its trackbed and the LB&HR had compulsory purchase powers, but the LBLR was laid entirely on rented land for which wayleaves were paid. Furthermore, if a light railway wishes to alter its name, route or gauge it needs a Ministry Order to grant the necessary authority. No such amending order was made for the LB&HR and Mr Walton (see above) said they did not apply for any Light Railway Order. It would appear therefore that, despite its title, the LBLR was not a proper light railway (unfortunately there is no legal definition of the term) but was in the same category as other industrial railways such as the lengthy lines in the Midlands ironstone field. There was however, the difference that the LBLR itself did not extend into the actual quarries; it was purely a carrier.

An undated document entitled 'Leighton Buzzard Light Railway Notes for Attention' survives and makes interesting reading. Although undated it seems to refer to the situation soon after the opening and may have been written on 5th January, 1920, apparently from the Secretary (Walton) to Arnold, who has added comments where appropriate. The items mentioned include:

a) Incomplete fencing at Page's Park and other places.
b) Insurance against Fire and Third Party Risks - Liverpool Legal General contacted.
c) Water supply to a connection in Vandyke Road £80. Urban Council would like an offer towards the expense as our supply and would not pay interest on outlay - Cannot agree to this, offer £30 contribution.
d) Ejectment orders for tenants at Billington Cottage and Billington Crossing - in Merry's hands, worry him to get permission.
e) Mac to be obtained for men working trains on Light Railway - at Leighton now.
f) Notices as to Trespassing on line and harming the Public at road crossings - in order.
g) Checkrails on main line for curves - watch and put in as necessary.
h) Petrol engine to be obtained for shunting at Billington terminus - bought for £265 to be put into running order by Mr Bland (Bland's garage still trades in Billington Road).
i) Are the boys responsible for Cutting and Training Hedges also cleaning out ditches - landlords state the Railway Co. must do this work - not sure, but where necessary do, to prevent a recurrence of the last flooding.

So the new light railway entered on its working life.

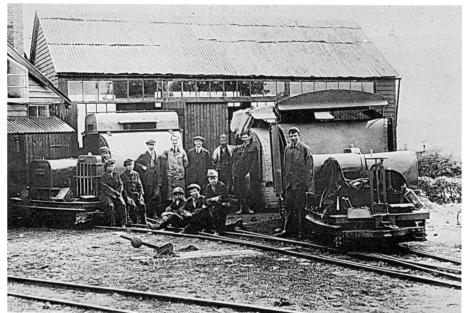

LBLR Billington Road Locomotive Sheds *c.* 1924, with two WDLR 20 hp (WDLR 2478 on the left), and three WDLR 40 hp locomotives - probably the entire motive power.   *Author's Collection*

Chapter Seven

Early Years

The LBLR began operations with two WD surplus Hudswell, Clarke 0-6-0WT, augmented at a very early date by a small petrol locomotive for shunting at Billington Road. Some notes, undated but apparently relating to mid-1920, show:

No 1 Steam Engine	4 trips to Double Arches @ 26 wagons (20 Arnold, 6 Garside). plus 1 trip to Chamberlain's Barn @ 25 wagons max.
No 2 Steam Engine	5 trips to Shenley Hill @ 26 wagons (14 Arnold, 12 Garside).
Lt Rly Petrol Engine	6 trips to Chamberlain's Barn @ 6 wagons
Joseph Arnold Petrol Engine	6 trips to Chamberlain's Barn @ 5 wagons

In the 13-week period 20th March to 10th June a total of 1,271 wagons were handled. The guaranteed daily traffic appears to have been a nominal 200 Arnold and 54 Garside wagons, which in reality was 241 wagons from Arnold (including 30 hauled by their own locomotive) and 84 from Garside. However, it seems that often the required number of wagons were not available so shorter trains then had to be run.

The first recorded accident occurred on Tuesday, 14th September, 1920 when a motor cyclist hit a train on Hockliffe Road (Leedon) level crossing (*see Chapter 10*).

Extensions of the water main, to the boundary of the town in Billington Road (costing £116), and by 235 yards in Vandyke Road (costing £214), were reported in the *Leighton Buzzard Observer* of 31st May, 1921. It was reported that half the cost had been paid by the Light Railway Company. This was presumably for locomotive use, to replace the well shown on an early photograph. Possibly locomotives also took water from the Clipstone Brook. However, reliable water supplies for locomotive use were soon to be unnecessary as the steam locomotives were sold on 16th August, 1921, having been replaced by 40 hp petrol locomotives (by the evidence of coal bills) from around March 1921. Thereafter, until the Preservation Society took control in the late 1960s, internal combustion reigned supreme. This undoubtedly contributed to a lack of interest in the line by many railway enthusiasts.

The *Leighton Buzzard Observer* used to publish reports of the LBLR Annual Meeting, and it is from these reports that the figures below have been obtained.

	1920 £	1921 £	1922 £	1923 £	1929 £	1934 £	1961 £
Traffic receipts	6042	6097	5326	6741	7985	9027	5434
(wagons)	(72617)	(73072)					
Rents/wayleaves	500	629	629	605	605	605	479
Fuel & Oil	1145	1186	914	997	1107	1216	-
Water	10	9	4	3	-	-	-
Wages	1237	1533	813	864	1513	1384	1786
Dividend		7½%			10%	12½%	10%

These figures shows the railway served the quarries well from its opening. In 1934 an additional locomotive had been bought 'they were so busy', and in that year the first Chairman, T. Bromham Bassett, died.

During the 1920s and 1930s several professional bodies visited the LBLR and the quarries. Reports of these visits appeared in the local press. Trade magazines also

A loaded sand train at Billington Road, hauled by WDLR 3104 (later LBLR No. 2). Note the lifting eyes on the second skip *c*. 1924. *Author's Collection*

An LBLR 40 hp locomotive on a *loaded* train heading north from Stanbridge Road with the level crossing in the distance. The most likely explanation is that the locomotive ran round its train at the nearby loop so it could be posed with the water tower (now demolished) behind it. Note the 2-link coupling and the doors open for ventilation, probably 1930s. *Author's Collection*

carried articles about the Leighton Buzzard sand trade.

The Institution of Sanitary Engineers made a visit to Leighton Buzzard on Saturday 4th September, 1921. After lunch at the Corn Exchange, about 60 members 'visited the sandpits of Messrs Arnold & Sons and G. Garside and traversed the Light Railway from end to end. The use of petrol locomotives was the most recent development, but the growing complexity of the trade, with its grading and washing, was noted' (*LBO* 6th September, 1921). The party also visited the Water Tower, Concrete Co., Bedfordshire Tile Co. and then had tea at the Corn Exchange.

The Institute of Quarrying made a similar visit on Wednesday 17th July, 1928. They met at 11 am at the Swan, Leighton Buzzard, and the itinerary was as follows:

Leighton Buzzard Sand Co	-	from loading gantry
Billington Road	-	Arnolds Sand Quarry
		Grovebury Sand-Lime Brick Works
		Garsides Washery
		Arnolds Washery
		Garsides Rackly Hill (if time)
Double Arches	-	Arnold & Garside
Lunch 1-1:30		
Shenley Hill	-	Arnold & Garside
	-	Vandyke Sand-Lime Brick
	-	Chances
	-	Arnold Chamberlain's Barn
Tea 4:30-5		

Even with official permission to visit all these sites they must have had quite a strenuous day!

Magazine articles about the Leighton Buzzard sand trade, and particularly Arnold's quarries, were published in:

Gardening World	3rd October, 1896
Quarry Managers' Journal	5th November, 1926 and August 1935
New Era Illustrated	June 1930
Cement Lime & Gravel	May 1934

In more recent times the LBLR featured in publicity for Motor Rail locomotives (*see* Chapter 9). The *Daily Mirror* of 29th October, 1969 had a short feature, with a photograph of F. & J. Arnold who had 'just sold sand to the Arabs'. This comprised various shipments of over 650 tons to water filtration plants at Tripoli and Tobruk.

Around 1964 the TV series 'Emergency - Ward 10' included an episode in which Arnold's locomotive No. 3 collided with a motor cyclist at Eastern Way level crossing, necessitating hospital treatment. Another Arnold's locomotive and its driver starred in the Mars 'Quarryman' TV commercial in November 1967.

The LBLR 1950-built locomotive shed on 22nd October, 1973, when it was Arnold's locomotive repair shop. The wooden hut housed the fuel pumps, the hatches being labelled P and T. The later diesel fuel tank is alongside. MR 7163 fresh from overhaul so carrying no number stands outside the shed, while the derelicts siding is occupied by No. 30 MR 8695 and an underframe. Note that all the track has been lifted except for a short length in the shed area.   *Author*

LBLR Billington Road Depot, looking south 10th April, 1961. Arnold No. 43 (LBLR 11) MR 10409 slowly lowers a loaded train down the bank into the yard, preceded by Arnold's Billington Road shunting locomotive in case of breakaways. A light engine stands on Garside's branch. From right to left the buildings are: the original LBLR steam locomotive shed (with extension), Arnold's corrugated iron locomotive repair shop, the LBLR 1950-built locomotive shed, Arnold's wagon repairs   *Author*

Chapter Eight

The Description of the Route

(*Note*: This description is written in the past tense, because the LBLR no longer exists. However, much of the route remains in use by the LBNGRPS, and modern features are described where appropriate. The quarry companies' installations are described later (see Chapter 13).)

The Leighton Buzzard Light Railway began (or, bearing in mind the main traffic flow, ended) at Billington Road (SP929240), about ¾ mile south-east of the centre of Leighton Buzzard, and a few yards north of the LNWR Dunstable branch level crossing. This double track branch was singled in 1965 and closed on 1st June, 1969.

The Light Railway began at the southernmost, and last survivor, of the three ungated level crossings over Billington Road. The LBLR was responsible for all three level crossings, but not for any track west of the road, which all belonged to Arnold or Garside.

The first level crossing served a gantry for loading standard gauge wagons in Arnold's Billington Siding. It also gave access to a former glass bottle works (later a sand lime brickworks). Three tracks crossed the road (two in 1926, and from mid-1968 until closure). Immediately east of the road the centre track divided. One branch joined the southernmost track and descended into Arnold's Pratt's Pit. The other branch, and northernmost crossing track, turned north, dividing to form three loops each about 100 yards long. Long sidings made trailing connections with each of the outer loops. The eastern loop and siding were latterly out of use owing to the proximity of Pratt's Pit. The other siding, between the loops and the road, gave access to the modern LBLR locomotive shed and repair shops.

This shed was built in 1949/50. Constructed out of bricks with steel framing, it measured 40 ft by 110 ft, the last 25 ft being the workshop. While there were three pairs of doors in the southern end, only two tracks were laid. The shed could hold about 20 locomotives. At its inner end was a small but well equipped workshop. Beside the approach track to the shed was the locomotive refuelling point. A small wooden shed covered the pumps. Hatches in the side wall were labelled 'TVO' and 'Petrol'. Later a rectangular tank for diesel was mounted on brick pillars alongside the hut.

When the LBLR ceased to provide motive power in 1958 this shed was taken over by Arnold to house main line locomotives, Billington Road shunters, and any spare quarry locomotives. All Arnold's locomotives were then repaired here. Previously Arnold's locomotives had been kept and repaired in a corrugated iron shed immediately north of the 1948 building, by the end of the loops. This was probably the structure built in August 1923 for £15 and extended the following June for £11 13s. 6d. (£11.67½).

After the closure of the main line in 1969 the tracks in the yard were lifted, but a single siding was left outside the shed. This was used to dump withdrawn and cannabilised locomotives. The workshop staff in 1977 was three men: one full time, one part time, and an apprentice.

North of the loops the single track began to climb and the branch to Garside's depot made a trailing connection. The gradient steepened to a maximum of 1 in 20 and the line turned sharply to the east to run beside Page's Park. At the end of the curve and top of the gradient a steeply graded branch (about 1 in 20) made a trailing connection. Originally this had served Garside's premises but served Arnold's washing plant instead once a new connection had been laid into Garside's in mid-1920.

In the angle between the main line and Arnold's branch stood the original LBLR

Seconds after taking the previous photograph there was a derailment. However, everything was soon back on the rails. Note the levers used to right the wagons, and the three LBLR locomotive sheds in the background. *Author*

LBLR Page's Park: Arnold No. 42 (LBLR 14) arriving. Note the painted out LBLR identification symbol (X) on the side of the cab, and the large wheels on Arnold's main line wagons. This is now the site of Page's Park station, 20th September, 1961. *Author*

A loaded train enters Page's Park loops, hauled by one of the modern 6 ton MR diesel locomotives, probably 10272 (LBLR 10). Note the check rail on the curve. Probably early 1950s.

Author's Collection

LBLR: The footbridge connecting RAF Stanbridge with the married quarters, 2nd January, 1969.
Author

Leighton Buzzard Concrete Works siding, with Arnold No. 43 collecting three empties to add to the train on the main line, 10th April, 1961.
Author

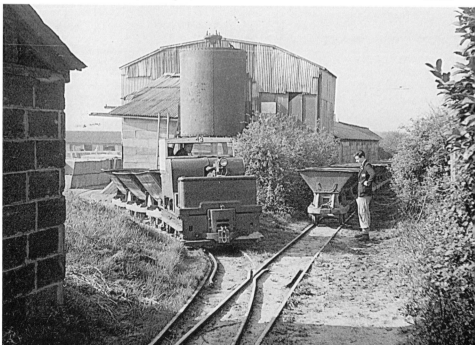

Arnold No. 42 (LBLR 14) MR 7710 crossing Stanbridge Road with empties whilst the driver's mate holds up the traffic with a red flag. Note the red hurricane lamp hanging from the handrail for use when visibility is poor, 10th April, 1961.   *Author*

Marley Tiles Loop, with the tile works on both sides of the line. Arnold No. 43 has left its train in the loop (note the sprag through the wheels of the first wagon) and is propelling a load of sand to the nearby concrete works, 10th April, 1961.   *Author*

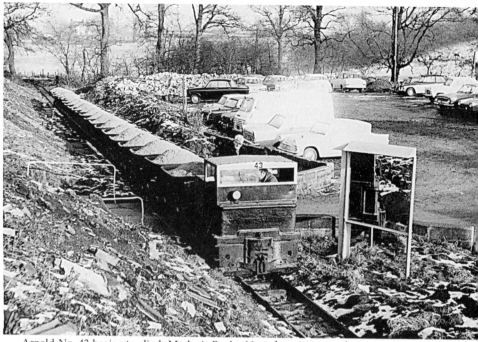

Arnold No. 43 begins to climb Marley's Bank. Note the mirrors so that road users could see approaching trains, and the blind curve at the foot of the bank, scene of a collision in 1962 (*see text*), 2nd January, 1969.   *Author*

Multilingual sign at the level crossing in Marley Tiles works. The languages are: English, German, Serbo-Croat and Polish.   *Author*

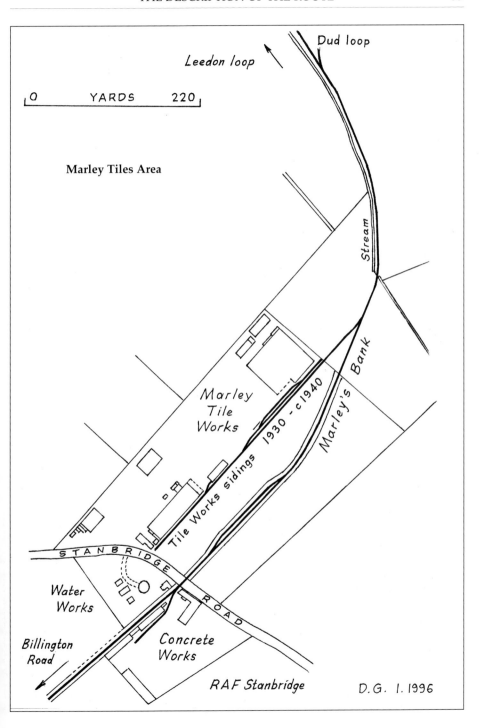

Dud loop

Leedon loop

0   YARDS   220

Marley Tiles Area

Stream

Marley
Tile
Works

Tile Works sidings 1930 - c1940

Marley's Bank

STANBRIDGE

Water
Works

ROAD

Billington
Road

Concrete
Works

RAF Stanbridge

D.G. 1. 1996

The result of a double breakaway to a Garside's train on Marley's Bank on 9th January, 1962 (*see text*). *P.R.Arnold*

Leedon loop and level crossing. LBLR No. 2 is in the loop with a loaded train and is waiting to be assisted up Marley's Bank by the modern 6 ton diesel (LBLR No. 10 or 11). A 20 hp locomotive stands in the loop on a rake of empties, 8th April, 1954. *G.H. Starmer*

locomotive sheds. Disused since the construction of the new shed in 1950 they were not pulled down until about 1966. The sheds were wood with corrugated iron roofs. Their concrete bases were still visible in the undergrowth in 1988.

The one nearest the railway, originally measuring 22 ft by 14 ft, was the original shed. It had a single track, off centre, which extended out of the far end. It is curious that a shed was built that was too short (by some 8 ft) to hold both locomotives! Possibly it was available and cheap. The shortness of this shed may also be the reason why the two steam locomotives faced in different directions, and why the shed had no smoke vents. If they were always stabled back to back the open sided cabs would have been protected and the chimneys would have been outside. There was a well beside the track just outside the shed which may have been the one marked on the 1901 OS map near a couple of buildings in field 457. An extension 11 ft long was later built on the approach track and doors fitted.

The centre shed measured 18 ft 6 in. by 12 ft, and was soon extended by 2 ft. Unlike the first shed it had windows on each side and at the ends. Possibly it was built for the first 20 hp shunting locomotive. The largest shed measured 36 ft by 13 ft, with three roads. There were windows above the doors and in the back. A pit was provided on the central road. This shed could hold three 40 hp locomotives and the central one two 20 hp ones after the extension was built, so this was probably the initial petrol fleet. After the steam locomotives had been sold two, later three, 40 hp locomotives could be kept in the original shed.

Just beyond Arnold's junction a lifting barrier was erected in the early 1960s. Made from a length of rail and pivoted about 18 in. above ground level, it could be padlocked horizontal and was to prevent children pushing wagons out of Page's Park loops. On level ground beside the park was a loop about 100 yards long (like all the others on the line), on the left (northern) side. This loop now serves the platform at Page's Park station. The platform is 90 ft long, made of broken stone faced with concrete blocks. Following complaints that Garside's trains waited here excessively long times, blocking the line, a second similar loop was laid on the right hand side of the line some time after 1926. In 1967 this southern loop was lifted, and the eastern point used to give access to the Iron Horse Preservation Society's shed and sidings.

The line curved slightly northwards and then ran more or less straight, between hedges at the edge of fields, climbing to a summit at Red Barn loop (660 yards). This loop fell out of use in the 1960s. The line fell at 1 in 60 past a housing estate, the married quarters for RAF Stanbridge. A steel footbridge with approach ramps was built in 1962 at the foot of the bank to link this estate to the main part of the station. In the early 1970s the Preservation Society lowered the track under the footbridge by a foot so that *Doll* could pass. When *Elf* entered service in 1980 its spark arresting chimney was found to be too high, so the footbridge was removed and replaced by a foot crossing. The main line was then lifted by two feet to make an easier, more even gradient. The track then levelled for the 200 yards to the Stanbridge Road level crossing (¾ mile). On the right, immediately before the crossing, was the Leighton Buzzard Concrete Co. Ltd Tower Works whose siding made a trailing connection. This had been laid in 1920 and rail traffic ceased on 10th September, 1968. Most of the siding was laid in bridge rail. Loaded wagons were uncoupled from the main train at the nearby loop (or at Leedon loop if the train was divided for the ascent) and pushed into the works. Opposite the concrete works stood the town's brick water tower.

After the crossing the line began to fall (1 in 80) as it passed through the first Marley Tile Works (opened in 1930, extended in 1935). There was a loop here. Sidings and a loop were laid into the works soon after it opened, but they disappeared around 1940

Arnold No. 42 (LBLR 14) crossing the meadows south of Clipstone Brook on 10th April, 1961. Note the low embankment, bridge (just beyond the last wagon), and bank up to Vandyke Road. This was taken close to the site of the present Appenine Way level crossing. *Author*

Arnold No. 7 MR 3862 a boat framed 20 hp petrol locomotive converted to diesel seen crossing the original Clipstone Brook bridge with a train from Chamberlain's Barn to Billington Road, 10th April, 1961. *Author*

and sand was then delivered by lorry. The sidings joined the LBLR near the foot of Marley's Bank. Up to 140 wagons daily used to be sent here from Double Arches. Beyond the loop the gradient steepened for 220 yards, averaging about 1 in 30 with a maximum of about 1 in 25 near the foot. There was a cutting about three feet deep on the centre section of the bank. Near the foot the line was crossed by a 1950s concrete road linking the two parts of the Marley Tile factory. This replaced older crossings nearby which were then abandoned. There used to be large numbers of foreign workers in Leighton Buzzard so these crossings were protected by notices in four languages (English, German, Serbo-Croat and Polish) reading 'BEWARE OF THE TRAINS. ON NO ACCOUNT IS THE LINE TO BE OBSTRUCTED'. The new crossing also had mirrors beside it to show approaching trains, because the railway was not visible from the road.

At the foot of Marley's Bank the line crossed a small stream (1 mile) and turned sharply with a check-railed curve to run slightly west of north, more or less level beside a hedge. After about 300 yards there was a second small bridge and a very short siding on the right entered by a facing point. This was the 'dud loop', and except when a train was passing the points were kept facing the siding to deflect runaways into the field. Leedon loop followed, crossed by a footpath, and the line reached Hockliffe Road (A4012) at Leedon level crossing (1¼ miles).

Still falling gently and running along the edge of fields, the railway continued northwards, before running across the centre of a field on a low embankment, which curved round to the north-west and brought the line to its major engineering feature, the Swing Swang bridge over the Clipstone Brook (1⅜ miles). This was a single girder of 15 ft span, with brick abutments and iron railings. The present bridge, built in the winter of 1974/75, is concrete faced with red brick and has a span of 26 ft, almost double the original.

This section, from Leedon crossing to the Clipstone Brook, now passes through the centre of a housing estate built in the 1970s. When the developers bought the land they were unaware that it was crossed by the LBLR, and drew up plans without reference to it! When the proposals became known the Preservation Society contacted the Council, and after the position was made clear the three parties concerned entered into negotiations. At first it seemed probable that the railway would have to be moved to a new alignment but eventually it was agreed that it could remain on its original route. However, the level of the new main road through the estate meant that in 1973 the previous low embankment was replaced by a shallow cutting for about six rail lengths either side of the road. The rebuilt section includes an ungated level crossing over Appenine Way, the major thoroughfare of the Planets Estate (so-called because many roads are named after astronomical features, e.g. Saturn Close). The cutting south of Appenine Way (Clipstone Cutting) was badly affected in 1977 by a ruptured land drain which caused the clay to become like jelly before repairs were effected.

A straight climb of about 1 in 50 brought the line up from the Clipstone Brook to the Vandyke Road. The level crossing (1¾ miles) was followed immediately by a long right-hand curve of about 70 ft radius leading into a shorter left-hand curve which brought the railway beside the road, separated from it by a hedge, the position it kept for the remainder of its route to Double Arches. This curve was known as the Co-op loop (the Co-op used to own the land on which the nearby schools are built). Originally there was a loop here, but since World War II this degenerated into a long trailing siding, mostly overgrown. By the siding points the branch to Arnold's Chamberlain's Barn quarries made a facing connection and curved sharply away to the left, running across the bottom of gardens of a 1950s estate.

The track climbed steadily for about 700 yards. Close to the summit was Bryan's loop

Vandyke Road level crossing with a train of Arnold's sand hauled by LBLR No. 2. The line has turned to run beside the road by the time it reaches the fence on the right, 13th April, 1957.
Author

Arnold No. 43 approaching Vandyke Road level crossing, showing the long sharp curve at the Co-op loop. The Chamberlain's Barn branch ran by the nearer hedge in the right background, 10th April, 1961.
Author

LBLR Co-op loop with a 20 hp petrol locomotive on a train for Billington Road while a train from Chamberlain's Barn to Stonehenge waits on the branch. Note the shape of the front handrail, July 1954.
F.H. Eyles

LBLR No. 5 (assumed) (MRTC 507 reconstructed by MR as 3848) passing Abraham's Farm along Vandyke Road, 8th April, 1954.
G.H. Starmer

A train of empties hauled by Garside No. 10 (LBLR 10) about to cross Shenley Hill Road. Abraham's Farm is in the distance, 20th September, 1961.   *P.R. Arnold*

LBLR No. 6 passing the Driroof Tiles works, with Stonehenge brickworks in the background, July 1954.   *F.H. Eyles*

and a permanent way hut (Bryan was one of the permanent way staff). The Preservation Society removed the loop and built a small platform there to mark the spot although no trains stop there. On the opposite side of the road was Abraham's Farm, a former brickworks closed before the LBLR was built. A dip and rise were followed by a descent to Shenley Hill Road level crossing (2⅝ miles). The descent continued for about 200 yards more to Arnold's Nine Acre (or Chances) Quarry and Stonehenge Brickworks(2¾ miles). On the other side of the road was the disused hollow of Garside's quarry. The original loop seems to have been on the quarry siding but later a loop was laid here in the main line where it crossed the forecourt of Stonehenge Brickworks (opened 1935). In the early 1950s the Driroof Tileworks was built between the level crossing and brickworks. The brickworks and tileworks sites were cleared in 1976/77 and Redland built a new tileworks there called Vandyke works. Old quarry stables close to the road at Stonehenge were converted to workshops by the Preservation Society. Many of the Society's locomotives and items of rolling stock are now stored here. In 1983 Stonehenge became the terminus for regular passenger services and a platform with runround loop was built in front of the brickworks.

A long climb through trees followed, with a maximum gradient of about 1 in 27. This section was laid with double track around 1945, but by the mid-1960s the western line had fallen into disuse following the reduction of traffic. The summit was by Mile Tree Farm and then there was a descent to Garside's Munday's Hill Quarry (3¼ miles) which had a loop. The quarry branch used to leave from this loop, but since 1966 it made direct connection with the main line a few yards further on.

The remainder of the route was more or less level. About 300 yards further on there was a triangular junction, laid in 1964 to serve Garside's new screening and drying plant about 200 yards north of the line. After another 100 yards a facing connection was made on the left. This track immediately divided. One line ran parallel to the main line and climbed to reach a wood and steel tipping dock, disused since about 1945. The other line continued straight to a corrugated iron building, formerly Garside's locomotive shed, and later used as workshops for repairing their excavators and other plant. Since 1964 locomotive repairs were done here too.

From the workshop junction a further 100 yards brought the line to Eastern Way level crossing (3½ miles). A few yards beyond the crossing was a pair of points, owned by the LBLR, which marked its boundary. The left-hand branch led directly into the yard of Arnold's Double Arches quarry while the right-hand branch curved, crossed a stream by a sleeper bridge, passed through a hedge and entered the yard of Garside's Double Arches quarry. This stream passes under the road in twin tunnels and so gives Double Arches its name.

The total length of LBLR main line was slightly over 3½ miles. Measurement of the 6 in. OS map gives a length of 6,300 yards (3.58 miles), while a survey my brother and I made in 1961 (with a length of thin rope supposedly 100 ft long) gave a length of 6,408 yards (3.64 miles). The contractors were paid for 8,193⅔ yards [sic!] - a little over 4½miles - but this included loops etc. as well as the Chamberlain's Barn branch. However, a mile total for these is not excessive, bearing in mind that there were seven intermediate loops (100 yards each) plus two more at Billington Road, and the Chamberlain's Barn branch was about 500 yards long. These give about 1,400 yards of extra track. The sign post at the junction of Mile Tree Road and Eastern Way gives the distance to Leighton Buzzard as 2½ miles.

The Chamberlain's Barn branch left the main line near the end of the sharp curve at Vandyke Road level crossing. It bore away sharply to the left, to run north-westwards at right angles to the road up the edge of a field. The 1926 map shows a loop on the

A loaded train passes empties hauled by Arnold No. 42 on the double track section, with Miletree Road on the right, and Kingsway Farm in the distance, 10th April, 1961.   *Author*

Garside No. 10 (LBLR 10) leaving Double Arches. Note the signal in the distance. The buildings on the left are Garside's repair shops (formerly Double Arches locomotive sheds). Beside them is the embankment to a disused lorry loading gantry. The large building in the distance is on Arnold's Double Arches site, 4th January, 1961.   *Author*

branch close to the junction, in addition to the loop on the main line. The loop on the branch was disused by 1946 but the points were not removed until the 1950s. In the late 1950s a housing estate was built in the fields west of the track, so the trains ran along the bottom of the gardens. Although disused from 1971 this track was still *in situ* in October 1973, but by then it was very overgrown. Originally the branch ran straight for about 600 yards close to Broomhills Farm before curving left into the pit which was being worked southwards. The LBLR boundary was probably where the branch entered the quarry, at a point about 500 yards from the main line junction. By 1937 the straight run had been cut to 250 yards. The line then bore sharply left to avoid the face which it skirted at a distance before running into the old part of the quarry nearer the road some 400 yards further on. Here there were screens and, close to the entrance, a loop by a tipping dock. Tracks led from the screens to the face, and to tips in the old parts of the pit. A locomotive shed stood on the edge of the quarry yard.

By 1947 the face had advanced southwards and had engulfed the previous line. The final access to Chamberlain's Barn quarry was then via a reversing point about 230 yards from the main line junction. From that time the LBLR finished at the last rail joint before the points, where the line ran through the hedge into Arnold's property. The approach track from the LBLR used the straight side of the reversing point and the line to the quarry yard was entered by a very sharp curve of about 12 yards radius. The line then ran just inside the quarry boundary to the yard. The approach track continued beyond the reversing point beside the boundary hedge. Originally it had been used to remove overburden, and in 1963 it became the start of the branch to New Trees quarry (q.v.).

The track of LBLR was originally laid with 28lb. per yard rails although 30lb. material had been agreed. The sleepers were cut locally and were of poor quality. The line was ballasted with ash. The finished track, 8,193⅔ yards, cost £12,030 13s. 8d. (£12,030.68). The Final Certificate was issued by the Consulting Engineers on 10th March, 1920. Latterly 30lb. rail was used, spiked to halves of ex-BR sleepers at 2 ft 6 in. to 3 ft centres. Ballast became hidden under sand droppings and grass. However, sections relaid by the Preservation Society would do credit to any railway and are well ballasted with broken stone.

At first six men were employed on track maintenance. Around 1950 the number fell to four, then to two by 1960, to one in 1966 and in 1968 to none. Repairs were then carried out by other staff as necessary, or when hard frosts stopped work in the pits. After 1958 quarry company staff had to report any derailments to the LBLR so that the permanent way gang could be informed. In later years the condition of the track deteriorated and left much to be desired in some places. Some of the old LBLR track still remained in 1990 on the section between Stonehenge and Munday's Hill used for rolling stock storage by the Preservation Society. The section had examples of the improvisation used when a replacement rail was slightly too short (by up to a couple of inches) for the space available. The latter-day LBLR solution was to lay the short rail and bridge the gap with a suitable offcut, held in place by the fishplates which were bolted to the two full rails! All locomotives carried a pair of 'V' shaped rerailing ramps which were sufficient for minor derailments.

When the Preservation Society did track repairs at Vandyke Road level crossing they found no less than three layers of track; seemingly it had been easier to lay new track over the top of the old and adjust the road/rail levels accordingly! So much for the elaborate provisions of the level crossings agreement! In 1982 the Society obtained grants to relay the whole line with new 40lb. rail.

In the quarries 20lb. rail was the rule, laid on steel or wood sleepers at about 3 ft 6 in. centres. The old horse- and hand-worked lines used lighter rail, about 10lb. per yard. A length of 50 cm (1 ft 7½ in.) gauge track survived in 1969, with the rails 4 metres (16 ft 6 in.) long and spaced by five steel sleepers.

Garside No. 10 (LBLR 10) about to cross Eastern Way. Garside's old drying plant and a lorry gantry (with shelter) are on the right. The junctions for Arnold's branch, and the LBLR boundary, are by the third wagon. Note the signal, 4th January, 1961.   *Author*

Chapter Nine

Light Railway Locomotives

Some correspondence between Joseph Arnold (at 124 Tottenham Court Road, London W1) and Robert Hudson of Leeds relating to the purchase of the initial locomotives has survived. An undated memo and the report of the Council AGM in April 1919 suggest that horse operation may have been considered but 'Mr Lamb was strongly in favour of locomotives.'

Arnold wrote to Hudson enquiring about locomotives on 8th May, 1919, at the time when Lamb was making the survey. Hudson replied on 9th May, offering three locomotives of type 'Poutagan', 600 mm gauge, at £1,225 each FOR Leeds (normal price £1,400). Arnold was interested, and asked Hudson to reserve two on 10th May. They had been delivered to the War Office and Hudson was taking them back again. Hudson replied on 12th May that they would do their best to hold two locomotives, but there was no guarantee as a considerable number of people were interested.

A second letter from Hudson on 13th May gave Arnold a potted history of the type. It had been introduced in 1914 and 77 had been built solely for the War Office (for use on forward railways in France and elsewhere, and at other military installations); they had not been allowed to supply private customers. A 1930 built example survives in preservation, *Bronllwyd* at Bressingham Hall, Diss, Norfolk.

Lamb & Co. seem to have made their own enquiries to Hudson, since (as already mentioned in Chapter 6) their letter of 14th May to Arnold suggested their contract should include the supply of 'two 6-wheeled locomotives at cost price viz £1,225 each FOR Leeds'. However, Arnold seems to have preferred to negotiate with Hudson direct.

Arnold's friend Fred Syme went to see the locomotives at Robert Hudson, a firm 'which I know very well', probably through his work for the Ministry of Munitions. He reported on 20th May that the gauge could be altered to 2 ft by moving the tyres on the wheels. He also suggested Hudson's for the supply of rails, wagons etc. Subsequently Hudson quoted for all permanent way materials at £902 per mile.

Hudson confirmed the price of £1,225 on 26th May, after Arnold and Syme had inspected the locomotives at Hudswell, Clarke's works in Leeds. (Robert Hudson supplied many customers with locomotives, but almost always sub-contracted the locomotives' orders, usually to other firms in the Leeds area.) Arnold was informed on 6th June that the gauge alterations were being put in hand and Hudson hoped that the locomotives would be needed within the three months. Arnold obviously wanted a different livery, but appears to have been unsuccessful as Hudson wrote on 17th June, saying that the low price included the standard War Office livery of dull black, not lined or varnished.

To paint the Engines Red would mean dismantling them, painting, re-erecting and then 'finish' painting. We estimate the cost of this would be at least:

£30-0-0 per Engine

and as we have the gauge of the Engines to alter to 24 in which alone will cost us:

£60-0-0 per Engine

we regret we cannot see our way to change the colour of the paint . . . .

Maker's photographs of 'Ganges' class 0-6-0WT as supplied to the LBLR.*R.N. Redman Collection*

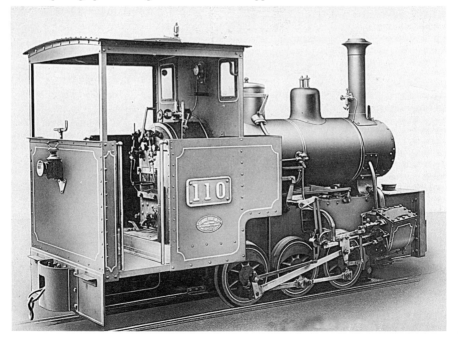

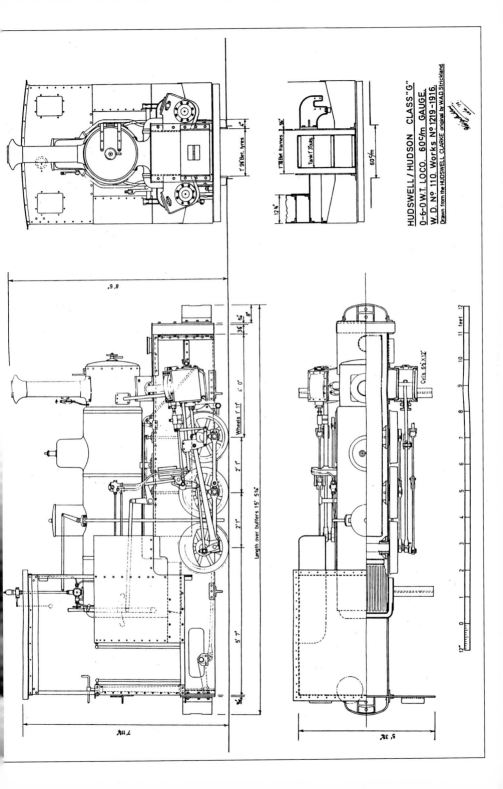

HUDSWELL / HUDSON CLASS "G"
0-6-0 W.T. LOCO. 60 c/m GAUGE.
W. D. Nº 110. Works Nº 1219 - 1916.
Drawn from the HUDSWELL CLARKE original by W.A.D.Strickland

One of the LBLR steam locomotives and the first 20 hp petrol locomotive MR 849 outside Billington Road shed, probably *c.* February 1920. Note the well. Underneath the WDLR numberplate (2570) the white lettering reads 'Messrs Arnold & Sons Billington Sidings Leighton Buzzard'. The bent frames of the petrol locomotive can be seen clearly.   *J. King*

WDLR 40 hp petrol locomotives at Billington Road, probably 1930s. Armoured type on left (LBLR Nos. 3 or 4), protected type on right (LBLR Nos. 1, 2 or 6). Note the raised steel plate covering a ventilation hole in the body at the right-hand end of each locomotive, and the ventilation gap under the body end plating.   *Author's Collection*

According to Hudswell, Clarke records these two 0-6-0 well tank locomotives, works numbers 1377 and 1378, were the last two of an order of 20 placed in June 1918 by Hudson for the War Office. They were numbered 3207 and 3208 in the War Department Light Railway (WDLR) list. Left on their maker's hands at the end of the war, they were regauged from 60 cm to 2 ft and sold to the LBLR for £1,000 each, leaving the works on 31st May, 1919 for delivery to J. Arnold & Sons, Billington Sidings, Leighton Buzzard.

The discrepancies between the two sources of information suggest that Hudson made £225 on each locomotive (less the cost of gauge conversion), that the gauge conversion was done within days of Arnold's visit to Hudswell, Clarke, and the surviving correspondence implies that Hudson would be liable for rent if the locomotives were stored for an excessive period in Hudswell, Clarke's yard after completion.

The locomotives were a standard Hudswell, Clarke design, 'Ganges' or 'G' class, supplied to a number of contractors and others since about 1910. They were of robust and simple construction. The six coupled wheels, 1 ft 11 in. in diameter, were closely spaced to give a rigid wheelbase of 4 ft 2 in. which, with the centre pair flangeless, enabled the locomotive to traverse a curve of only 35 ft radius. Two outside cylinders, 6½ in. diameter by 12 in. stroke, drove the rear coupled wheels. Outside Walschaert's valve gear was fitted. The water tank was between the frames and held 110 gallons. This and the lack of foot plating caused the boiler to appear very high pitched. The boiler barrel, 5 ft 6 in. long, 2 ft 1 in. in diameter, was made of ⅜ in. steel plates and supplied steam at 180 psi. There were forty-five 1¾ in. OD steel tubes giving a heating surface of 109.2 sq. ft. The firebox was of best ⅜ in. copper plate, the crown and sides being one piece, with a heating surface of 18.3 sq. ft and a grate area of 3.75 sq. ft. The dome was fitted with a pair of Pop type safety valves, and a sandbox was also mounted on top of the boiler. Side bunkers held 16 cu. ft of fuel. The 'driver's shelter' was open above the waist except at the front. The locomotives were 15 ft 5½ in. long over buffers, 5 ft 4 in. wide over cab and 8 ft 6 in. high to the top of the chimney. In working order they weighed 6 tons 17 cwt. The tractive effort at 75 per cent boiler pressure was 2,970lb.

At Leighton Buzzard the two black steam locomotives do not appear to have been numbered, although they were referred to as 'No.1' and 'No.2 Steam Engine'. They did not last long, however. Various reasons for their demise were given by old employees. It has been said that they were heavy on repairs, being especially liable to steam pipe fracture and to the abrasive effects of sand in the axle-boxes and valve gear. Then they were said to have been unsteady, often rolling off the track, or spreading the rails on curves. This was attributed to their weight, but the track may not have been that well laid in the first place. Their lack of water capacity was another alleged problem, water having to be taken at Swing Swang bridge as well as at the termini. Lastly, the smuts were said to contaminate the sand. Certainly sparks caused a fire at Leedon, probably the reference in the 1921 accounts to 'Compensation for crop damage £15', despite the provision of spark arresters. Having said this, the type had been popular on the WDLR systems!

The LBLR soon sought alternative main line motive power. An undated note, probably from early 1921, reads:

Engines -	new Hudson	1600)	spares very expensive
	second-hand	900)	
40 hp Petrol	575		
20 hp	400		

Following successful trials, two 40 hp Motor Rail & Tramcar Co. 'Simplex' petrol

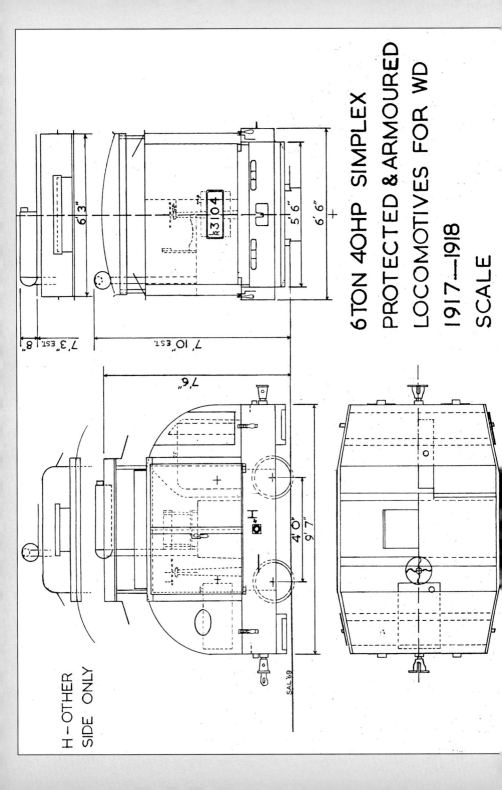

6 TON 40HP SIMPLEX
PROTECTED & ARMOURED
LOCOMOTIVES FOR WD
1917—1918
SCALE

R3104

6'3"
5'6"
6'6"
7'3" EST. 8"
7'10" EST.
7'6"
4'0"
9'7"
H
SAL '69

H – OTHER
SIDE ONLY

32/42 hp Motor Rail Locomotive

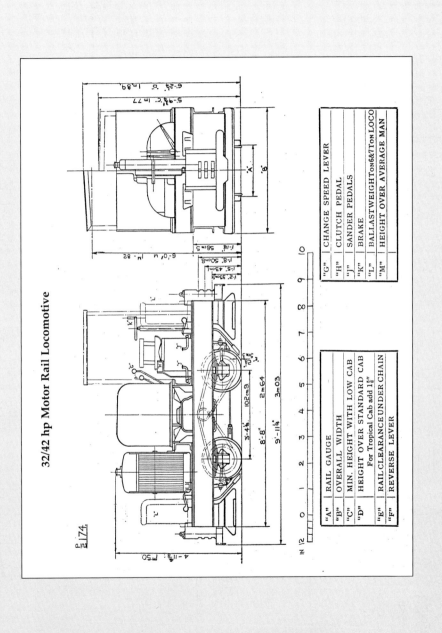

P.174.

"A"	RAIL GAUGE	
"B"	OVERALL WIDTH	
"C"	MIN. HEIGHT WITH LOW CAB	
"D"	HEIGHT OVER STANDARD CAB For Tropical Cab add 1⅛"	
"E"	RAIL CLEARANCE UNDER CHAIN	
"F"	REVERSE LEVER	

"G"	CHANGE SPEED LEVER	
"H"	CLUTCH PEDAL	
"J"	SANDER PEDALS	
"K"	BRAKE	
"L"	BALLAST WEIGHT on 6 & 7 Ton LOCO	
"M"	HEIGHT OVER AVERAGE MAN	

LBLR No. 1 entering the loop at Stonehenge, while another train follows closely behind (a short working to Stonehenge?). The double track section began here, 8th April, 1954. *G.H. Starmer*

LBLR No. 3 waiting in the loop at Stonehenge. Note the limekilns in the background and the former stables (now LBNGR workshops) behind the locomotive, 8th April, 1954. *G.H. Starmer*

locomotives were purchased for £900 in 1921 and the steam locomotives (only two years old) were sold to the dealer R.H. Neal on 16th August, 1921 for £1,150. They were resold to Bryant & Langford Quarries Ltd, Portishead, Somerset where they ended their days. Coal bills from the local firm of Labrum were £75 in December 1921, £45 in April 1921 and were then much smaller, suggesting that the use of steam locomotives was discontinued around March 1921, assuming the bills were paid in arrears for fuel delivered over the previous months. The loss on the sale of the steam locomotives of £1,069 (after allowing for one year depreciation) was written off at £133 10s. pa over the next nine years.

Some general notes about the Motor Rail & Tramcar Co., its subsidiaries, and its post-World War I competitors may be helpful before continuing with the LBLR locomotive history.

The success of the Motor Rail & Tramcar Co. (Motor Rail from 1st May, 1931), undoubtedly lay in the 20 hp 'Simplex' petrol locomotive developed for haulage on the 60 cm gauge War Department Light Railways (WDLR) laid to serve the front line in World War I. As described in W.J.K. Davies' book *Light Railways of the First World War* (David & Charles 1967) haulage on the main supply routes from standard gauge railheads to forward areas was entrusted to steam locomotives, but their weight and exhaust made them unsuitable for use on the battered tracks close to the front. The 20 hp Simplex was found to be ideal and some 675 were constructed. After the war the LBLR and the sand quarry companies bought examples of these handy locomotives. As any steam locomotive was betrayed by its exhaust, more powerful internal combustion locomotives were also developed for main line use. These designs included the 40 hp Simplex used on the LBLR, of which 329 were built.

After the war many ex-WDLR Simplex locomotives were available. Many were bought by Motor Rail, refurbished as necessary and resold. A new works number might or might not be given, and this data might or might not be recorded accurately. Other firms, notably F.C. Hibberd and the Kent Construction Co., also bought Simplex locomotives and spares. Some were resold as they stood, some were rebuilt, some locomotives were built using a mixture of new parts and Simplex spares, some were totally new but to the basic Simplex design. Enthusiasts have had a lot of trouble as a result! Furthermore, Motor Rail had two subsidiary companies, Petrol Locomotive Hirers and, later, Diesel Locomotive Hirers. The hire fleets obtained new locomotives and also bought second-hand ones which were then reconditioned by Motor Rail, sometimes being given a new works number in the process. Some hire locomotives were subsequently sold to their hirers instead of a 'new' locomotive.

Both WDLR Simplex designs continued in commercial production after World War I. Indeed, the basic layout and appearance of the majority of narrow gauge Simplex locomotives built up to the 1960s hardly changed from the 20 hp WDLR design.

The first petrol locomotive used on the LBLR belonged to the contractor, Lamb & Phillips. It was a 2½ ton 20 hp 4 wheel Simplex locomotive, ordered from the Motor Rail & Tramcar Co., Bedford on 1st August, 1919 'for immediate delivery' (i.e. two or three days from stock) to Billington Road. Lettered L&P on each side, it had works number 1856 and cost £585. Its subsequent fate is not recorded, but it seems certain that it remained in the Leighton Buzzard area. Details of 20 hp Simplex petrol locomotives, as used by both Lamb & Phillips and the LBLR, are given in Chapter 15.

The respective accounts show that the LBLR bought a petrol locomotive in January 1920 for £265, and so did Joseph Arnold & Sons. The most likely explanation is that both companies bought a locomotive and that buying two enabled them to gain a discount. I suspect Arnold's friend Fred Syme with his contacts in the Ministry of Munitions may have been behind the deal, or possibly the locomotives were brought from Kent Construction (who sold one to the LBLR in 1924). Arnold's involvement could also account for the lettering 'Messrs Arnold & Sons' on the LBLR locomotive. A second-hand WDLR locomotive obtained direct from surplus sources could well require attention, hence the note already mentioned 'to be put into running order by Mr Bland'.

Lamb & Phillips were required to 'guarantee the stability of the works for six months' which would have expired around the end of May 1920. They could well have kept their own locomotive on site for this task. On 12th June, 1920 they last ordered spares for it. These could have been to put it in good order prior to, or immediately following, sale, possibly to Garside who bought his first locomotive in May 1920.

On the other hand Arnold could well have bought a locomotive for £265 and thus been in a position to suggest the price if the LBLR had decided to make an offer for Lamb & Phillips' locomotive. Again, Bland would be an obvious choice to repair a locomotive already on site. The contractors' spares order in June might have been at the end of a guarantee period, or even an error by Motor Rail.

A photograph taken around 1924 (from the evidence of two 20 hp locomotives) appears to show the entire fleet. Both 20 hp locomotives had WDLR number plates so neither could have been Lamb & Phillips' locomotive, but by then there had been at least one collision so it could have been disposed of. One informant said the contractor's locomotive had definitely gone to the LBLR.

If neither Garside nor the LBLR bought the contractor's locomotive then it could have languished at Leighton Buzzard, to be purchased by Arnold in 1921 (*see Chapter 15*). On balance I think that Garside bought it in May/June 1920. If it later lost its works plate, as did so many quarry locomotives, it could have been one of the unidentified locomotives dumped at Billington Road. The only drawback to this is that I had very little difficulty in assigning running numbers to Garside's known purchases. Possibly it was written off in the 1930s and replaced by a new locomotive.

The first LBLR order for Simplex spares was dated 15th February, 1921 and probably refers to a 20 hp locomotive. Published reports of the LBLR annual meeting show locomotive purchases as follows:

	20 hp	40 hp
1920	1 L&P(?)	
1921		2 @ £900
1923		1 @ £359 3s. 0d. ex Kent Construction*
1924	1 @ £380 (1st April) 2213+	1 @ £400 (2nd May) 3674+ (No 1)
1931 & 1933	one locomotive hired from Petrol Loco. Hirers	
1934		1 @ £260 3848+ (No 5)

Notes: * or £350, on 30th May. Perhaps the difference is carriage.
              + MRTC works number.

The initial two large petrol locomotives were soon followed by two more, and another two were brought in the mid-1930s. In 1946 two 40 hp locomotives were bought for spares but the fleet was obviously in need of replacement, not least to substitute efficient diesel engines for the thirsty petrol ones. Locomotives (power unknown) were also hired from Petrol Locomotive Hirers in June 1931 and October 1933.

The WDLR 40 hp Simplex, used for main line haulage by the LBLR, weighed 6 tons. The steel frame was 6 ft 6 in. wide for about half its length, tapering to 5 ft 6 in. at each end, with deep plates almost to rail level along each side. The tapered frame with deep side plates could have been designed to clear obstructions away from the track. The locomotive was about 1 ft 3 in. wider than the standard WDLR wagons, so where a locomotive could pass the train could also. Length over buffers was 11 ft 1½ in., over headstocks 9 ft 6 in. The locomotive was carried on 1 ft 6 in. diameter wheels, on a 4 ft wheelbase. A sandbox was provided for each wheel.

The driver sat centrally on top of the engine, facing outwards, to see easily in either direction. The seat was hinged to give access to the engine beneath. To his right was a rectangular 20 gallon petrol tank and to his left the radiator, both on the locomotive centre line. The radiator was mounted longitudinally so that it was equally efficient in either direction. Gear and clutch controls were in front of the driver and a vertical pillar handbrake, which acted on all wheels, was between him and the petrol tank. The maker's plate was on the engine cover behind the driver's legs. Thin iron weights were bolted underneath each end of the frame to increase adhesive weight, and they also supported the locomotive in the event of derailment. A step was rivetted on the frame in front of the driver.

The engine was 4J0 type with four water-jacketed cylinders. This comprised two 2J0 cylinder blocks (as used on the 20 hp locomotives) with a common crankcase, thus making many engine spares common to the two types. The engine drove a Dixon Abbott patent gearbox, giving two speeds, 3.4 and 8.2 mph, in each direction, via an inverted cone type clutch situated in a large flywheel. Final drive was by roller chains to each axle. At these speeds the tractive effort was 2,550lb and 1,372lb respectively, giving haulage capacities of 79 and 46 tons on the level. A socket for the starting handle was fitted in the steel frame plate behind the driver.

Running costs could be reduced by substituting paraffin for petrol. This obviously required an additional fuel tank and controls. The engine was started on petrol, and when it was hot the driver would change to paraffin (so-called Tractor Vaporising Oil). The change of fuel caused a 20 per cent loss of power in top gear.

The basic locomotive described above left the driver, and the vulnerable petrol tank and radiator, totally exposed. Accordingly, the WDLR locomotives could be fitted with one of three types of interchangeable body to provide varying degrees of protection.

The open or weather protected type had heavy curved steel plates mounted at each end to protect the petrol tank and radiator. A sheet steel roof attached to four pillars mounted on the end shields kept off the worst of the rain.

The protected type was similar, with the addition of double steel doors on either side to protect the driver, and steel shields on the ends of the cab roof to reduce the size of the window opening. With a reduction in the amount of air openings, extra provision was made for engine cooling air. A hole was cut in the shields at each end, on the right when looking at the locomotive, so the two holes were diagonally opposed. A plate slightly larger than the hole, curved like the shield, was fastened with spacers to cover the hole but about 2 in. away from the original plates.

The armoured type was more like a little tank! It was similar to the protected type, but the cab roof was a flat steel plate, with small sliding steel vizors in the sides and ends of the 'turret' to give the driver some vision. The roof also had a ventilation plate similar to those on the ends.

The LBLR had examples of the protected version (Nos. 2, 5, 6) and armoured version (Nos. 3, 4). Examples of the protected version are preserved at the Imperial War Museum, Duxford, Cambridge and at the Leeds Industrial Museum, Armley Mills, Leeds.

There are no LBLR locomotive records, so the following description of its stock is based mainly on photographs and the observations of enthusiasts since 1945. As most of the early locomotives appear to have been obtained through army surplus dealers,

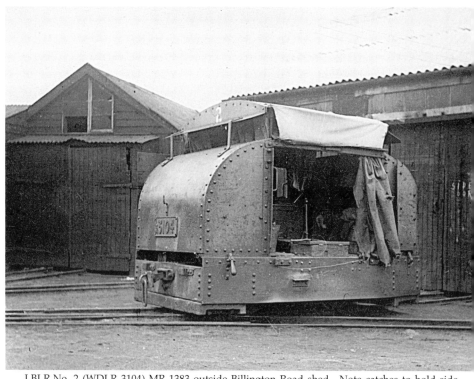

LBLR No. 2 (WDLR 3104) MR 1383 outside Billington Road shed. Note catches to hold side doors open, canvas sheeting to keep out draughts, and (*above*) the short extension to the second shed, 17th November, 1945.   *A.G. Wells*

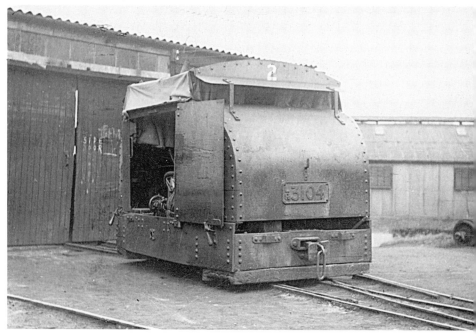

Motor Rail's excellent records have not been able to shed much light. Only three were purchased direct from Motor Rail, one of armoured type, later LBLR No. 1, on 3rd May, 1924. The success of the first big petrol locomotive caused the company to buy more. The evidence of the largest locomotive shed suggests that the original (1921/22) fleet numbered three, and a fourth was bought in 1924. Two more came in the mid-1930s to handle the growing traffic.

About 1923 a LBLR 20 hp locomotive which had been in an accident and bowed its frame was sold to Joseph Arnold & Sons for use in their quarries. This might explain the purchase, from Motor Rail, of a reconditioned 20 hp WDLR locomotive on 12th March, 1924 and the departure of Lamb & Phillips' locomotive if the LBLR had owned it. The 20 hp petrol locomotives, used for shunting and light trains, had a canopy in later years with tarpaulins for extra protection. The driver's mate sat on the bonnet. In the early days the words 'Leighton Buzzard' were painted on the bonnet sides.

The third locomotive purchased from Motor Rail was another 40 hp one, ordered on 31st May, 1934 for £260. It had been reconditioned by them, having worked previously for Manchester Waterworks. This locomotive (No.5) and another obtained around 1935 were bought to cope with the increasing traffic, and were presumably the cause of the shed nearest the main line being extended by 11 ft.

A.G. Wells visited the line in November 1945, when there were six 40 hp locomotives and two 20 hp ones. A year later E.S. Tonks found six 40 hp, four 20 hp and two more 40 hp ones bought from Mowlem, the contractors, for spares. In May 1958 D. Semmens noted six 40 hp and two 20 hp (plus the modern locomotives) so that it would probably appear that the normal post-war stock, and hence probably the pre-war stock too, was six large and two small locomotives. The two extra small ones, observed by Mr Tonks, could have been purchased to help with the heavy post-war traffic until more satisfactory locomotives could be obtained. Mr Semmens discovered that numbers 4 and 6 (old) were the Mowlem's locomotives, number 4 then being used for spares and number 6 scrapped a year before, while the new 6 was also withdrawn as it was prone to derailments. The stock is summarised, as far as it is possible to do so, in the table at the end of the chapter.

The 40 hp locomotives had been converted in the late 1930s to run on TVO (paraffin) after starting on petrol, which cut the fuel costs considerably, although some power was lost too. This enabled the locomotives to remain in use for as long as they did. There were plans for fitting them with diesel engines after World War II, but this was not done, modern diesel locomotives being purchased instead. However, some of the old locomotives were in use to the end of 1958, so completing 40 years of service. On the LBLR the armoured doors were usually kept open for the driver's comfort and safety, and a tarpaulin hung across the opening. After 1945 electric car headlights were fitted; previously railway type oil lamps had been used after dark, hung from a central lamp bracket.

At first the livery was grey, later it was changed to green (grey was the standard WDLR livery, and Motor Rail's standard livery was green). Running numbers do not appear to have been carried at first, and were later allocated in an apparently arbitary order. (Date of purchase of 40 hp locomotives: Nos. 2, 3 or 4, 6 in 1921/22; 1 in 1924, 5 in 1934 and 4 or 3 not known, but probably around 1935). The numbers were painted on the cab ends or bonnet covers. The 20 hp locomotives were numbers 7, 8 and 9. Perhaps the WDLR numbers carried were sufficient identification in the early years and some locomotives retained their old cast WDLR number plates to the end. In addition, each main line locomotive (including the diesel ones purchased in the 1950s) had a distinctive paint scheme to permit identification at a distance. This is described in

Chapter 10. In 1948 the book value of the locomotive stock was £3,015.

The company's first new locomotive since 1919 was a 2½ ton 20/28 hp diesel dispatched from Motor Rail's works on 28th November, 1950. No. 9 cost £742 and was built to a rail-gauge of 600 mm i.e., 1 ft 11⅝ in., not 2 ft. It replaced a similar 2½ ton diesel locomotive which had been hired from Diesel Locomotive Hirers Ltd. The hired locomotive may have been on the LBLR since May 1950 or even since March 1948. The construction of all 2½ ton locomotives is described in Chapter 15. Electric headlights were fitted. However, the original engine gave a great deal of trouble and in February 1951 it was replaced by a new one.

Two more new locomotives followed, both 6 ton 32/42 hp models for main line work. No.10 left Motor Rail's works on 1st May, 1951, and cost £1,325 complete with cab and battery lighting. The second, No.11, was ordered in October 1953, and delivered on 14th January, 1954. The price had risen to £1,454. Three similar locomotives, but only weighing 5 tons, were purchased second-hand from the dealer G.W. Bungey Ltd., Heston, Middlesex in October 1956. They were numbered 12 to 14 and had been built originally for a gravel pit near Wrexham worked by Sir Alfred McAlpine.

These large locomotives had frames of heavy steel channel, well braced. The centrally mounted cold starting solid injection two cylinder Dorman 2DL diesel engine developed 32 hp at 1000 rpm and 42 hp at 1500 rpm. A large diameter single plate clutch transmitted the power to a patent gearbox giving three speeds of 2.9, 4.75 and 7.56 mph at 1000 rpm. The final drive to the wheels was by heavy roller chains. The driver sat sideways at one end and at the other was a central longitudinal radiator. Hinged sheet steel covers protected the engine. Cabs were optional on Motor Rail narrow gauge locomotives but all the modern LBLR ones were fitted with standard cabs. One side was open (closed by a tarpaulin) while the other was closed but fitted with a half height emergency and inspection door. Sliding windows were fitted back and front, and the roof was slightly ridged. Electric headlights were fitted at both ends.

The 5 ton locomotives had a tubular handrail across the front. This was not necessary on the 6 ton version which had cast iron ballast weights 2 ft high, and 3 to 5 inches thick, bolted to either end of the frame. Both models had flat transverse weights under the ends of the frame for ballast and to prevent damage to the gears when the locomotive was derailed, by limiting the distance it could fall. Overall dimensions were 8 ft 8 in. long over frame (9 ft 11¼ in. over buffers) 4 ft 11 in. wide and 6 ft 2½ in. high. The 18 in. diameter wheels had a wheelbase of 3 ft 4½ in. The modern locomotives were painted medium green with the upper half of the cab white.

The LBLR provided facilities for Motor Rail to test prototypes, which were often photographed on the line for catalogue illustrations. A new lever brake was first fitted to a normal locomotive in April 1954, and No. 21500 was tested on the LBLR. It was shown on the cover of a Motor Rail brochure with a train on the gradient up to the old locomotive sheds at Billington Road. The brake had been developed to reduce the length of locomotives, so that they could be lowered down narrow shafts. This problem was particularly acute in South Africa, and the first lever braked locomotive had been built in September 1953. In September 1955 the prototype of a new design of 50 hp locomotives, No 11001, was on trial. A photograph of it on one of Arnold's trains near Leedon was used in the brochure. Production models had a slightly different frame from the first four built. A standard locomotive, No 8725, built in 1940, and owned by the Motor Rail subsidiary Diesel Locomotive Hirers Ltd was experimentally fitted with a 3 cylinder Perkins 3/152 engine, and automatic transmission. It was on trial in December 1961 and January 1962. In June 1973 Motor Rail tested the remotely controlled locomotive 123 U123 to make a video of it in operation.

While some locomotives were scrapped over the years, most survived to 1958 even if not in regular use. When I made my first visit to the line in 1957 only one of the old WDLR 40 hp locomotives was at work. I was shown the others lined up inside the Billington Road shed. However, falling traffic and the organisational changes it caused altered all this. When haulage became the responsibility of the quarry companies as from 1st January, 1959 the modern locomotives were shared between Arnold and Garside (Arnold 1 x 2½ ton, 2 x 5 ton, 1 x 6 ton), (Garside, 1 x 5 ton, 1 x 6 ton) and the rest were hauled out and dumped at the south end of Billington Road yard, where they were scrapped on site by Smith of Watford around February 1959. He had some difficulty with the armour plate!

Withdrawn LBLR locomotives awaiting scrapping at the southern end of Billington Road yard, 3rd January, 1959. No. 4 MR 468, with No. 1 behind and No. 3 on the right.   *Author*

Leighton Buzzard Light Railway Locomotives

Notes: A - armoured
P - protected
n/s - not shown
s/s - scrapped or sold, actual disposal not known
me - manuscript entry in makers records - not always dated and often jotted in random order if undated.
IJ - Ian Jolly comment.

First spares ordered 15/2/1921; first identifiable spares are on 30/4/21 when there is an order for 'Chain double links and 2 pins 40 hp and 20 hp'.

LBLR	Type	Works No.	Ex Works	WDLR	Notes
-	0-6-0WT	HC1377		3207)	Ordered 6/18 by WDLR but not delivered. Regauged to 2 ft gauge before delivery. Ex-works
-	0-6-0WT	HC1378		3208)	31/5/19. Sold to R.H. Neal (dealer) 16/8/21, then to Bryant & Langford Quarries Ltd., Portishead, Somerset.
-	4wP 2.5T	MRTC 849	1918	LR2570	To LBLR 1/20. Later No. 9? s/s.
-	4wP 2.5T	MRTC 1856	n/s		20 hp New Lamb & Phillips Ltd. Ordered 1/8/19. s/s (to Garside 5/20?)
-	4wP 2.5T	MRTC 1757	8/1/18	LR2478	20 hp New to WDLR. To LBLR 1/20? To J. Arnold & Sons Ltd c. 1923 following collision.
-	4wP 2.5T	MRTC 2213	12/3/24	LR2406	20 hp New to WDLR as MRTC 1775. Purchased from French Disposals Board per pooling arrangements with Wm Jones (1/4/22) and reconstructed as MRTC 2213. £380 delivered Billington Road. Replacement for MRTC 1757? s/s.
1	4wP 6T	MRTC 3674	3/5/24	LR2316	40 hp New to WDLR as MRTC 595/1917. Purchased by MRTC ex-French Disposals Board and Rebuilt as 3674. MRTC's records indicate that the locomotive still had its original body - 'flexible upward exhaust, armoured canopy and side doors'. Cost £500. Scrapped by Smith of Watford c. 2/59 at Billington Road.
2	4wP 6TP	MRTC 1383	17/12/18	LR3104	40 hp New to WDLR. On LBLR by c. 1921. Scrapped by Smith of Watford, c. 2/1959 at Billington Road.
3	4wP 6TA	MRTC 478	26/3/18	LR2199)	40 hp New to WDLR. Both of these purchased by LBLR c. 1921? Both scrapped by Smith of
4	4wP 6TA	MRTC 468	26/3/18	LR2189)	Watford c. 2/1959.
5	4wP 6TP	MRTC 3848		LR2228	40 hp New as MRTC 507 to WDLR in 1917. Purchased by MRTC from Manchester Waterworks and reconstructed as MRTC 3848 - ordered by LBLR 31/5/34 - no ex-works date given. Scrapped by Smith of Watford, c. 2/1959 at Billington Road.
6	4wP 6TP	MRTC 1299	29/7/18	LR3020	40 hp New to WDLR. Purchased c. 1921. Scrapped by Smith of Watford, c. 2/1959 at Billington Road.
4?	4wP 6T	MRTC 3675	1/10/24	LR3005	40 hp New to WDLR as MRTC 1284/1918. Subsequently rebuilt as MRTC 3675 and supplied to W.G. Armstrong Whitworth, Tarunga, New Zealand. Fitted with side doors and light canopy. Purchased ex-Mowlem 1946 for spares - Mowlem number 27. Scrapped.
6?	4wP 6TP	MRTC 1283	1918	LR3004	40 hp New to WDLR - delivered to Belgian Government. ex-Mowlem number 26. Cabless. Scrapped.

No.	Type	Works No.	Date
7	4wP 2.5T	MRTC	
8	4wP 2.5T	MRTC	
9	4wP 2.5T	MRTC	
–	4wD 2.5T	MR 8682	19/3/42
9	4wD 2.5T	MR9547 60 cm £483.18.7 Ordered 4/8/50	28/11/50
10	4wP 2.5T	MR(TC)	
10	4wD 6T	MR 10272	27/11/51
11	4wD 6T	MR 10409	14/1/54
12	4wD 5T	MR 7932	29/10/41
13	4wD 5T	MR 7933	29/10/41
14	4wD 5T	MT 7710	9/6/39

20 hp Ex ? in 1930s. Scrapped by Smith of Watford c. 2/1959.

20 hp Ex ? in 1930s. Scrapped 1950.

20/28 hp 2.5 tons 2 ft gauge 4wDM New to Diesel Loco Hirers Ltd. Ordered 16/10/41. Ex-Works 19/3/42 on hire to John McGeoch & Sons. Overhauled for DLH 29/1/42, 12/10/42, 28/4/43, 13/10/43, 3/3/48, 17/5/50. This date ties in with following entry on MR's Spares Order Sheet for LBLR '18/7/50 Put loco 8682 in order'. The loco may well have been on the LBLR for up to two or more years - i.e. since last overhaul (IJ) Maker's delivery note (8/11/50) for MR 9547 says 'Delivery Loco 9547 and collect Loco 8682 on loan'. MR 8682 '1/12/54 Sold to Inns & Co. Ltd. Was on hire and has been purchased' - PLH records.

20/28 hp new to LBLR with steel cab and batteryless electric lighting. Maker's delivery note (8/11/50) for MR 9547 says 'Delivery Loco 9547 and collect Loco 8682 on loan'. To J. Arnold & Sons Ltd 3/12/58, 41. PRESERVED by Ian Jolly, Mold, Clwyd 15/1/79. MR 9547 was ordered on 18/8/50 on the Contract Sheet and on 4/8/50 on Material list. (NOTE this date was AFTER the date MR 8682 was sent on loan - IJ).

20 hp Ex ? Scrapped by Smith of Watford, c. 2/1959 at Billington Road.

2 ft gauge. New to LBLR with cab and batteryless electric lighting. Ordered 2/5/51. To George Garside 3/12/58, 10.

2 ft gauge. New to LBLR with cab and batteryless electric lighting. Ordered 6/10/53. To J. Arnold & Sons Ltd 3/12/58, 43. PRESERVED by LBNGRS c. 4/72.

32/42 hp 5 ton 3 speed 2 ft gauge £688 less 5%. New to Sir Alfred McAlpine & Sons Ltd, Pant Farm Gravel Pits, Gresford, Wrexham, Denbighshire. Ordered 7/10/41. (To Great Stanney Plant Depot, Ellesmere Port?) Seen in yard of G.W. Bungey Ltd 14/10/56. me 22/10 'Now owned by Leighton Buzzard Light Railway as phoned - Mr Gaskin'. To George Garside 3/12/58, 12. To Hopkins England, Woburn Sands 2nd half 1965 - resold to Jonallen, Singapore 8/66 as No. 1.

32/42 hp 5 ton 3 speed 2 ft gauge £688 less 5%. New to Sir Alfred McAlpine & Sons Ltd, Pant Farm Gravel Pits, Greford, Wrexham, Denbighshire. To Great Stanney Plant Depot, Ellesmere Port to Hartington Quarries Ltd, Derbyshire R19. Seen in the yard of G.W. Bungey Ltd 14/10/56. me 22/10/56 owned by LBLR' per phone Mr Gaskin. To J. Arnold & Sons Ltd 3/12/58, 44. PRESERVED by LBNGRS c. 3/75.

32/42 hp 5 ton 2 ft gauge (channel frame) £536 less 5%. New to Sir Robert McAlpine (Midlands) Ltd, Pant Farm Gravel Pits, Gresford, near Wrexham, Denbighshire, Ex-Works 9/6/39. To Great Stanney Plant Depot, Ellesmere Port. Sold to Derbyshire stone Quarries Ltd, Hopton Quarry, Derbyshire me Derbyshire Stone'. R10. Seen in yard of G.W. Bungey Ltd 14/10/56. To LBLR by 10/56. To Joseph Arnold & Sons Ltd 3/12/58, 42. PRESERVED Cadeby Light Railway, Leicestershire 12/5/79.

Chapter Ten

Operations and Accidents

The heavy traffic carried by the LBLR was handled with the minimum of regulation. There was only one signal, and no recognised method of single line working was used. Trains ran as required, and a sharp lookout was kept for traffic in the other direction. The line ran through fairly open country so trains could usually be seen or heard while some distance apart. As speeds were low this was not quite as hazardous as it sounds, but collisions were not unknown. Loops were provided from the outset at approximately half mile intervals. If two trains met between loops the empties had to give way and reverse to the next loop, although if the loaded train had just passed a loop it might reverse. Between Chamberlain's Barn and Stonehenge two loaded trains could meet, in which case the one from Chamberlain's Barn had to give way. Trains kept to the left at loops when they crossed, and the loaded train had the straight track; when not crossing all trains used the straight road.

Until 1958 almost all traffic over the LBLR, except some sand to Stonehenge from both Double Arches and Chamberlain's Barn, was hauled by LBLR locomotives which worked into the various quarry yards and into the washing plants at Billington Road. The 40 hp locomotives were used for main line traffic. The 20 hp ones were used for light loads, collecting wagons, and for hauling sand between quarries. Shunting within the quarry companies' premises (quarries, washing plants, Billington Road gantry) was done by Arnold's and Garside's horses or locomotives. In 1920 some of Arnold's traffic from Chamberlain's Barn was hauled by their own locomotive (*see Chapter 7*) but this does not seem to have lasted long.

The normal load handled by one of the large locomotives was 24 loaded wagons (about 30 tons of sand) while the small locomotives owned by both the LBLR and the quarry companies took 10 or 12 wagons. Six ton bogie open wagons were used to carry sand in bags from Arnold's drying and grading plant at Double Arches to Billington Road. These were taken as 'equal to four' loaded sand wagons and were always marshalled next to the locomotive. A round trip from Billington Road to Double Arches took 1¼ hours minimum.

The railway handled a considerable traffic. During the periods 1934-1940 and 1945-early 1950s Arnold dispatched 300 wagons daily and Garside 100-150, i.e. over 100,000 tons annually. Even in the late 1950s it was carrying 250 tons daily (60,000 tons yearly), and in 1961 three big locomotives (two Arnold and one Garside) were in daily use. However, by mid-1968 rail traffic had dropped drastically, usually only a single train (or occasionally two) was required from Double Arches to Billington Road, and even these became less frequent by the end of the year.

Working was organised in 'trips' of 72 wagons, and normally there were four trips daily. This required a minimum of three 40 hp locomotives (or the equivalent in 20 hp). Unfortunately, a 20 hp petrol locomotive could only manage 10 wagons, so an extra journey was necessary. The small locomotives were also used for light winter work and short runs such as from Chamberlain's Barn to Stonehenge. Locomotives made three or four round trips daily. At its busiest, 4½ trips daily were tried, and also making trips of 80 wagons, but this was unsuccessful due to the shortage of empty wagons in the quarries in the mornings, and too many for unloading at Billington Road in the evenings.

When Marley Tiles received sand by the LBLR it took up to 140 wagons daily, almost half the total traffic. The Concrete Works took at most six wagons daily. When the empties were collected the train was left on the main line just clear of the points. Full wagons were marshalled at the rear of Billington Road trains. These stopped in the Marley Tiles loop and the wagons pushed to the works. If the train had been divided for the ascent, then the wagons were pushed up from Leedon loop, or else they would be in the middle of the train when it re-formed. If the whole trainload was for Marley Tiles, the train was divided at Leedon loop. Half was taken to the tile works and tipped. The empties were pushed back to the loop and the second half collected. When this had been tipped and the wagons pushed back to the loop the locomotive ran round ready to haul the train back to the quarry.

In general the gradients favoured loaded trains, with the exception of the steep bank, maximum about 1 in 25, through the Marley Tiles Works. All trains were supposed to have rear assistance up the bank, or divide, to reduce the strain on the couplings, but certainly after the quarry companies took over operation this rule does not appear to have been observed strictly, although if a driver was caught ascending unassisted he might be reprimanded. Unassisted ascents were also said to stretch the locomotive driving chains. Trains were divided at Leedon loop and half was hauled up to the Marley Tiles loop, where the wagons were left while the locomotive returned for the remainder. If, as was commonly the case, there were several loaded trains following each other, the first was banked by the locomotive off the second, its train being left in Leedon loop. By the time the second locomotive returned to collect its train, the next loaded train was about to arrive and the cycle was repeated. A variation of this was to have a locomotive on banking duty only. From around 1946 the last wagon of Garside's trains was fitted with a sprag, a short length of old rail fastened loosely in the coupling pocket, which trailed behind, bouncing over the sleepers. If a coupling broke, the sprag dug into the ground and stopped the train before it could run far.

A fatality occurred in 1951 at Marley Tiles loop. A boy fell and was run over while he was taking out the pin to uncouple two locomotives.

Garside - Billington Road: No. 12 (LBLR 12) (MR 7932) hauling a train of empties out of the washing plant. Note the LBLR identification code on the cab. Bland's garage (with parked car) is on the right, early 1960s.   *F. Jux*

A 5 mph speed limit was observed past Stonehenge to keep trains under control down the bank from Munday's Hill. Further precautions had to be taken at Billington Road where the level crossings into the quarry company depots were all approached by steep gradients. Loaded trains stopped in the loops beside Page's Park. Arnold's trains used the line nearest to the Park; Garside's used the side furthest away. The main line locomotive ran to the back and waited until a 20 hp quarry locomotive had arrived and coupled on to the front. Then, with a locomotive at each end, the train was taken slowly down the gradient into the depot. This procedure also had the effect of putting the main line locomotive into position to haul back the empties. Trains of empties from Arnold's washing plants were banked up to the Park by a 20 hp locomotive. Following the closure of the washing plants, when only the southern tipping dock was in use, the Billington Road shunter was used to double-head Arnold's trains from the Park down the bank into the yard by the locomotive shed.

Trains could be seen from Billington Road as they approached Page's Park loops. To cut waiting time there to a minimum, the LBLR 40 hp locomotives had different shapes painted on their cabs for easy identification from a distance. Since on any day a given locomotive hauled trains of only one company, the ownership of any trainload could be quickly determined, and the appropriate quarry locomotive sent to meet it. This scheme appears to have been introduced in the late 1940s/early 1950s, and lasted until about 1960, by which time traffic had fallen considerably and delays did not matter so much. Usually the LBLR had four locomotives on Arnold's traffic and two on Garside's.

Main line locomotives carried a crew of two, driver and assistant, often a boy. In the 1930s Arnold paid their boys 24s.0d. or 32s.6d. per week. The boy coupled up the train, changed points and flagged the train over the ungated level crossings which had gates across the railway only. He rode in or on the front of the locomotive, hence the handrails on the radiator and across the front. At crossings he ran ahead with his flag, or (on winter mornings) a red oil lamp to open the gates and hold up the traffic. After the train had crossed the road it stopped to allow the boy to regain the locomotive. In LBLR days, if a locomotive was at a quarry waiting for a load at lunch time the crew were collected by the company car and taken to Billington Road where there was a rest room. Crews tended to keep to the same locomotive.

Locomotive Identification Codes

LBLR No.	Arnold/Garside No.	
(1)		White central panel to cab-front sheet and a white square in the centre of the end.
2		White horizontal stripe across end; ends of cab-front sheet white.
3		Number above white horizontal stripe across end.
4		Number below white horizontal stripe across end. White circle either side of vizor.
(5)		None; but locomotive a distinctive shape.
6		White horizontal stripe across end, and white cab-front sheet.
10	G10	None; but locomotive a distinctive shape until 11 *et seq.* bought.
(11)	A43	White rectangle on upper half of cab side.
12	G12	White triangle on cab side.
13	A44	White rectangle with circle cut out on upper half of cab side.
14	A42	White X on upper half of cab side.

( ) Number not carried.

From the mid-1960s many quarry locomotives operated across Eastern Way and they did not carry a second man, so from 1965 a flagman was permanently on duty there. However, by 1977 a flagman was used only when wagons were being pushed across the road. The sole LBLR signal, a fishtail arm mounted on a rough, unpainted 30 ft pole, stood beside this crossing. It was visible from the end of the double track near Munday's Hill, and combined the duties of point indicator for the two quarry branches with that of a warning of approaching loaded trains. The line blocked indication was the arm pointing straight up. The signal was not greatly used, and was derelict by 1961. In 1954 the arm was divided into five approximately square panels, three red and two white, but later it was completely red.

Operation remained very similar after 1958 when the quarry companies took over haulage of their own trains. Most main line traffic was handled by 40 hp locomotives and 20 hp ones shuttled between the various quarry premises and Stonehenge brickworks. For a time in the mid-1960s Arnold operated the main line in two sections, either side of the Co-op Loop (Vandyke Road level crossing), in order to handle New Trees traffic (see Chapter 13).

Most railways have accidents, and the list which follows, while not complete, gives an indication of mishaps which have befallen the LBLR.

At an early date a 40 hp locomotive met a 20 hp one, WDLR 2478, head on. The impact bowed the frame of the smaller locomotive upwards slightly and thereafter it needed special brake blocks. Around 1923 it was sold to Joseph Arnold & Sons, but it was not scrapped until the 1950s. The entry in the 1923 accounts to Insurance 'damage to engine £115' may refer to this. There is the suggestion of another collision by the order of one 6-ton locomotive buffer in June 1928. In May 1965, a train from New Trees to Double Arches met a loaded train from Double Arches to Billington Road near Abraham's Farm, a short distance along Vandyke Road east of the Chamberlain's Barn branch junction. The 6-ton main line locomotive was unharmed but No. 34 on the New Trees train bent its chassis and was scrapped.

Two youths each lost a foot as a result of accidents in 1935. On 28th May a 16 year old was riding on 'a train of sand lorries' [sic] when he fell off near Double Arches and the wheels passed over his right leg, almost cutting off the foot. His foot was amputated on the spot by the local doctor, assisted by his dispenser who administered the anaesthetic, and the unfortunate boy was then taken to the Royal Bucks Hospital. The driver of the train was unaware of the accident until he reached his destination (LBO 4th June, 1935). In September a 14 year old lorry driver's mate released two wagons at Chamberlain's Barn. He 'was caught by one of them and his foot crushed'. He was removed to Bute Hospital, Luton, where part of his leg was amputated (LBO 24th September, 1935).

Marley Tiles bank has been the site of several runways. In the early days a coupling broke and the train ran as far as the Hockliffe Road crossing before derailing and crashing into a cottage adjoining the line, luckily without loss of life. Subsequently the cottage was purchased by the railway and demolished, apart from a few buildings which served as a linesman's hut. A 'dud loop' was later laid just beyond the foot of the bank, the point always being left set for the siding to deflect any runaways into the field.

Once the crew of a following light engine heard some runaways careering down the hill, although the light was not sufficient to see them. Fortunately they were able to jump clear before the collision which left wagons piled high on the locomotive.

In August 1962, Garside No. 10 with a loaded train met one of Arnold's locomotives on a train of empties at the blind corner on the bridge at the foot of the bank. Arnold's driver, followed by three wagons, jumped into the brook, while Garside's driver sat tight. There was no personal injury but many wagons were destroyed. A similar accident happened at the same spot in 1964 when Arnold No. 43 on a loaded train met a loaded Garside's train, carrying sand away from Billington Road depot before it was closed down. No one was hurt, and little damage was done, but a little while later No. 43 suffered from a broken crankshaft, possibly as a result of the impact.

A double break-away occurred on 9th January, 1962. A Garside's train was ascending the bank when a coupling broke. The sprag derailed the last three or four wagons before they ran far. As the train continued up the bank there was a jerk which snapped the locomotive coupling and the rest of the train ran back into the derailed wagons causing more wagons to be derailed.

Collisions with road vehicles at level crossings occurred from time to time. The first one, reported as 'An Exciting Incident', occurred on Tuesday 14th September, 1920 when the railway was not yet a year old. At 10 am a motor cyclist was going down Hockliffe Road and

> . . . . his attention was diverted by some cattle. When he had negotiated these he was too late to avoid a train of sandwagons which had already reached the crossing. He swerved in the direction in which the train was going, and striking the (steam) engine broadside he was thrown over the handlebars and into the cab, but beyond a few bruises he was unhurt.' The new motor cycle was carried along by the train and wrecked. 'The engine driver knew nothing of what was happening until a spectral form sailed in through the cabin window and fell fondly on his neck . . . . it took a few moments to explain that it was only an ex-flying man doing a new stunt! (*LBO* 21st September, 1920).

A lorry crashed into a train of Arnold's empties at an unspecified crossing on 2nd December, 1947. The locomotive driver escaped with a severe shaking, although the locomotive and three wagons were derailed. The lorry driver was unhurt. 'Flagmen who were on the spot when the crash occurred and other employees of the railway quickly cleared the roadway'. At Hockliffe Road crossing a van was rammed by a train in February 1958. The van driver was injured, but the locomotive was undamaged. A lorry collided with a locomotive here one foggy morning in 1960. In 1961 a car hit a train in the early morning, the flagman's oil lamp having gone out. In 1965 a train of Arnold's empties, contrary to regulations, was being propelled by a 20 hp locomotive over Eastern Way crossing before there was a permanent flagman, and it hit a car. Also in 1965, at 3.45 one Sunday morning a car ran into a locomotive at Eastern Way. On 28th November, 1968, a train from New Trees collided with a Stonehenge employee's car at the brickworks entrance. The car driver admitted he failed to look for a train before crossing the line.

The only brakes on a train were on the locomotive. Once these failed while a loaded Arnold's train of 16 tipping wagons and 2 bogie opens was descending from Munday's Hill, and the train ran out of control to derail on the points at the entrance to Stonehenge.

When blocked by a heavy fall of snow the line was cleared by hand, assisted by a snowplough, with additional help from Garside's snowplough. Arnold and Garside paid £28 and £12 respectively for LBLR snow clearance in February 1940. In the severe winter of 1962/63, Arnold's trains ran with a locomotive at each end, while Garside's trains were double-headed.

Chapter Eleven

Later History

Traffic steadily increased over the years. The LBLR supplied the motive power and maintained the track, while the quarry owners provided their own wagons. The usual dividend paid until the early 1950s was 15 per cent, fluctuating to 17½ per cent and 12½ per cent in good and bad years. The line's heyday was in the period between 1934 and 1939, and in the years following 1945 when petrol restrictions discouraged road traffic and the demand for sand boomed. It was necessary to lay double track between Stonehenge and Munday's Hill in the late 1940s. This may have been known as Harry Jeff's loop. Arnold dispatched up to 300 wagons daily and Garside 200, making some 20 train loads. In 1948 the company purchased the freehold of the depot at Billington Road and built a new locomotive shed and workshops, completed in 1950 at a cost of £3,018. This, and a length named Miletree Furlong, was the only land owned by the LBLR, although a piece near Leedon had been sold sometime after 1945. Wayleaves, costing about £550 pa, accounted for almost all of the route.

The Registered Office was moved to 6 Church Square, Leighton Buzzard from 27th May, 1948. During the war all sign posts, place names etc had been removed to confuse invaders. The company plate had therefore been amended to read 'Light Railway Company Limited', to the subsequent confusion of at least one enthusiast!

Between 1950 and 1954 three new diesel locomotives were purchased, and in 1956 three more, second-hand. The old Simplex petrol locomotives then tended to languish in the shed at Billington Road.

As post-war restrictions on road transport were eased, decreasing quantities of sand were sent away by rail. This trend was accelerated when British Railways suffered from a 17 day strike in June 1955. This caused many of Arnold's and Garside's customers to have their sand delivered by road, and they continued to use road transport afterwards. In many cases, especially Garside's customers, the sand was loaded at the quarry. Often the customers sent their own lorries, so that the quarry companies had decreasing control over the time when a load should be ready. LBLR traffic fell disastrously, and the dividend fell to below 10 per cent. As a result, operation was re-organised on 3rd December, 1958.

From this time the LBLR owned and maintained the track and the quarry companies hauled their own traffic, paying tolls (2s.4½d. per wagon in 1968) to the LBLR. The ex-WDLR locomotives which had served the line well for nearly 40 years were all withdrawn for scrap and the six modern ones sold, four to Arnold and two to Garside, as this was roughly the proportion of traffic handled. Following the change, there were usually two of Arnold's large locomotives and one of Garside's each making about three journeys a day, the last leaving Double Arches around 3 pm.

As the founders died so their shares were divided, often passing to people with no connection with the sand trade. The rights of the non sand-pit owner shareholders were safeguarded by a special resolution passed on 2nd February, 1948, which amended the articles to provide for a board of six Directors, three to represent sand merchant shareholders and three to represent the remainder. The sand merchant Directors had to be customers for the time being of the railway. In 1950 there were 38 shareholders, with holdings ranging from 18 to 1,701 shares. The issued capital in 1959 was £15,100; for many years it had remained at the £15,000 originally issued.

A special resolution, on 27th July, 1949, gave the company power to distribute to its members any surplus from the realisation of capital assets (as distinct from revenue or business profits) and defined such surplus as meaning monies over and above a sufficiency of assets to cover all liabilities including paid up capital.

The LBLR had bought investments in addition to distributing its profits. In 1942 it had £3,300 in defence bonds and a building society. In 1947 this had risen to £5,200, and by 1953 there was £6,500 in the building society. Interest from these investments helped maintain the dividend. The money realised by the sale of its locomotives and workshops was invested too, so that following 1958 most of the LBLR dividend was obtained from these investments, not from its railway operation. The company's accountants were Keens, Shay, Keens & Co of 14 Church Square, Leighton Buzzard.

Garside's traffic continued to fall, so that the LBLR became increasingly Arnold's railway. On 1st January, 1963, Arnold purchased all LBLR shares at par and the railway became a subsidiary, its registered office now being Arnold's office. Such Garside's traffic as used the railway was still hauled by Garside's locomotives but tolls were paid to Arnold. Near Kingsway Farm the LBLR ran on Garside's land, so Arnold paid Garside the wayleave, while Garside in their turn paid tolls to Arnold for their trains. The section, from Munday's Hill to Eastern Way, later became a private road for Garside's dumpers. The rails are said to still lie beneath its sandy surface.

The old sand plants at Billington Road became less and less economic to run. Garside built a large modern drying and grading plant at Eastern Way, which came into use in 1964. Its traffic to Billington Road ceased completely by the end of the year, but trains still shuttled continuously between Munday's Hill and Double Arches quarries and the new plant, from which all sand was dispatched by lorry.

Arnold built a washing plant at Double Arches in 1963. Water was readily available and the new plant could be built without interfering with the existing equipment. Furthermore, the Billington Road site was cramped, and it was easier to dispose of reject sand in the pit than to have to haul it back to Double Arches. Following this, Arnold's main line traffic fell; only sand for dispatch by rail was taken to Billington Road. One large locomotive making three daily journeys handled this traffic. The upper section remained busy as there was the shuttle service between Double Arches and Stonehenge and also the trains from New Trees to Double Arches.

Following various reappraisals and modernisation of methods, British Railways increasingly gave the impression of being interested solely in train load traffic. Wagon load sand traffic steadily diminished and, as a consequence, the tonnage hauled to Billington Road over the LBLR dropped further. By 1969 a single train from Double Arches was usually sufficient, and even that did not run every day. Early in 1969 British Railways announced that they wanted to close the remnants of the Dunstable branch serving Billington Road and Grovebury sidings as it lost £26,000 pa.

Arnold stopped sending sand to Billington Road at the beginning of May 1969 but BR did not close the sidings until 8th December, 1969. The last inwards consignment was a withdrawn container bought by the Preservation Society.

After the closure of Billington Road sidings the only traffic south of Vandyke Road was Arnold's locomotives travelling to and from the workshops and it was not economic to retain the whole railway just for them. The enthusiast group, the Iron Horse Preservation Society, established in 1967, therefore agreed to take complete responsibility for this section, including wayleaves and rates, as from 1st May, 1969. The Society then had the sole use of the section and Arnold's locomotives etc. went to and from the workshops by road. The future of the section from Vandyke Road crossing to Stonehenge was also uncertain in 1969. It was then only used by trains from New Trees quarry taking coarse sand to Double Arches for washing, but it was uneconomic to retain it in the absence of any Billington Road traffic. Arnold therefore applied to the

County Council for permission to use lorries instead, running along Shenley Hill Road, and the company was eventually successful. New Trees trains ceased running in July 1971.

Beyond Stonehenge the future of the railway seemed secure in 1969 as the brickworks took a lot of sand from Arnold's Double Arches quarry, and the section beyond Munday's Hill carried heavy traffic for Garside as well. The closure of the Stonehenge Brickworks in the spring of 1977, however, meant that the only traffic over the LBLR was Garside's, on the section between Munday's Hill and Double Arches.

The Preservation Society were therefore able to obtain the section from Vandyke Road level crossing to Munday's Hill. This was mainly used for access to the Society's shed and workshops at Stonehenge. By 1983 regular passenger trains were operating from Page's Park to Stonehenge. The former double track to Munday's Hill had been used by the occasional enthusiasts' special train, but its main function was to store the Society's wagons.

In 1969 I wrote that,

The whole line may survive if the Iron Horse Preservation Society achieves its aim of running regular passenger services over the LBLR. The existing wayleaves expire in 1979 and some landowners are believed to be unwilling to renew them when the time comes. This date may mark the complete closure of the line, or of large parts of it. Much depends on the use the quarry owners make of the northern section - many quarry railways have succumbed to dumper trucks and/or conveyors in recent years - and on the success or otherwise of the Iron Horse group.

The success of the Preservation Society can be gauged from the following chapter.

Iron Horse Preservation Society fan trip, 3rd March, 1968. The second train, two of Arnold's class 'D' wagons hauled by No. 7 MR 8723 waits at Page's Park. The frame of MR 5875 (now LBR brakevan No. 6) is in the foreground. *P. Nicholson*

Garside's crane behind the IHRPS shed Page's Park. The road into Pratt's Pit is in the middle distance, 13th August, 1968. *Author*

Chapter Twelve

Preservation

The decline of the LBLR during the 1960s, particularly the section from Billington Road to Vandyke Road, has already been described. Of the remainder, the Vandyke Road to Stonehenge line was secure only until such time as Arnold obtained permission to use lorries at New Trees Quarry. Stonehenge could receive sand by lorry and that then left the Munday's Hill to Double Arches fragment . . . . The writing appeared to be on the wall. However, this situation was altered by the activities of some railway enthusiasts who saw the railway in a different light.

On 9th January, 1967 there was a meeting at the home of L.C. Brooks in St Albans 'to discuss the possibilities of a narrow gauge railway somewhere in the vicinity, but no progress was made' (*IHRR News No. 1*). Subsequently, Brooks and B.J. Harris (of Hemel Hempstead) decided 'to go it alone'.

A few days later they visited Arnold's quarries 'with a view to purchasing materials only to discover that far from scrapping the line, Arnolds intended to keep it running for another 12 years at least' (i.e. to 1979, when leases for the route expired). Brooks and Harris had an interview with J. Arnold on 17th January, 1967 and obtained permission to run trains over the line at weekends. The three men discussed plans in more detail on 21st February. On 20th March Garside gave permission for the Iron Horse Railroad to use some sheds at Billington Road for storage etc. A bank account was opened in the name of the Iron Horse Preservation Society soon afterwards.

Initially the Preservation Society seems to have been more of an informal supporters club, although 'a small, but hard working, labour force attended Leighton Buzzard every Sunday. Throughout the summer the work of digging, painting, mending and overhauling continued'. Four Simplex diesel locomotives had been purchased from St Albans Sand & Gravel Co., and wagons obtained from Colne Valley Water Board at Watford.

Brooks and Harris 'had been responsible for the capital and the whole operation was really a business which, it was hoped, would make a profit'. Also 'it was the wish of the principals to run their railway as an American style narrow gauge operation' (*IHRR News No. 1*). However, with the need for more money and more people to take a share of the responsibility, it was decided in October 'to turn the project into a real Society, which had hitherto been in name only . . . . Therefore, a meeting was held in the Garside's shed in October, a committee was formed and a membership subscription started on the spot'. (Subscriptions: adult 30s. (£1.50), junior 15s. (£0.75.) The first true Society function was a film show in the Arcadian Hall, Leighton Buzzard, on 11th November, 1967. *IHRR News No. 1* finished by advertising 'FAN TRIP Sunday 3 March 1968. Our first fan trip from Pages Park, departing 10 am. A trip over the whole line using Messrs Arnolds gondolas. Fare 10s. (50p)'.

The local paper gave advance publicity on 27th February, 1968 under the headline 'The "Iron Horse" is rarin' to go!' The paper said that 'The Iron Horse Preservation Society is operating a 'Fan Trip' over the Leighton Light Railway on Sunday - and hopes it will be the first of many to provide passengers with an idea of what the Wild West railroad used to be'. The report of the event, in the issue of 5th March, began 'The sun beats down on the mining town of Leighton Buzzard . . . . two men ride in from the Shenley Hills and head for the Red Lion saloon . . . .' A more factual account followed. The first train, of three bogie wagons was hauled by a 'blue, yellow and red painted locomotive with the society's badge emblem on its side'. The Society's crest comprised a white prancing horse on a red circular background, surrounded by a golden ring with the words IRON HORSE RAILROAD, LEIGHTON BUZZARD in black. The reporter wrote 'Not many Leighton people will have seen the town from this viewpoint before'. The enthusiasts inspected Arnold's sidings at Double Arches for three-quarters of an hour while the train was prepared for the return journey. The second train was passed during the return journey.

The second issue of *IHRR News* (August 1968) reported the official opening of 'our first regular passenger train service' on 29th June, timed to coincide with Leighton Buzzard Carnival. The Society entered a float for the carnival and gained third prize for 'an old steam locomotive, complete with cowcatcher, headlamp and bell . . . . using an old oil drum for the boiler and a tipper chassis for the main frame . . . . and covered with glue and paper'. The Carnival Queen (Miss Margaret Powell) was one of the first passengers and the event was a 'tremendous success - trains were full to capacity!'

The vertical boilered locomotive *Chaloner* preserved privately some years before at Kings Langley, had been loaned to the Society and was in steam all day. A 2 ft bubble car conversion *Rail Taxi* had also been loaned. Less glamorous, but of vital importance, one of Garside's corrugated iron sheds had been dismantled, moved across Billington Road and re-erected to house the Society's stock at Page's Park station.

The track had received minimal maintenance in later years and the Society said that much effort would be required to bring it up to an acceptable standard. Loose fishplate bolts which permitted a rail to 'turn on to its side and bite into the sleepers' seem to have been a particular problem. The first season's traffic figures were an estimated 7,000 passenger journeys.

The first AGM was held on 28th September, 1968. The retiring Committee included Harris as 'Hon. Sec.' but did not include Brooks. Harris seems to have 'faded out' over the following winter, as the June 1969 issue of the newsletter had a 'Report from Acting Secretary in the Society's Business Feb-May 1969'. This report said that Garside's buildings had been vacated in February, following the sale of the land to a London property firm. In May the Society took over from Joseph Arnold & Sons Ltd the lease of the line from Page's Park to Shenley Hill, at a rent of £150 per annum. This had been agreed in principle in 1968 when it became known that the BR exchange sidings were to close. The Society still had an agreement to operate over the rest of the line as before.

Two additional steam locomotives had been obtained by the IHRR Society, *Pixie*, which arrived on the line on 7th December, 1968 and *Doll*, which arrived from Bressingham on 9th August, 1969. By June 1969 there were two bogie open coaches, rebuilt from wagons, and two 4-wheel knifeboard coaches on loan. A field telephone line was being laid from the engine shed to Stanbridge Road, and plans were in hand to extend the shed itself. The first special train for a railway society was run on 27th April, 1969, when *Chaloner* hauled a train to Leedon and back.

The second AGM, held on 20th September, 1969, heralded significant changes. A new Management Committee was elected and the Society's name changed to the Leighton Buzzard Narrow Gauge Railway Society Limited. The newsletter - soon to be called *Chaloner* - was made quarterly (previously there had been only three newsletters in eighteen months). The American image was also dropped at this time.

The new Society continued to improve the track, relaying and realigning as necessary. A curve at Leedon had to be slewed 'to remove kinks'. The track near the footbridge first had to be regraded to improve the approach to Stonebridge Road crossing (1969). In the spring of 1971 this section was lowered by a foot to increase the clearance under the bridge for *Doll* (optimistic as this locomotive did not finally enter service until 1992!) and *P.C. Allen*.

Additional locomotives, steam and diesel, were obtained as the opportunity offered, sometimes by the Society, sometimes by its members. New coaching stock was built. Initially all passenger trains had to have a brake van at the rear. Even when all passenger stock had been fitted with safety chains (by September 1970) there was still need for the brake vans to help control trains on the gradients. Brake vans were converted from Motor Rail locomotives with the engine removed and a new body fitted.

Accommodation became a pressing problem. The original shed was soon extended. Supplementary accommodation was obtained in the form of an ex-BR type 'BD' container in December 1969 which had been condemned at Wolverton works. It was delivered to Billington Road sidings on Thursday 4th December, 1969. A hired crane loaded it on to two type 'D' bogie wagons, which were then hauled by Arnold's No. 38 to Page's Park depot. The container was then jacked and slid into position on the Saturday. Meanwhile the empty main line wagon had been collected by the 'pick-up' on Friday, 5th December. The Society thus took delivery of the last consignment made to Billington Road sidings, as BR closed the Dunstable branch to freight as from Monday, 8th December, 1969 (passenger traffic had ceased on 2nd July, 1962).

The lease for the former stables at Stonehenge was obtained in the summer of 1970. This large stone building was converted into a locomotive shed, workshops and stores, and was operational by the Spring of 1972. A small turntable laid in the floor immediately inside the entrance gave access to three roads and enabled seven locomotives to be housed under cover. While less convenient operationally, Stonehenge was more secure. Page's Park shed was frequently broken into by vandals.

Initially trains ran to Stanbridge Road, then they were extended down Marley Bank to Leedon. During 1970 the last train of the day was extended to Vandyke Junction. Enthusiasts' specials were run to Double Arches and regular Saturday services began. It was sometimes necessary to have two locomotives in steam. During 1971 the LBNGR joined the Transport Trust, an association for the preservation movement. This was followed in 1973 by joining the Association of Railway Preservation Societies.

In 1972 land south of the Clipstone Brook was sold for development. For a time it looked as though the railway would be cut to half its length. However, the 'Urban District Council agreed to secure the land on which the tracks run from Billington Road to Vandyke Road to ensure that the railway will continue' (*LBO* 2nd May, 1972). A new bridge over the Clipstone Brook was required. The eventual reconstruction of this bridge by Anglia Water was delayed and completion was a month behind schedule. As the deck of the new bridge was at a slightly higher level than before some 150 yards of track had to be raised. Due to the delay, society members were only able to relay the track the day before the resumption of public service on Good Friday 1975. Stock marooned at Stonehenge had to be taken to Page's Park by low loader in readiness (*LBO* 8th April, 1975). During 1974 trains had continued to run through the building site which was the new estate, where Clipstone Cutting had been constructed to bring the railway down to the level of a new road.

At an Extraordinary General Meeting on 17th March, 1973 it was unanimously agreed to become a Limited Society in accordance with the Industrial & Provident Societies Act 1965 (*Chaloner* 15). (The same issue gave notice of planned tests of a remotely controlled 7 ton Motor Rail diesel locomotive with hydrostatic transmission.) In 1975 the LBNGR obtained charitable status with its tax advantages.

A publicity film 'Steam Train to Stonehenge' was made in 1973 and released in 1974. Subsequently it was also released on video. However, the condition of the track forced the railway to suspend all passenger trains between Vandyke Road and Stonehenge in 1977, for an indefinite period.

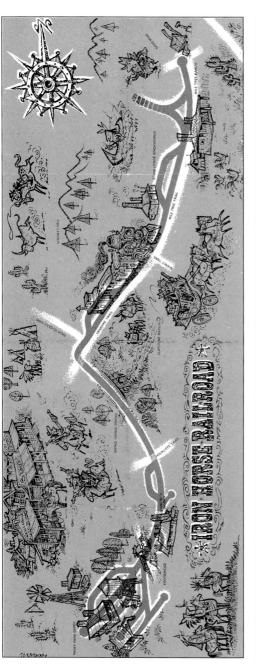

GRADIENT PROFILE

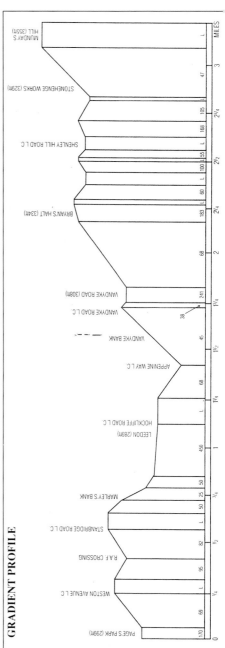

During 1975 and 1976 Page's Park station was improved, first by the purchase of a second-hand Terrapin building to house the booking office, shop, refreshments etc. and then by the reconstruction of platform 1. Page's Park and, from 1983, Stonehenge, are the only stations with platforms. The request stops which existed at various times at each level crossing and at Munday's Hill never had platforms. Passengers alighted directly on to the ground.

Trouble was experienced in 1977 with waterlogged track in the new Clipstone Cutting. The problem was traced to a broken land drain. Following the necessary repairs no further trouble has occurred here. The locomotive *Chaloner* was extensively renovated in readiness for its centenary celebrations. Subsequently in 1979 it had a spell on display at the National Railway Museum, York.

The future of the railway was secured in March 1979 when the South Bedfordshire District Council honoured an undertaking given by the former Leighton Buzzard UDC 'to secure the line of the railway for perpetuity', by securing the leases for the land used (*LBO* 21st June, 1977, 23rd March, 1979). By early 1982 all the leases had been renewed with the Council, Arnold, English China Clay (Garside), Marley Tiles, Redland, and others including some charities. The line was safe for another 25 years.

Page's Park engine shed was extended in 1979. Throughout the 1970s the track had been progressively relaid, using second-hand rail obtained from various locations in the UK. New sleepers replaced rotten ones and the track was ballasted. Some ballast came from BR and some was new limestone to give a good foundation. The standard timetable in 1979 had a service on Sundays, Bank Holidays, and some Saturdays. Trains left Page's Park for Vandyke Road every hour from 11 am to 5 pm. The journey took 20 minutes each way, with five minutes to run-round at Vandyke Road.

Until now the majority of passenger trains had only run as far as Leedon, or, later, Vandyke Road. Not only was the journey comparatively short it was also mostly in the built up area. It became obvious that the regular passenger service needed to be extended to Stonehenge which had not seen even enthusiasts' specials since 1977, owing to the condition of the track. Work on the Vandyke Road to Stonehenge section began in December 1979, relaying and cleaning 50 years accumulation of fallen sand (*LBO* 12th December, 1979).

The 'Return to Stonehenge' appeal was launched in 1981 with a target of £7,500. Some £2,500 had been raised by early 1982, when Bedfordshire County Council awarded the railway in March a grant of £4,000 on condition that the railway immediately spent the money on materials. This included 825 standard gauge sleepers, to be cut in half, 1 tonne of rail spikes, 560 fishplates with 1,200 bolts, and 120 tonnes of ballast. A government sponsored Youth Opportunity Programme (for unemployed young people) was set up and its members (two supervisors and twelve young persons) did the work. They began track lifting at Vandyke Junction on 7th June and reached Shenley Hill Road on 23rd June. A contractor then regraded the trackbed while the YOP team cut and drilled sleepers in readiness for track laying, which began on 5th July and was back to Vandyke Junction on 28th July. The team then worked at Leedon loop and on Vandyke Bank before being disbanded in December 1982.

The Stonehenge extension opened to passenger traffic during the 1983 season, delayed slightly by a period of heavy rain which caused subsidence at two places on the regraded formation. The original platform at Stonehenge was a simple earth and timber structure against the roadside hedge. The new one was faced with concrete slabs built on the loop, facing the road. Also in 1983 work began on platform 2 at Page's Park. This work was completed in 1986 by the Church Community Programme (for unemployed people), who finished it in a week and then went on to modify the layout in Page's Park

COMPARATIVE TRACK LAYOUT – Part 1

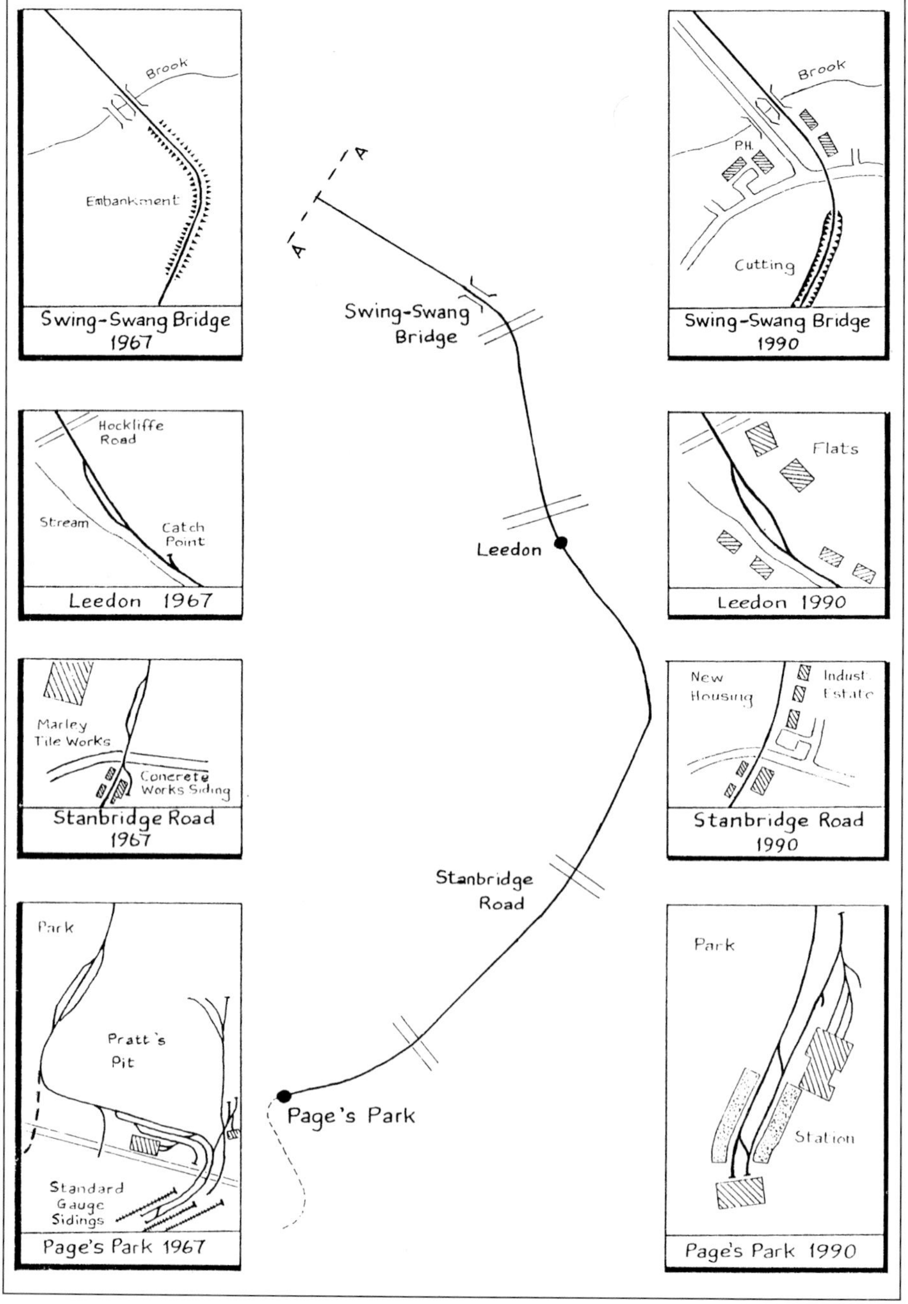

Brook
Embankment
Swing-Swang Bridge
1967
Hockliffe
Road
Stream
Catch
Point
Leedon 1967
Marley
Tile Works
Concrete
Works Siding
Stanbridge Road
1967
Park
Pratt's
Pit
Standard
Gauge
Sidings
Page's Park 1967
A
A
Swing-Swang
Bridge
Leedon
Stanbridge
Road
Page's Park
Brook
P.H.
Cutting
Swing-Swang Bridge
1990
Flats
Leedon 1990
New
Housing
Indust.
Estate
Stanbridge Road
1990
Park
Station
Page's Park 1990

COMPARATIVE TRACK LAYOUT – Part 2

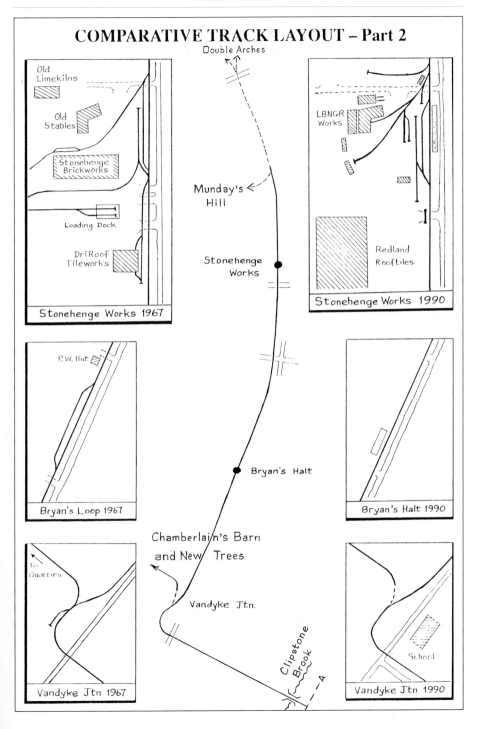

Double Arches

Old Limekilns

Old Stables

Stonehenge Brickworks

Loading Dock

DriRoof Tileworks

Stonehenge Works 1967

LBNGR Works

Redland Rooftiles

Stonehenge Works 1990

Munday's
Hill

Stonehenge
Works

P.W. Hut

Bryan's Loop 1967

Bryan's Halt 1990

Bryan's Halt

Chamberlain's Barn
and New Trees

To Quarries

Vandyke Jtn.

Vandyke Jtn 1967

School

Vandyke Jtn. 1990

Clipstone Brook

A

Chaloner and Rail Taxi at Page's Park December 1968. Note the Iron Horse crest carried by each.

P. Nicholson

Rishra and *Damredub* entering the original Stonehenge Works station in 1984. *LBR*

P.C. Allen crossing Appenine Way *en route* to Stonehenge on its first run following heavy repairs, 20th June, 1992.   *LBR*

An engineer's train in Clipstone cutting. Note the air brake pipe on Arnold No. 43, steel-bodied side discharge wagons from British Industrial Sand (Nos. 116, 122, 121, ?), permanent way mess van (2) and a 20 hp Simplex in the rear.   *LBR*

Page's Park station in the early 1990s, looking from the buffers. The locomotive and carriage sheds can just be seen behind the train. *LBR*

A visiting locomotive, ex-Polish 0-6-0WTT *Naklo* from the South Tynedale Railway (Cumbria), storms alongside Vandyke Road in 1992. *LBR*

yard, built the diesel shed there and then rebuilt the lean-to at Stonehenge which sheltered *Doll* ('the Doll's house').

The Department of Transport has oversight of all public passenger carrying railways in the UK, from BR down to pleasure lines in parks. In the early 1980s it was announced that all passenger trains had to be fitted with continuous brakes under the control of the driver and guard. No longer was it sufficient to rely on hand brakes on the locomotive and brake van.

This situation presented real problems. Suitable braking equipment had to be purchased or made and then fitted to locomotives and rolling stock. Initially only two locomotives, one steam and one diesel, were fitted with continuous brakes and there was concern that the service would be jeopardised if either broke down, but continuous brakes were essential if the railway was to continue operating passenger services.

Chaloner returned from display at the National Railway Museum, York in 1984 and it was decided to celebrate the event with a Steam Up and Gala Day on 24th June. All four available locomotives (*Chaloner, Rishra, Pixie, Elf*) would be in steam and special trains run. The event was a great success and raised much needed funds for the brake equipment. Subsequently similar events have been held with equal success. Sometimes the LBNGR diesel locomotives are the main attraction. One of the biggest special days was in September 1986 when nine different steam locomotives were used to haul passenger trains during the course of the weekend, carrying 1,406 passengers.

The braking system eventually chosen and fitted to the railway's locomotives and rolling stock used many components intended for use on heavy lorries. Standard components reduced costs and it has proved very reliable in service. Mike Satow, President of the LBNGR, designed and manufactured a prototype air pump in 1987. This has been adopted and even export enquiries have been received for it. Descending Marley's Bank now is not as hazardous as it used to be. The first locomotive fitted was *Feanor* in 1984, then *Elf*, and gradually other members of the fleet.

Two other problems dogged the railway in the 1980s. Worn bogies and wheels under carriages had to be replaced. This was done using 14 new sets obtained from Poland in 1987. The other problem was the track itself. Although most of the rail laid before the Society took over had been replaced, the replacement rails were themselves second-hand from other industrial systems, for example Knostrop Sewage Works, Leeds, and often had a life of only a few years. In 1979 relaying was quoted in the local paper as costing £40 per yard.

The railway negotiated with the local authorities, Bedfordshire County Council and South Bedfordshire District Council. The result was that sufficient brand new 40lb. rail to relay the whole line was ordered from British Steel. It was delivered in 1988 and 'no better 21st Present could have been obtained'. Part of the deal, which was financed equally between the two councils and the LBNGRS, involved the formation of a trading company, called Leighton Buzzard Railway Limited, initially to deal with the transactions involved in purchasing the rail but now used to operate the railway itself. Such co-operation between the Councils and Railway serves to show that the railway is seen as a valuable asset to the area.

Following their success on other preserved railways, the LBR introduced Santa Specials in the weeks leading up to Christmas in 1988. The trains ran as far as Leedon. Each child received a present from Santa and adult passengers were given a mince pie and hot drink. Like the Steam and Gala Days they have become a regular feature. Their popularity can be gauged from the numbers of passengers carried; 1,874 in the 1994 Christmas period.

Also in 1988 work began cleaning the site for new workshops at Stonehenge on the edge of the Twenty One Acre Quarry site. A museum policy was also drawn up and exhibits began to be acquired, including two 10RB face shovels from Garside's Munday's Hill Quarry.

A start was made extending Page's Park locomotive shed during 1989. The railway also provided test facilities for a small diesel locomotive built by Alan Keef (No. 28) for the Milton Hall Brick Co., Southend. This was followed by the use of his new steam locomotive (AK 38) on 1991 Santa Specials whilst on trial at Leighton Buzzard.

The 25th Anniversary of the Society was celebrated in 1992. The climax was a special Steam Gala on the 12th and 13th of September. The report in the Narrow Gauge Railway Society newsletter *Narrow Gauge News* (issue 193) read:

Thirteen steam locomotives and seventeen internal combustion locos first assembled at Page's Park. Shafts of sunlight broke through the swirling clouds of smoke and steam trapped under the trees which shelter the station. Both main tracks were filled with locos for the cavalcade. This started with eight steam locos individually making their way off followed by the 17 diesel and petrol machines with the last five steam locos bringing up the rear. The engines on parade had connections with 10 different countries and this was nicely acknowledged by each steam loco flying the flag of its former home alongside the Union Jack.

A second run-past of only the steam engines was briskly followed by the departure of the first of an intensive service of eight mainly double-headed trains which left throughout the afternoon at 40 minute intervals. The one exception to doubling up was the train hauled by the massive and splendid *Naklo*, with its crew wearing Polish issue railway hats. *Katie* also doubled up with diesel No. 43 MR 10409/54 providing the braking power on one run. The final passenger service to leave was a special charter for Scania Trucks. Afterwards there was an amazing spectacle when all 17 diesel and petrol machines travelled as one train to Stonehenge Works with many of them providing power and all of them providing horns!

List of locomotives in order of procession on Saturday, 12th September, 1992

Montalbahn	O & K 6640/1913	(West Lancs Light Rly)
Doll	A. Barclay 1641/1919	
Bronhilde	Schwartzkopf 9124/1927	(Bredgar & Wormshill)
Katie	Arn Jung 3872/1931	(Bredgar & Wormshill)
Rishra	Baguley 2007/1921	
Chaloner	DeWinton 1877	
Pixie	Kerr, Stuart 4260/1922	
Peter Pan	Kerr, Stuart 4256/1922	
-	Baguley petrol 2095/36 or 3002/37	(West Lancs Light Rly)
No 24	Motor Rail 4805 or 11297	
Sarah	Ruston & Hornsby 223692/1943	
	(ex Far Ings Tileries)	
Thorin Oakenshield	Lister 11221/1939	
-	Lister 37170/1951	
No. 41	Hudson Hunslet 2536/1941	
T.W. Lewis	Ruston & Hornsby 375316/1954	
Poppy	Ruston & Hornsby 408430/1957	
Gollum	Ruston & Hornsby 217999/1942	
RAF Stanbridge	Ruston & Hornsby 200516/1940	
No. 44	Motor Rail 7933/1941	
Festoon No. 21	Motor Rail 4570/1929	
Caravan No. 36	Motor Rail 7129/1938	
Arkle No. 13	Motor Rail 7108/1937	
Damredub No. 17	Motor Rail 7036/1936	
Falcon	O & K 8986	
Feanor No. 18	Motor Rail 11003/1956	
Woto	Bagnall 2133/1924	(Patrick Keef)
Elf	O & K 12740/1936	
Naklo	Chrazanow 3459/1957	(South Tynedale Rly)
P C Allen	O & K 5834/1913	
Barbouilleur	Decauville 1126/1950	(Chalk Pits Museum)

The railway is firmly established. While speculation about the future is fruitless, it is certain that the policy of improvement and service will continue on the operating railway, and the museum project is only just beginning. The intention is to build new workshops at Page's Park and then convert the old stables to a museum covering the role of narrow gauge railways in industry. A large part will be devoted to the local sand industry. Locomotives, rolling stock, maps, books, photographs, etc. are being collected. The museum building will include toilets and a cafe, and passengers will visit it on arriving at Stonehenge, or break their journey there if the proposed extension of services to Munday's Hill materialises.

Already interim heritage displays have been established for visitors to see. Particularly popular are the Industry Train Displays, featuring authentic wagons and up to 10 internal combustion locomotives. Peat, munitions, sand and forestry are among the industries represented, and a running commentary is provided to explain the significance for visitors. Displays by the 10RB quarry excavator were introduced in 1995.

As one of the top tourist attractions in Bedfordshire it is necessary constantly to improve facilities. For example, new toilets and café building are due to open at Page's Park in 1996.

Passenger Figures (Bookings)

1969	1,912 in first two months, 5,891 total
1970	6,325
1974	approx 12,000 (23,334 passenger journeys)
1975	approx 10,000 (19,871 passenger journeys)
1978	11,695
1980	12,491 (19,923 passenger journeys)
1986	13,819
1994	17,412

Arnold - Billington Siding: Loading main line wagons from the gantry in the 1930s. Note construction - brick pillars, steel girder frame and wooden floor.   *J. Arnold & Sons*

Arnold - Billington Siding: No. 7 MR 8723 crosses Billington Road with a train for the gantry. Note the three tracks across the road. Arnold's blacksmiths and wagon repairs on the right, 8th January, 1962. *Author*

Arnold - Billington Road washing plant on a misty morning, looking north. The trees on the right are in Page's Park. The tracks in the foreground continued to a reversing neck, and then a steep gradient brought them to road level. Note the shed for the low level shunting locomotive, 8th January, 1960. *Author*

Chapter Thirteen

Quarry Systems Connected to the LBLR

Billington Road Depot and Pratt's Pit
Arnold - Gantry (Billington Siding) (SP928240)
Arnold - Pratt's Pit (SP930242)
Arnold - Washing Plant (SP927242)

Joseph Arnold & Sons Ltd had two premises west of Billington Road. The southernmost, in use until 1969, was an elevated wood and steel platform on brick piers from which both unwashed and bagged sand could be loaded into main line wagons standing on Billington Siding (laid 1903). It had a track along each side and was approached by a double track extension from the LBLR. Horses were used to haul wagons up on to the 'bridge' until 1938/1939, when they were replaced by 20 hp locomotives. Wagons were pulled up on to the tip and pushed back down into the empties road in the LBLR yard. The usual tipping point in recent years was on the inside of the bend of the gantry, the locomotive setting back to tip. In the last months of operation the main line train was divided and its locomotive gave banking assistance up the 1 in 15 gradient to the tip for each half in turn. After the closure of all the loops in the yard due to excavation in Pratt's Pit, gravity shunting had to be done to run the locomotive round its train. A ground level line was provided by the tip for incoming coal and stores, but by 1969 it had not been used for years. This gantry was closed in May 1969.

Pratt's Pit east of Billington Road was served by rail until 5th August, 1968, when a concrete road to the face was brought into use. About 15 ft of overburden covered 30 ft of sand. In 1967/1968 the western face was worked, and was brought so close to the road that one loop in the LBLR yard had to be lifted and another closed. Sand was brought up either to the main line tip (Billington Siding), or to a lorry tip beside Arnold's smithy (this required two reversals), or to a factory north of the main line tip. This factory was first a glass bottle works (making jam jars), with sand brought in by LBLR, then in the 1930s the Grovebury Sand-Lime Brick Works operated by Grovebury Brickworks Co., (the Portland Cement & Limestone Products Ltd in 1929) used the site. This works made sand lime bricks (like Stonehenge Brickworks) and took about 90 wagons a day from Pratt's Pit. About 1950 the site was sold to a firm making jute sacks and the site was again for sale in 1961. Although long disused, tracks could then still be traced in concrete roads and through thick grass.

Arnold's locomotive repair shops used to be housed in a corrugated iron shed approached from the LBLR terminal loops, but in 1958 the company took over the former LBLR shops and the old building was later demolished in the early 1960s. A brick building beside the southernmost level crossing housed the smithy and wagon repair shop. The building remains in use as a workshop for repairing quarry equipment.

The washing plant stood north of Garside's depot in an awkward corner of Gregory Harris's old sand pit, adjacent to Billington Road. The approach from the LBLR was down a short stretch of about 1 in 25 gradient beside Page's Park, across the road and round a very sharp check-railed curve, which brought the track parallel to the road. Originally the line turned south after crossing the road, to serve Garside's premises. However, after a new connection had been laid for Garside in June 1920 the track turned north and served Arnold's plant, probably built in the late 1920s. Incoming sand was tipped into storage hoppers beside the line. Loaded trains had a locomotive at each end, the main line one at the back ready to take the empties away, and a 20 hp one at the front.

Arnold - Billington Road: Loading sand at Arnold's Harris Siding with No. 33 MR 4708. Note the steel plates put inside the wagons to reduce spillage, 22nd October, 1959. *Author*

Arnold - Billington Road washing plant: No. 41 (LBLR 9) MR 9547 working hard taking two skips up to road level, 10th April, 1961. Note the exhaust! *Author*

Arnold - Billington Road: A loaded train is about to descend to the washing plant, headed by No. 41 (LBLR 9). At the rear is No. 43 which brought the train in. It has run round and coupled on, to provide braking and in readiness to take the empties away, 10th April, 1961. *Author*

Arnold - Billington Road: A 20 hp locomotive brings up a rake of empties in the 1930s. In the foreground are the approaches to the LBLR locomotive sheds, with the main line curving on the far right. This is now the forecourt of the LBR station. *Author's Collection*

Arnold - Billington Road: Billington Road shunter No. 4 MR 7201 pilots a train hauled by No. 42 (LBLR 14) MR 7710 down into the yard to provide extra braking power. Note the sheeted WDLR bogie open wagon of dried bagged sand next to the locomotive, 8th January, 1962. *P.R.Arnold*

Garside - Billington Road: Loading bagged sand into a BR steel sand wagon. Note bogie flat wagon hauled by cabless locomotive No. 14 *Devon Loch* MR 7145, 8th January, 1960. *Author*

This was attached at Page's Park loop where the large locomotive had run round. The 20 hp locomotive stayed to bank the empties up to Page's Park and to catch any breakaways.

Beyond the hoppers the line fell at about 1 in 10 to a short reversing neck (capacity a Simplex and two wagons) which gave access to the bottom of the plant. On this level was a corrugated iron shed for one locomotive, a tipping dock for loading main line wagons at 'Arnold's Harris Siding', and a line to a dump for reject sand. When a horse had been used for shunting below the washers and screens its back was covered by a waterproof sheet. Occasionally washed sand was brought up the incline. The washers and screens were horizontal rotating drums of wire mesh. Much labour was involved and the plant became uneconomic, so in 1964 a new washer was built at Double Arches. This site was then abandoned and dismantled, it was sold in 1969 and became (along with Garside's site and Billington Siding) Page's Industrial estate.

Billington Road Depot
Garside (SP928241)

The approach to George Garside's depot branched off the LBLR just before the loops in Billington Road yard and turned into a check-railed curve to cross the road. This connection to the LBLR seems to have been laid in the first half of 1920. Before that Garside had obtained access using the level crossing which later served Arnold's washing plant. The change was made by mutual agreement as a meeting of the LBLR on 16th June, 1920 reported a new connection at Billington Road, 'jointly for Joseph Arnold and George Garside', which included 120 yards of track, including a level crossing, setts, and gate. The total cost was £120 4s. 0d. Garside gained an easier approach to their depot and Arnold gained rail access to their former Union Street/Billington Road quarry site.

After crossing the road the track ran through a brick shed, used to house the locomotives after work, and this gave access to a long level stretch. The line led across a weighbridge and continued to a wood and steel gantry from which main line wagons were loaded. Nearby were nine brick bins for sand storage. Loaded trains, with a 20 hp locomotive leading and a 40 hp one at the back, were brought to a stand with the big locomotive just across the road. The 20 hp one, which had been attached in Page's Park loop while the 40 hp one ran-round, then shunted the train.

A junction near the weighbridge led back towards the road. Between the locomotive shed and an inclined ramp for loading lorries (rarely used) was a siding which led into one locomotive repair shop (this building was later used by the Iron Horse). Another siding served a second locomotive repair shop. The main track passed two hoppers for the washing plant before entering the drying, grading and bagging plant built in the late 1920s. A trailing connection was made with the line serving the brick wagon repair shop and smithy, outside which stood a wooden lifting tripod. Outside the far end of the bagging plant the track finished, very close to Arnold's line. Often one or two locomotives were stored there. Originally it had continued over the road up to the main line at Page's Park.

The 1926 25 in. OS map shows a junction with the line from Page's Park, which had been turned to run northwards parallel to the road although no washing plant had then been built.

The low level of the washing plant was approached by a long gently falling line which ran back from a junction near the main line tipping gantry. It was laid with light rail.

Garside - Billington Road: Locomotive graveyard and crane, 12th April, 1961. *Author*

Garside - Billington Road: No. 16 *Ribot* MR 7149 below the washing plant, 8th January, 1960. *Author*

The line ended in a tip for rejects. By the washing plant two tracks diverged into some bushes near the edge of the old flooded pit. This was Garside's locomotive graveyard. From about 1950 to the early 1960s withdrawn locomotives were dumped here and left, often for years, before their remains, shorn of all useful components, were cut up. Ten or more locomotives, mainly unidentifiable, might be found here at one time. Doug Clayton found 25 derelicts here in May 1958!

In the 1950s, with increasing quantities of sand being loaded at the quarries, Garside used the LBLR only for the sand which had to be dried. As this was mainly dispatched by lorry too there was little justification for any plant at Billington Road. Accordingly new premises were constructed at Double Arches, and Billington Road was closed at the end of 1964. The Iron Horse Preservation Society was given the use of one shed and the rest was abandoned. The level crossing and its approach were lifted but most of the track remained *in situ* until 1968 when the site was sold for re-development.

Chamberlain's Barn Quarry
Arnold (SP926264)

Joseph Arnold & Sons Ltd opened a large quarry, Chamberlain's Barn, on the northern edge of Leighton Buzzard beside Heath Road in 1910. Much of the sand left by road but the quarry was connected to the LBLR from the outset. The branch left the main line just beyond the Co-op loop at Vandyke Road crossing and turned sharply through a right angle to run directly away from the road along the edge of a field, later a 1950s housing estate.

The original branch from the LBLR had run straight into the centre of the quarry, close to Broomhills Farm. As the face advanced southwards the connection had to be re-aligned. At about 250 yards from the junction at Vandyke Road, on entering Arnold's property, the line curved westwards to run round the southern edge of the quarry and then into old workings near the road before reaching the quarry yard.

The quarry continued to be worked southwards and in the period 1931 to 1936 an Anglo-Saxon cemetery was uncovered. In early January 1932 two burials, a man and a woman, together with a shield boss, spear, beads and a pot 'grave goods' were discovered. While the initial discovery was made by quarrymen the site was subsequently excavated by Mr Fred G. Gurney of Eggington. For years the items were displayed in Arnold's London office but in 1956 they were given to Luton Museum and Art Gallery.

Eventually the face threatened the rerouted connection, so in 1947 the eastern section was relaid. A direct connection to the LBLR was no longer possible, probably because Arnold could not obtain a wayleave for the necessary curve in the corner of the access field. Instead, the LBLR branch was connected to a quarry line (formerly used to remove overburden) running northwards above the eastern edge of the pit. A trailing connection, with an extremely sharp curve of about 12 yards radius, gave access to the new line laid immediately inside the southern boundary hedge. The LBLR boundary was then on the connection from Vandyke Road, at the last rail joint before the points. The reversing neck later became the start of the branch to New Trees Quarry (q.v.).

The original LBLR connection ran direct into the quarry yard, where tracks ran to the various faces. The later connections also came into the quarry yard, although it had been moved nearer the road. Here were screens, a washer and storage sidings. The original (late 1920s) barrel washer was replaced by a screen and bucket dewaterer type on the same site, itself replaced in 1984 by a floatex plant. A branch with a loop served a

Arnold - Chamberlain's Barn: No. 6 MR 7403 and a Priestman excavator are seen behind Broomhills Farm, 14th August, 1968. *Author*

Arnold - Chamberlain's Barn: No. 6 MR 7403 arriving at the screens while No. 36 MR 8756 waits to return to the pit, 12th August, 1969. *Author*

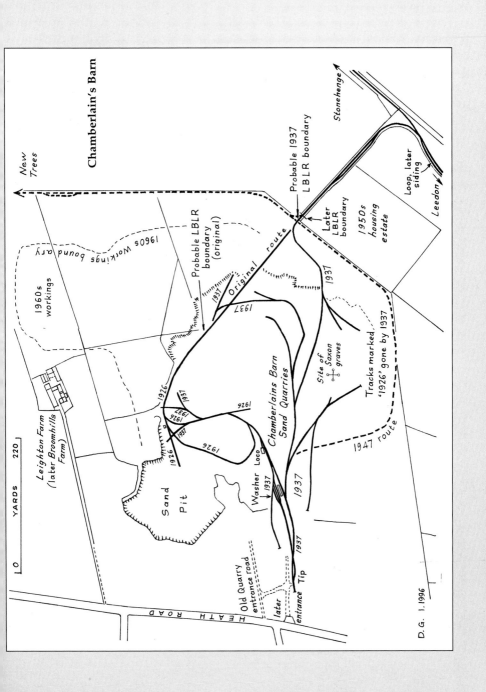

Chamberlain's Barn

New Trees

1960s Workings boundary

1960s workings

Probable LBLR boundary (original)

1937

Original route

1937

1937

Probable 1937 LBLR boundary

Later LBLR boundary

1950s housing estate

Stonehenge

Loop, later siding

Leedon

Leighton Farm (later Broomhills Farm)

1926

1937

1937

1926

1926

1937

1937

1937

1926

1926

Sand Pit

Washer

Loco

1937

Chamberlains Barn Sand Quarries

Site of Saxon graves

1937

1937

Tracks marked '1926' gone by 1937

1947 route

YARDS 0 220

Old Quarry entrance road

later

entrance Tip

HEATH ROAD

1937

D. G. 1.1996

Arnold - Chamberlain's Barn: Loading a lorry at the gantry by the entrance *c.* 1940. Note wartime blackout fitting on one headlight.   *Joseph Arnold & Sons*

Arnold - Chamberlain's Barn: An air compressor for rock drills mounted on a skip frame, 8th January, 1960.   *Author*

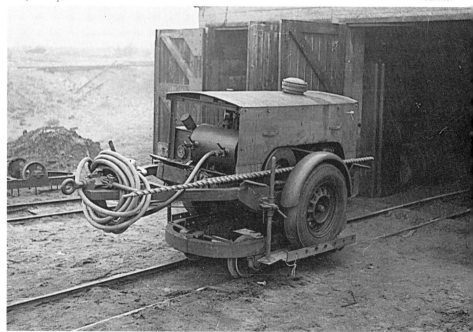

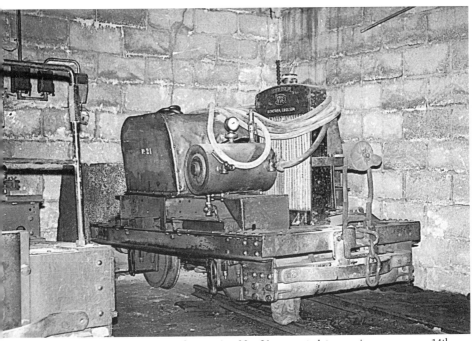

Arnold - Chamberlain's Barn: MR locomotive No. 21 converted to an air compressor, 14th August, 1968. *Author*

Arnold - New Trees: A train of empties crossing Shenley Hill Road with No. 21 MR 7215 leading and No. 34 MR 9547 at the rear. Note the fuel tank by the gate, 12th August, 1969 *Author*

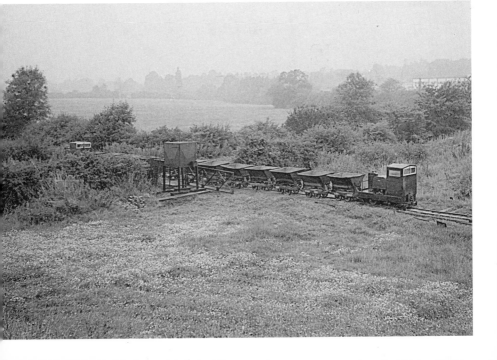

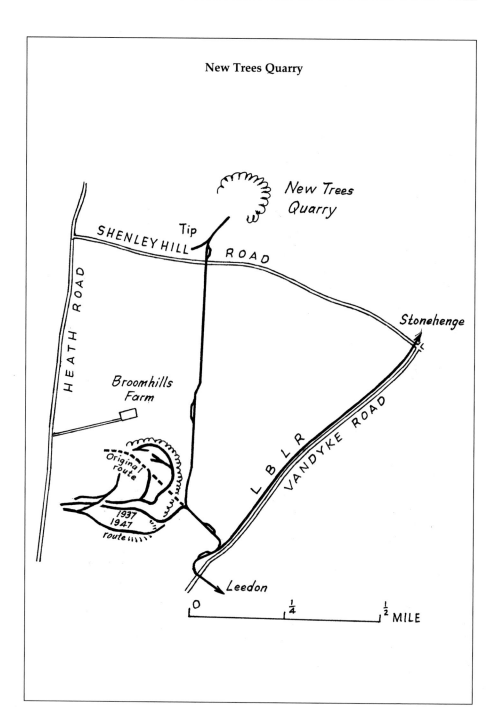

New Trees Quarry

New Trees Quarry

Tip

SHENLEY HILL ROAD

HEATH ROAD

Stonehenge

Broomhills Farm

Original route

L B L R

VANDYKE ROAD

1937 1947 route

Leedon

0   ¼   ½ MILE

loading dock for lorries near the gate. The original wooden locomotive shed was replaced in the 1950s by a new shed, constructed of concrete blocks with a corrugated iron roof, built beside it. The new shed had two roads and measured 41 ft 6 in. by 18 ft. The wooden shed was then used to store the mobile compressor for rock drills, and associated drilling equipment, which was needed when patches of hard sand were encountered and had to be blasted. The sheds were demolished in 1974 after the quarry railway had been superseded by dumpers.

During the mid-1960s the layout at the screens was simplified following the erection of a new washer. The face, which in 1960 was close to Broomhills Farm, was extended northwards behind the farm in 1964.

Locomotives were introduced around 1925. In 1968 the quarry had five locomotives allocated to it, three in use, one spare and one converted to an air compressor. Two trains of four wagons operated between face and washer. One would be loaded by an excavator, starting with the wagon nearest the locomotive, and then hauled to the washer. The driver then left his train for the other which was pushed back for loading. A shunter moved the loaded wagons past the hopper, tipped them then took the empties on to the through line to leave the hopper road clear for the next loaded train. The third locomotive moved loaded wagons from beneath the washer up to the lorry tip and stock pile by the entrance. Some shunting beneath the washer was done by hand.

LBLR locomotives, even the large ones, used to work as far as the sidings by the screens. Some sand was still worked to Billington Road in 1969 and some went out to Stonehenge and Double Arches, hauled by 2½ ton locomotives, but much of the sand went by lorry to the nearby Anchor tile works. In mid-1969 a direct road was made from the washer to the tile works, and the washer was altered to accommodate lorries. Anchor then collected its own sand. The connection to Vandyke Road was broken near the screens around June 1969, but the track round the southern side of the quarry remained in position for some years. The last traffic to use this route was the occasional train of sand to Stonehenge Brickworks.

The railway in this quarry was last used on Friday 27th July, 1973. During the following holiday fortnight the washer was altered and a 6 cu. yd Matbro' Goose dumper was introduced. By 1977 the only signs of the railway were half a dozen wagon bodies and a pile of track.

New Trees Quarry
Arnold (SP931275)

A new quarry was opened on the west side of Shenley Hill in the summer of 1963. Permission to operate the quarry was granted only on condition that the sand was removed by rail as the road was still made of water bound macadam which could not withstand heavy lorries. This quarry has not been in continuous production.

The quarry was reached by a branch which continued northwards from the Chamberlain's Barn reversing point, running between the quarry and hedge. An overgrown loop marked the summit of a gentle climb. The loop saw little use due to bad points and was removed in June 1969. At the field corner the track passed through the hedge to run on the eastern side, and a ¼ mile straight stretch of falling gradient brought the line to a level crossing over Shenley Hill Road. Just before the crossing was a trap siding. This level crossing was only ⅝ mile by road over the hill from the LBLR level crossing near Stonehenge Brickworks but it was nearly three times as far by rail.

The falling gradient continued beyond the level crossing past an elevated fuel tank

Arnold - New Trees: A loaded train leaving the pit, hauled by No. 21 MR 7215 and banked by No. 41 MR 5839. Note the additional ballast weight under the frame of the leading locomotive to bring the weight up to 3½ tons, 22nd October, 1973.   *Author*

Arnold - New Trees: The tip beside the road, with Nos. 21 MR 7215 (*left*) and 41 MR 5839 (*right*), 8th September, 1973.   *Author*

and through a loop. A trap siding guarded the steep descent into the pit, where the face was worked eastwards. A 24RB excavator with ½ cubic yard bucket was used in 1973. The steep gradient meant that two locomotives had to be used to haul sand out of the pit.

All sand excavated was taken to Double Arches for washing. As the quarry extension was laid in light rail only 20 hp locomotives could be used. The usual locomotives were numbers 34 and 41, which were ballasted to 3½ tons to improve adhesion. They ran one at each end of the train of about 16 wagons, which solved the problem of reversal at the Co-op loop. When returning with empties the rear locomotive was not coupled but followed a few yards behind the last wagon. Initially the two 20 hp locomotives, one at each end, hauled the wagons as far as the Co-op loop. There a 40 hp locomotive took over, which had arrived on a train from Double Arches. A second 40hp locomotive brought empties for New Trees from Billington Road, and returned there with the train of washed sand from Double Arches. Thus the main line was worked in two parts, with both 40 hp locomotives returning to Billington Road in the evening. However, when the fall in traffic required the attention of only one 40 hp locomotive, the system was changed so that the 20 hp locomotives worked through to Double Arches, and were shedded there instead of at Chamberlain's Barn.

Following the closure of Billington Road depot in 1969, Arnold applied for permission to substitute lorries for the trains carrying New Trees' sand to Double Arches. Permission was initially refused, but was eventually granted in 1971. Trains ceased running to Double Arches about July 1971 and the branch was lifted soon after by a Northampton firm. In 1978 overburden was being dumped on the former route.

Although now isolated from the rest of the system the railway within the quarry remained in operation. A tipping dock was constructed near the entrance to load the lorries, and a siding was laid nearby to store spare locomotives. No shed was provided. The allocation was four locomotives, two in daily use, one spare and the fourth unserviceable.

The sand was conveyed to the tip in trains of six skips with a locomotive at each end due to the steep gradient out of the pit. When loading the train one driver left his locomotive in neutral and operated the excavator while the other driver positioned each wagon for loading.

The railway system seems to have remained in operation until the late summer of 1978, probably until the annual holiday shutdown. It was reported in use on 18th July (MR4803, 9547 working, MR5859, 8994 out of use) and a report on 23rd November read 'no change' but this probably referred to the locomotive allocation. It was definitely out of use by 22nd February, 1979 although three locomotives still remained on site (MR9547 had gone). By December 1979 only a couple of skips and a few lengths of track remained.

Miletree (or Twenty One Acres Quarry) and Nine Acres (or Chance's) Quarry
Arnold- Twenty One Acres (or Miletree) Quarry (SP942276)
Arnold - Nine Acres (or Chance's) Quarry (SP938276)

These quarries were worked by Joseph Arnold & Sons for many years. Miletree Quarry had had a 3 ft gauge horse operated system in the 1890s and an undated map shows this tramway serving Nine Acre. Presumably the routes diverged near Sandpit Cottages. The wagons were brought from the quarry along a rising embankment to a tip beside Miletree Road, a distance of about 550 yards. The 3 ft gauge was replaced by 2 ft

Arnold - 9 Acre: An early photograph. Note the horses and skip for removing overburden.

Joseph Arnold & Sons

Arnold - 9 Acre: Screening sand at the quarry face c. 1940. Note the tarpaulin screen and awning fitted to the 20 hp petrol locomotive.

Joseph Arnold & Sons

gauge once the LBLR was opened. Six 'contractors wagons 3 ft gauge' were advertised for sale on 3rd December, 1919. The 1926 map shows the embankment and tip without any track, but this tip was again used by the 2 ft gauge by 1937. Although it again fell out of use in the early 1960s the tip and embankment were not demolished until the site was redeveloped in the late 1970s.

Nine Acre (Chance's) Quarry had about 15 ft of overburden and Twenty One Acre had 20 to 30 ft of clay overburden. According to Quarry returns, Nine Acre was operational in 1904 to 1907, and then idle until 1925.

In 1926 there was a loop close to the LBLR and the quarry branch then divided in two. One line almost doubled back on itself and led to Parrott & Jones quarry (q.v.). The other turned north through a right angle and served Arnold's Twenty One Acre quarry, opened early 1920, the face in use being near the eastern boundary of the site, close to the later lime kilns. A building which could have been a locomotive shed is shown. The quarry entrance was opposite Mile Tree Farm. After working out the deposits of silver sand the quarry was closed in the late 1930s and was later partially filled in by Luton RDC who used it as a tip. In 1926 Nine Acres appears not to have been in use.

In 1937 the layout was much the same as 1960. Nine Acres was in use again, working a lower bed of sand or 'compo'. The earlier track petered out in old workings of Twenty One Acre, disused from the early 1930s. A new line made a trailing connection with the loop, turned to run beside the stacking yard for the brickworks (q.v.) and continued into the pit. Beside the stacking yard was the old embankment and siding to the tipping dock. A new facing connection for sand from Double Arches was laid into the LBLR east of the brickworks. This line ran through the works yard, past the brickworks hoppers. Near the LBLR there was a diamond crossing over the route to the old workings. By the hoppers was a loop, and a double track branch to the lime kilns. Behind the brickworks, beyond the loop, the line curved to join the other route to the pit by the quarry's wooden engine shed.

After rail traffic ceased the Preservation Society used the engine shed as a store for a time. It was then abandoned but was still standing in May 1988, hidden in the undergrowth at the back of the works. The stables for the quarry horses, a sturdy building built of 'conks', later became the workshops for the Preservation Society. In 1937 there was a loop by the main line junction with a building spanning a short length of both loop tracks. No trace of either remained in 1960.

The quarry tracks were on two levels, curving in opposite directions round the pit. The layout was simplified in the mid-1960s. When the lowest level of sand had been reached on the western edge of the pit the face was worked eastwards in the 1960s by dragline. A screen was built in the pit. Sand was loaded at a high level siding, taken round the lip of the quarry, down a steep gradient, locomotive trailing, to the screen, then brought out for dispatch. Three loaded wagons was the maximum that could be hauled out of the pit by a 2½ ton Simplex. Waste sand from the screen was tipped in the pit from a conveyor; formerly skips were used to take the rejects to the tip. Overburden was also tipped in the pit.

In later years some sand was sent out over the LBLR but most left by road. It was tipped on to stockpiles by the brickworks entrance where a front loading shovel loaded it into lorries. Three locomotives were usually allocated here.

Sand continued to be excavated and sent by rail to Double Arches until December 1972. After that the railway was only used internally but this did not last long. Sand was tipped at the screens for Tilcon LSM Mortar, which had a corner of the site for five years in the mid-1970s. A little sand was also sent by dumper to Double Arches for screening and washing.

Above: Arnold - 9 Acre: The screening plant in the pit. From left to right, No. 35 MR 7126 is collecting screened sand, No. 33 MR 7037 is tipping raw sand, No. 27 is collecting reject sand, 12th August, 1969. *Author*

Right: Arnold - 21 Acre: The Bucyrus steam excavator loads clay overburden in the 1930s. Note the locomotive which does not appear to be a standard MR product. Possibly it is one of Arnold's unrecorded purchases (*see text*).
Joseph Arnold & Sons

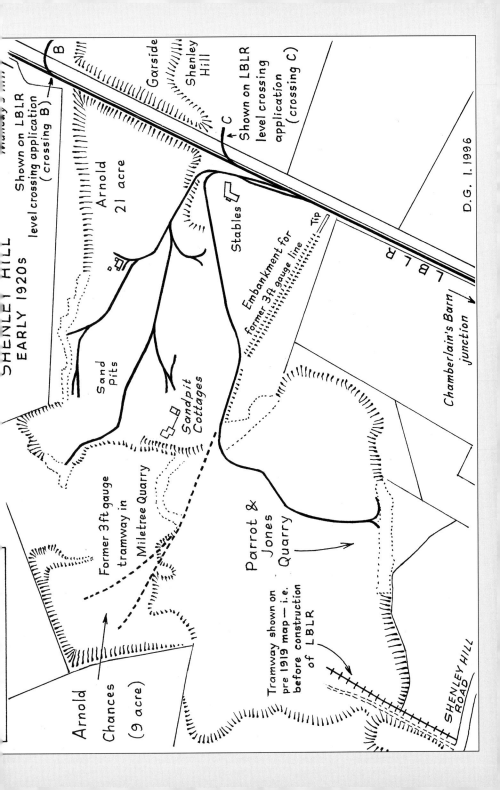

SHENLEY HILL
EARLY 1920s

Shown on LBLR
level crossing application
(crossing B)

B

Garside

Shenley
Hill

C

Shown on LBLR
level crossing
application
(crossing C)

D.G. I. 1996

Arnold
21 acre

Stables

Embankment for
former 3ft gauge line

Tip

L B L R

Chamberlain's Barn
junction

Sand
Pits

Sandpit
Cottages

Former 3ft gauge
tramway in
Miletree Quarry

Parrot &
Jones Quarry

Arnold
Chances
(9 acre)

Tramway shown on
pre 1919 map — i.e.
before construction
of LBLR

SHENLEY HILL
ROAD

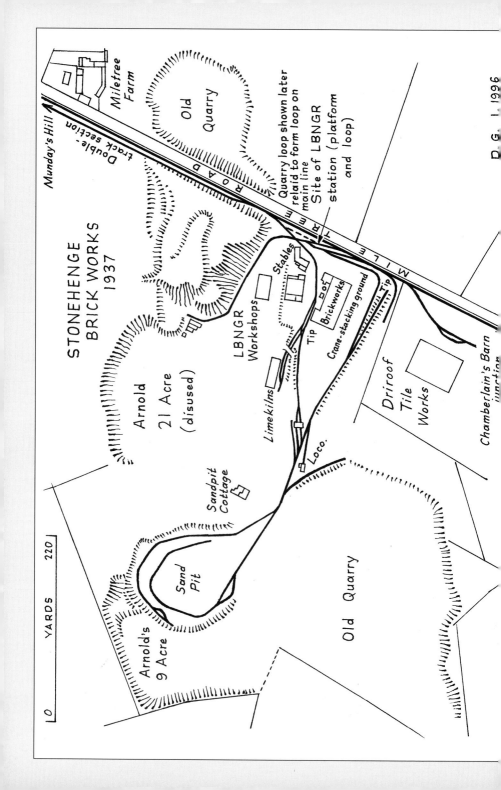

STONEHENGE
BRICK WORKS
1937

Munday's Hill

Miletree Farm

Double-track section

Old Quarry

ROAD

MILE

Quarry loop shown later relaid to form loop on main line

Site of LBNGR station (platform and loop)

D. G. 1. 1996

Arnold 21 Acre (disused)

LBNGR Workshops

Stables

Limekilns

Loco.

Brickworks

Tip

Crane-stacking ground

Tip

Sandpit Cottage

Sand Pit

Arnold's 9 Acre

Old Quarry

Driroof Tile Works

Chamberlain's Barn junction

YARDS   220

0

Shenley Hill
Parrot and Jones (SP938274)

Parrot and Jones, engineers, of North Street, Leighton Buzzard owned several small sand pits. The largest was between Nine Acre Quarry and Shenley Hill Road. An undated early map shows a tramway from Shenley Hill Road into the quarry. In 1926 it was connected to the LBLR by a 300 yds-long branch from the Nine Acre loop, and there was another 200 yds of track in the pit. This firm is said to have owned a 10 hp Planet locomotive. Certainly there was a sufficiently long haul to justify one.

By 1937 the pit was derelict, possibly a victim of the recession, and became very overgrown although the railway is still shown on the 1938 6 in. OS map. In the 1960s odd lengths of 20lb. rail could still be found. Also in the undergrowth were a 2 ft gauge prefabricated point and an end tipping wagon chassis. One curiosity on the southern edge of the site, close to a rough access track, was a length of 2 ft 2 in. gauge track. This was probably a relic of a horse worked system before the LBLR was built, as the map which accompanied the LBLR level crossings application showed a railway about 200 yards long from the pit westwards to Shenley Hill Road. In 1988 the site had become a Civic Amenity Tip for domestic rubbish.

Stonehenge Brickworks
(SP941274)

Under the headline 'Sand Lime Bricks - the New Leighton Works - High Output Expected' the *Leighton Buzzard Observer* of 30th July, 1935 gave a comprehensive description of the new brickworks whose construction was nearing completion on Vandyke Road. The works were being built for Vandyke Sand Lime Bricks Ltd, Chairman Mr Arthur Blackman, Mayor of Hastings, 'whose knowledge of building trade requirements is of an exceptional character'.

The works were built on the north side of the road and at right angles to it, with the axis approximately north-west - south-east. The machinery incorporated the latest German patents. The plant was laid out so that there was a smooth flow from the input of sand and lime at one end to the output of finished white bricks emerging from the other. Along the south-west side of the works was a stockyard, served by an overhead travelling crane whose rails were 59 ft apart and 340 ft long. Within the plant and in the stockyard the bricks were carried on about 200 2 ft 6 in. gauge flat trollies.

A large boiler, with mechanical stoker and self cleaning firebars, raised steam at 210 psi. The chimney was 103 ft high. The steam was required for the brickmaking process as well as to drive a twin cylinder steam engine 'of very fine small size compared with those of thirty of forty years ago' which produced 145 hp at 550 rpm. The company generated its own electricity, although it could also use the public supply. The machinery was driven by shafts and belts 'a practice which is explicable when one remembers that the works must be operated as a whole or not at all'.

The sand required came 'from the very edge of the works'. Chalk from the company's quarries at Edlesborough, five miles south-east of Leighton Buzzard, was taken to Stonehenge and burnt in a battery of lime kilns at the north-east corner of the works. In later years lime was obtained from the Tottenhoe Lime & Stone Co. Ltd (two miles from Edlesborough) and eventually it came from Buxton. By the time the works closed the limekilns had long been out of use although they were not demolished until the 1970s. The later Tilcon LSM Mortar plant was built on the site of the limekilns. Water was

Stonehenge Brickworks: Arnold No. 19 MR 4805 tips sand from Double Arches. Note the tip for lime (brought in by lorry) on the left and the derelict lime kilns on the right, 12th August, 1969.
Author

Garside - Munday's Hill: The 10RB shovel loads a train hauled by No. 17 *Damredub* MR 7036, while No. 16 *Anglo* MR 7149 waits. Beyond is the excavator driver's locomotive No. 13 *Arkle* MR 7152, 22nd October, 1973.
Author

supplied to the works from a new borehole, 8 in. diameter and 210 ft deep.

Sand and lime were tipped into separate hoppers in the north-east wall of the works. Elevators and conveyors took the raw materials to a huge rotary iron drum, where they were mixed in very carefully controlled proportions, to ensure a uniform, high quality product. Steam was admitted to hydrate the lime and the sand - lime mixture was then transferred by paddle creeper (a type of conveyor) to the presses where the bricks were made. The new bricks were loaded on to trollies and run into autoclaves, iron cylinders larger than the plant's boiler. The autoclaves probably accounted for the curious proportions of the trollies, 3 ft 4 in. long by 5 ft 7 in. wide. After sealing the autoclave steam at 210 psi was introduced to complete the chemical process, combining the sand and lime into calcium silicate. The finished white bricks were then taken to the stacking ground to mature.

The intended production was between 100,000 and 150,000 bricks per day, production being expected to start 'in a week or two' i.e. mid-August 1935. Ten diesel engined lorries had already been purchased for deliveries 'with others to follow'.

In 1968 the brickworks took 50 wagons loads daily from Nine Acre pit, while Double Arches supplied 47 wagon loads for the brickworks and 20 for the neighbouring tileworks (q.v.). Arnold's locomotives Nos. 19 or 26 shuttled continuously to and from Double Arches with this traffic, hauling about eight wagons each time. Driroof Tiles emptied wagons themselves as required, but Arnold's drivers tipped brickworks wagons on arrival and then returned for more.

Redland Tiles bought the works in 1976, and the adjoining Driroof Tiles factory. Both were closed in the spring of 1977 (Double Arches had ceased supplying sand in February) and the site was redeveloped as a modern tile works. The chimney was felled on 21st June, 1986.

Driroof Tiles
(SP939272)

Driroof Tiles built a factory immediately west of Stonehenge Brickworks in the early 1950s. It made tiles from sand and cement. The plant was served by a siding from the LBLR. A loop on this siding entered the building to serve the tip for incoming sand.

The works was closed in early 1977 and in May were being demolished to permit the construction of Redland's new Vandyke Works for manufacturing tiles.

Mile Tree Road (or Shenley Hill)
Garside (SP942276)

This quarry appears to have been very short lived, and may have been opened to meet World War I's demands. It was operational in 1919 as it accounted for two of the level crossings on the LBLR application. The quarry was on the opposite side of the road to Arnold's quarries, close to Mile Tree Farm. The site, a grassy hollow, is still clearly visible from the road.

Access into the southern end of the quarry was direct from the LBLR with a level crossing over Mile Tree Road, just east of the connection to Arnold's Twenty One Acre quarry. The northern end was served by a line with a level crossing close to Mile Tree Farm. In view of the lack of any rail connection to this quarry on the 1926 map, it is possible that these branches and level crossings were not made. Soon production was

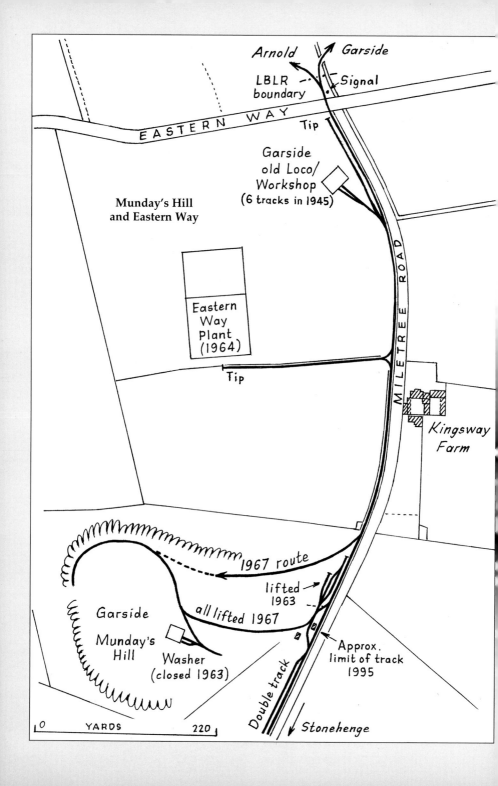

concentrated on Munday's Hill and Double Arches and this quarry closed. Perhaps the sand here was of indifferent quality, as this was the only pit on the east side of the road.

Munday's Hill
Garside (SP942279)

George Garside opened this quarry in 1925. The early layout is not known but the site would suggest that it began as a pit close to the LBLR and gradually worked away into deeper cover. By 1990 some 60 ft of clay overburden was being removed by self propelled scrapers. Beneath the clay was a thin bed of ironstone, grit and phosphatic modules, then 15 to 20 ft of silica sand. Below this was a very fine clayey sand called 'compo' used for building and plastering.

In 1960 a facing connection was thrown off the LBLR just beyond the end of the double track. The track ran parallel to the main line and then divided into a loop and siding at a three-way point. It is probable that loaded wagons were pushed up from the quarry to the fulls siding, while trains of empties from Billington Road ran into the loop. The main line locomotive could then have been released by the other loop road and would have been able to return almost immediately to Billington Road with the loaded wagons. Adjacent to the three-way point was a trailing connection to the quarry, which descended at about 1 in 20. At the foot of the gradient, out of sight of the road, was a screening plant with several sidings. The main track continued to the face, one end of which yielded yellow sand and the other end white.

The layout by the LBLR was altered to a simple loop in 1963/64 so that trains could run from the quarry to the Churchways (Double Arches) washer without reversal, and the gradient out of the pit was reduced. The screen in the pit was then closed and dismantled. Later, in 1966, a new connection was laid from the LBLR into the quarry, a few yards on the Double Arches side of main line loop. The old route was abandoned, although the loop remained in use for locomotive parking while drivers rested in the brick hut by the road. Two faces were then worked at different levels, producing sand of a variety of colours from silver to red-brown.

This pit was worked in close conjunction with Double Arches quarry which supplied locomotives. Operation of all Garside's premises in this area is described in the Double Arches section.

Eastern Way Installations
Garside - Drying Plant (SP941284)
Garside - Sheds (SP943284)

A modern drying and grading plant was built beside Eastern Way at Double Arches to replace the Billington Road plant. Designed in 1963-64, it was brought into use in January 1965. A triangular junction, with both curved sides check-railed, gave access to a 200 yds-long branch to the plant, where the track divided to serve a tip and the plant input stockpile hoppers. The Eastern Way side of the triangle later fell out of use. Train operation will be described later in the Double Arches section.

Depending on production requirements suitable sand was excavated and taken to the Eastern Way plant. Munday's Hill quarry produced white and brown sands of coarse to medium grade, and Churchways quarry produced fine grade sands. Sand from both quarries was washed at Churchways.

Garside - Munday's Hill: No. 15 *Brown Jack* MR 7148 climbs out of the lower level of the quarry, 2nd January, 1969. *Author*

Garside - Eastern Way: No. 29 *Ayala* MR 7374 at the tip. Note the wagon loaded with 'conks', 14th August, 1968. *Author*

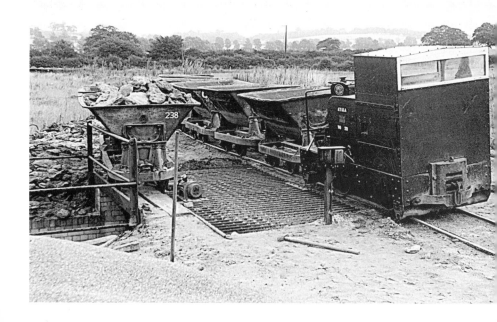

The washed sand was first dried by oil fired rotary driers in the southern part of the building. The dry sand was then conveyed by bucket elevator into one of a pair of 100 ton storage bins, one for white sands and one for brown. Dried sand from these bins was taken by a pair of conveyors, one for each colour, to the central section of the building for grading. The grading machines had two sets of wire mesh, so producing three grades of sand. The meshes could be changed to give different gradings. A conveyor took the graded sand to a second set of storage bins at the northern end of the building. The graded sands could be delivered loose into lorries, or regraded into subgrades and bagged for dispatch. These operations took place in the north end of the building. Some twenty different grades of sand could be produced, suitable for applications ranging from water filtration to laboratory testing of cement.

A short distance from the junction for the drying plant was Garside's original Double Arches area locomotive shed. This was a corrugated iron building with six parallel roads each holding one locomotive. In the 1950s it became the base for repairing quarry equipment. The two fitters here kept a locomotive which they used to reach any breakdown. Their locomotive was an old petrol one, with a vice and tool boxes bolted to the frame to form a mobile workshop. Around 1960 it was No. 21 *Tosca*; later No. 21 *Festoon* was used for this duty. However, breakdowns became less frequent as old equipment was replaced, and the vice was removed in mid-1967. A standard diesel locomotive, No. 34 *Kilmore*, was used in the late 1960s and No. 13 *Arkle* in the mid-1970s. After the move from Billington Road in 1964 locomotive repairs were carried out here too. Remains of withdrawn locomotives were stored on the embankment to the nearby lorry gantry after Billington Road had been vacated.

A track from the locomotive shed / workshops junction led to an elevated steel tipping dock just beside the Eastern Way level crossing, which used to be used for loading sand from Munday's Hill. It fell out of use about 1945, lorries being loaded from gantries at Double Arches instead.

Double Arches Quarries
Garside - Depot (SP944285)
Garside - Churchways Washer (SP941292)

At the eastern end of the LBLR the track divided just after crossing Eastern Way. Garside's quarries were reached by the right-hand branch. This crossed a small stream, which marks the boundary of Arnold's and Garside's property, passed through a hedge and entered the quarry yard. The original pit, now flooded and used as a spoil tip, was at the further end of the yard. The 1926 map shows only a single track into the quarry.

In the early 1930s a new quarry, Long Stretch, was opened beside the Watling Street, and this was worked until 1950. Also around 1930 the present quarry, Churchways, was started, the workings being adjacent to Arnold's Double Arches quarry.

To reach the new quarries a railway was laid beside the old workings. For about ¼ mile from the end of the yard the line was in a cutting through a wood. Then it curved slightly to run in the open to the junction for the quarries. In 1960 most of this main line, about 600 yards in all, was double track, but following the reduction of traffic in the late 1960s the empties road became relegated for use as a siding for surplus wagons, and was mostly lifted in the early 1970s.

The line divided just beyond the end of the double track. The left-hand branch crossed a stream and divided again, the main line descending into Churchways quarry while the sidings on the right served the input side of the washing plant. This washer

Garside - Double Arches: No. 34 *Kilmore* MR 7105 inside the locomotive repair shop. It just fits! Note the emergency door on the cab, 14th August, 1968.   *Author*

Garside's snow plough as fitted to No. 37 *Gay Donald* MR 7108 standing in Double Arches yard. A second plough lies on its side. The line to Double Arches quarries went through the break in the trees, just visible above the locomotive's cab, April 1969.   *C. Daniels*

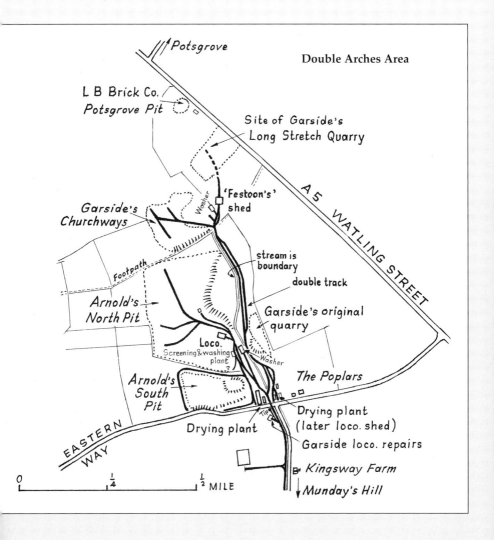

Potsgrove

Double Arches Area

L B Brick Co.
Potsgrove Pit

Site of Garside's
Long Stretch Quarry

A 5 WATLING STREET

Washer

'Festoon's'
shed

Garside's
Churchways

stream is
boundary

double track

Footpath

Arnold's
North Pit

Garside's original
quarry

Loco.
Screening & washing
plant

Washer

Arnold's
South
Pit

The Poplars

Drying plant
(later loco. shed)

EASTERN
WAY

Drying plant

Garside loco. repairs

Kingsway Farm

Munday's Hill

0   ¼   ½ MILE

Garside - Churchways Washing Plant: No. 13 *Retrial* MR 5870 shunting. *Festoon's* shed can be seen in the distance, on the line to the former Long Stretch quarry, 4th January, 1961.   *Author*

Garside - Double Arches: No. 13 *Retrial* MR 5870 on the double track section from Churchways pit to the quarry yard, 4th January, 1961.   *Author*

had been enlarged in 1964 to handle sand from Munday's Hill as well. Until 1960 sand was excavated in Churchways by a dredger, which pumped sand and water to a hopper in the quarry from which the skips were loaded. Latterly sand was dug by excavator and loaded directly into wagons.

The right-hand branch also crossed the stream and threw off a pair of sidings to the left which served the output side of the washing plant. The main line continued across another stream and formerly served Long Stretch quarry. Following the closure of this quarry a wooden shed was built over the track just beyond the stream. Originally the shed was used for excavator spares, and from about 1967 it was used to hold the last petrol locomotive, No. 21 *Festoon*.

The buildings beside Eastern Way originally contained a drying plant. Following the opening of the Eastern Way plant and the move from Billington Road they housed only the wagon repair shop and the locomotive shed serving all Garside's installations in this area. The previous quarry locomotive shed was a low two road corrugated iron structure near the eastern gate, demolished in the late 1960s. Two elevated tracks served a stockpile and a gantry by the gate for loading lorries. A simple corrugated iron shelter formed a windbreak on the lorry gantry and a similar one was to be found at the quarry washer. Although the function of buildings changed the layout was not greatly altered by the move from Billington Road.

Neglecting *Festoon* stored in the quarry, and *Kilmore* in the fitters' shop, Double Arches had an allocation of seven locomotives in 1968, of which about five were in daily use as follows: one worked from Churchways quarry to the washer; one shunted at the washer; two worked from Munday's Hill to the washer, and one worked from Munday's Hill to Eastern Way or to the lorry tip. Munday's Hill was then the busier pit. By 1973 traffic required three locomotives daily on sand trains, plus one more to take the driver of the 10RB ⅓ cubic yard excavator to and from his work. Empties waited in the former Munday's Hill loop if a loaded train was due out of the quarry.

In 1977 the operating pattern had changed. White sand was taken trom Munday's Hill to Churchways washer, then to Eastern Way for drying. Yellow sand from both Churchways and Munday's Hill was taken to Eastern Way for drying and grading. Locomotive usage at this time was:

One locomotive hauled brown sand from Munday's Hill to Eastern Way - the driver operated the excavator and loaded his own train.

One locomotive hauled white sand in 12-wagon trains from Munday's Hill to Churchways, where another man operated the washer.

Two locomotives worked white sand from Churchways washer to Eastern Way. The driver of the full train drew into the locomotive shed siding then walked to the level crossing to protect the train of empties being propelled back to the quarry. He then returned to his own train and hauled it over the road.

The excavator at Churchways was operated by the locomotive driver whose train usually comprised 10 wagons. The track being level, it was safe for him to leave the locomotive brake off so that he could move the train with the excavator by slewing the machine and racking out the bucket arm, thus bringing more empties within reach. Trains from Munday's Hill had six or seven wagons. Those to the drying plant from Churchways had 15 wagons, although 10 wagon trains were operated before the expansion of Munday's Hill. The lorry gantry held five wagons.

In 1969 it was said that this busy system was unlikely to be replaced by conveyor belts in the foreseeable future. The sand was worked selectively and conveyors to each feeding point would have been expensive. Locomotives were cheap to run and had a long life.

Garside - Double Arches: No. 13 *Retrial* MR 5870 at the lorry gantry. Note the screen, 4th January, 1961. *Author*

Garside - Double Arches: Trains pass in the quarry yard. The driver of the loaded train (No. 29) from Churchways to Eastern Way is just returning to his locomotive having signalled the empties (No. 31) across the road, 27th July, 1977. *Author*

Arnold - Double Arches: A loaded train hauled by a LBLR locomotive is ready to leave. The screening plant can be seen in the distance,   *Joseph Arnold & Sons*

Arnold - Double Arches: An empty train pushed by No. 22 (MR petrol, unidentified) crosses South Pit. Note the skips on the overburden tip in the right background, and in the far distance, 8th April, 1954.   *G.H. Starmer*

Arnold - Double Arches: Hand loading sand. Petrol locomotive No. 23 stands by, 8th April, 1954.

G.H. *Starmer*

Arnold - Double Arches (North Pit): Loading sand by dragline. No. 26 MR 4701 heads the train, 12th August, 1969.   *Author*

Arnold - Double Arches No. 1 MR 8683 leaves the face shovel, 22nd October, 1973.   *Author*

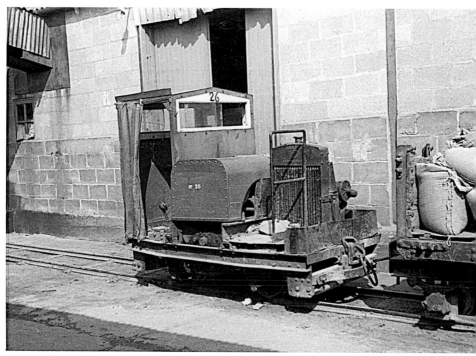

Arnold No. 26, believed to be FH 1917 at Double Arches, 10th April, 1961.   *Author*

Arnold's Double Arches locomotive shed and workshop. No. 4 MR 7201 and No. 18 MR 7188 stand outside. Nearby is the rectangular tank from a steam excavator water carrier, 22nd October, 1973.   *Author*

However, within 10 years the railway had gone. An enthusiast reported in October 1980 that a dumper was expected on trial 'in a few months', to work alongside the railway. The last sand train ran on 2nd June, 1981, from Churchways quarry to Eastern Way. The economic effects of advances in dumper and excavator technology did not permit the quarry railway to continue. By September the track was lifted or buried and large Volvo dumpers operated between the quarry faces and Eastern Way, using the former LBLR track bed which became a private sandy road. A visitor on 13th September, 1981 reported 'Track beds bulldozed out to produce roads for dumpers and for the most part it is difficult to realise that a railway operated here a few months ago.' The workshops had been demolished and No. 29 *Ayala* stood on the site, with 25 skips on the LBLR trackbed nearby. Four locomotives languished in the shed: Nos. 13 *Arkle*, 17 *Damredub*, 31 *Mill Reef*, and 34 *Red Rum*. They were the last of the many locomotives used in the Leighton Buzzard sand quarries. Three had remained in daily use to the end.

Double Arches
Arnold (SP943285)

Arnold's main quarries were served by the left-hand track from the junction at the end of the LBLR. By 1926 there were several loops in the quarry yard and a long siding parallel to the road, presumably for loading carts or lorries. The first workings were well away from the road, beyond the 1943 engine shed. In 1930 the face was 600 yards long and 20 ft to 30 ft high, making it one of the largest sand pits in the country. South Pit, near the road, had been opened in the mid-1920s and was the only pit in the early 1960s, the North Pit having finished about 1960. By that time only a shoulder high ridge of sand separated it from Garside's workings in Churchways quarry. North Pit reopened in December 1966 and is still in use.

In 1969 a Roman well was discovered in the northwest end of the pit. Subsequently excavation showed the well to have a shaft 40 in. diameter, lined with stone to give an internal diameter of 14 in. Found in the shaft were two water ewers, one 12.5 in. high and 11 in. in diameter and the other (which showed signs of repair) 8.5 in. high and 8.25 in. in diameter.

The main line cut diagonally across the quarry yard before resuming its former direction in a large marshalling yard. Trailing connections served the drying and bagging plant. A large building here had been used for the LBLR opening speeches. This could not have been the drying plant if Bedford Silica Sand Mines Ltd (q.v.) were indeed the first to offer dry graded sand in 1928. The 'Old Shed' designed for drying sand was in operation by 1930. The long low building had large doors at the rear for loading sand, which was spread over the heated floor. Sidings were laid past the doors. Rotary barrel driers were installed in the mid-1930s, and were superseded by fluid bed driers in 1986. On Friday 4th December, 1931 there was a fire in the drying and bagging plant which caused £500 worth of damage (*LBO* 8th December, 1931). The drying kilns used to be coke fired. Fuel for them and coal for the excavators (introduced around 1930) was brought up in the bogie open wagons to a stockpile by the original wooden engine shed which stood near the drying sheds. It was demolished about 1960. The loading bays had verandahs which gave them a vaguely Continental appearance. Facing connections gave access to the ramp for the new washer, erected in 1963 to deal with the extra sand from New Trees as well as to replace the old Billington Road washers, and to a siding for the washed sand dump. Wagons were usually loaded with washed sand by a tractor shovel instead of from the sand hopper.

Arnold - Double Arches: A hydraulic drag shovel loads sand. The locomotive is No. 40 MR 7153, but no number has been painted following the last overhaul, 27th July, 1977.   *Author*

Arnold - Double Arches: No. 36 MR 8756 waits with empties in a short siding for No. 8 MR 7215 to pass. At the time, No. 8 had recently returned from Stone pits, 22nd October, 1973.

Author

Arnold - Double Arches Quarry Yard: (*left to right*) tip for primary screen, locomotive shed and workshop, approach to North Pit (seen in the distance), washing plants, link to LBLR (*right foreground*), December 1969.
Joseph Arnold & Sons

Arnold - Double Arches: A lorry loads at one of the gantries beside Eastern Way. In the right distance a train of empties approaches. In the left distance is the gantry beside the level crossing which Garside's used to use for sand from Munday's Hill, 8th April, 1954.
G.H. Starmer

Arnold - Double Arches: WDLR bogie wagons loaded with bagged sand are seen under the veranda outside the drying shed, 4th January, 1961. *Author*

Arnold - Double Arches: A train from New Trees crosses Eastern Way, hauled by No. 34 MR 9547 with No. 41 MR 5839 in the rear, 14th August, 1968. *Author*

Beside the road were three lorry loading docks and bins for stockpile sand. Moving away from the road, on the west side of the yard, was the line into the South quarry which began in cutting through an old spoil tip then descended on a long embankment. Half way along the yard was the primary screening plant, served by a steeply inclined line. At the far end of the yard double track to the North pit descended past the 1943 locomotive shed.

This shed was constructed of concrete blocks and had two storage roads plus a single road workshop alongside. The total capacity was 11 locomotives. In 1965, 14 locomotives were allocated to this quarry, several being stabled overnight under the verandahs of the drying plant.

Drivers tended to keep to one locomotive. Trains were normally about five or six wagons. There was almost always something moving in the yard as about 10 locomotives were in daily use. Double Arches provided the motive power for 10 or 12 trains daily to Stonehenge (Nos. 19 or 26), and also to New Trees (Nos. 34 and 40). Until about 1950 five or six more locomotives were used on overburden removal.

The connection to the LBLR was removed in April 1977 to give a large concrete hardstanding area for lorries being loaded with bagged sand by fork lift truck. Rail traffic in the quarry ceased around the end of 1977. A visitor in January 1978 found MR4803 moving occasionally and men cutting up wagons. MR7153 was working in July. The solitary yard shunter, MR8540, was finally taken out of use about 16th November, 1978 when the quarry finally went over to dumpers. A visitor on 23rd November found that the quarry had converted to dumpers the previous week (although Garside's quarry produced three locomotives hard at work on this date and, in fact, their system remained in use until June 1981). The quarry yard was cleared of most track within a week, leaving 10 locomotives marooned in the shed. Arnold advertised 'Narrow gauge equipment - locos, skips and track' for sale in the *Contractors Journal* (23rd November, 1978). News of the closure appeared on the front page of *Narrow Gauge News*, issue 117. Under the bold headline LEIGHTON BUZZARD: SAND LINE CLOSES it continued 'Joseph Arnold & Sons sand quarries have ceased to use rail transport . . . .'. The last locomotive, MR4805, did not go for preservation until May 1983, long after everything else had gone.

The quarry continues in operation. Old workings were being used as the Double Arches landfill site, operated by F.R. Cawley Ltd in 1988. It was still being filled in 1994.

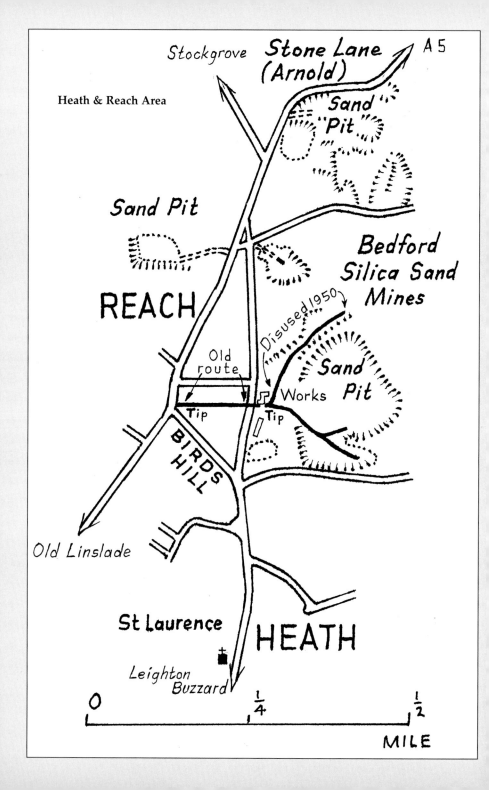

Chapter Fourteen

Other Quarry Systems
Not Connected to the LBLR

Bedford Silica Sand Mines Ltd, Reach Lane Quarries, Heath & Reach
(SP926284)

The adjoining hamlets of Heath and Reach, about two miles north of Leighton Buzzard on the main road to Woburn (A418) were made into a single civil parish in the last quarter of the 19th century. Of the several sand pits in the vicinity of the village, the largest is situated to the east of Reach Lane linking Heath and Reach.

This pit has been in production since around the turn of the century. The 1914 Bedfordshire Trade Directory gives Christopher Claridge, Sand Merchant, Heath & Reach. He was still the proprietor for the 1922 quarry returns. Around 1923 the Waste Recovery Syndicate Ltd, Silver Sand merchants took over operation, but the Syndicate did not operate for long. Bedford Silica Sand Mines Ltd 'speciality dried and graded sand' started work here about 1928. Although the 1928 edition of the trade directory still showed the Waste Recovery Syndicate the quarry returns showed Bedford Silica Sand Mines Ltd. This company was the first to dry and grade sand in this country, the necessary plant being opened in 1928. The railway was laid at about the same time, no doubt to deal with the increased output of the new process and to ease transport from quarry to works. Previously horses and carts had been loaded at the quarry face.

The track layout was in the form of a 'Y', with the drying plant at the centre. The two arms led eastwards to the sand pit, although the northern one had been disused since about 1950, and lifted in 1953. A pair of Motor Rail dumpers were then used to carry the sand from the quarry instead. The track comprising the stem of the 'Y' ran westwards for 200 yards downhill, on an embankment of gradually increasing height, to a wooden tipping dock beside the main road. This section was abandoned in 1939 when a brick tipping dock was built beside the works. The embankment remains, overgrown, at the bottom of the gardens of a housing estate, while the tip itself was removed and a house, 32 Birds Hill, was built on the site in 1960.

A railway was also used to transport overburden until 1936 when it and the remaining barrow runs were replaced by a Smith (Rodley) excavator and a dumper. A small portable screen fed by bucket conveyor was installed in the pit at about the same time. Men then shovelled sand into the conveyor hopper instead of directly into the wagon.

The railway was operated by gravity, with two or three horses to haul wagons back uphill. Trains comprised three or four wagons with the leading one fitted with a platform at one end, on which a man rode to apply the screw brake when necessary. About one quarter of the Hudson side tipping wagons were brake fitted. After the screen was introduced, a loop was laid in the pit with the delivery chute from the screen above one track. Empty wagons were left on the other and pushed by hand under the chute as required. Previously there had been a number of short spurs to the different parts of the face, reached by points or by turning plates. Some of the points were of conventional design; others were made to fit on top of the permanent track, so that a temporary spur could be laid in without cutting the main line at the junction.

The horses were replaced after World War II by two second-hand 2½ ton Motor Rail diesel locomotives purchased in 1946 and 1948. They hauled trains from the pit and pushed the empties back. Loads of screened but undried sand were pushed onto the tipping dock. In 1961 there were 58 Hudson wagons (not all in use). The track was 20 lb. and 30 lb. rail, laid on halves of ex-BR sleepers. The railway was then nearing the end

Bedford Silica Sand: Hand excavation of sand and overburden. Note the barrow run on planks and trestles, and the quarryman half way up the sand face, 1934. *Bedford Silica Sand Mines*

Bedford Silica Sand: A horse drawn train passes the first sand drying and grading plant in the country, 1928. *Bedford Silica Sand Mines*

Bedford Silica Sand: A quarry scene in 1934. Note the man controlling the rake of loaded skips with the handbrake, a skip on overburden removal, and a spare turning plate (in lieu of a point) in the foreground. *Bedford Silica Sand Mines*

Bedford Silica Sand: From top to bottom; a bulldozer towing a scraper to remove top soil, a shovel loading a dumper to remove clay overburden, men shovelling sand from the face, a locomotive (probably MR 8588) on a train by the screens. *Bedford Silica Sand Mines*

Bedford Silica Sand: The tipping dock by the main road in 1928, with the works in the distance. Note the brakes on the leading wagon and the two horses. *Bedford Silica Sand Mines*

Bedford Silica Sand: The drying and grading plant in 1948. A locomotive (probably MR 8588) stands with a train on the tipping dock. The line to the former tip by the main road went through the gate in the left distance. *Bedford Silica Sand Mines*

of its life, since it could not supply the elevated high-capacity bunker necessary if the plant was to increase its output and efficiency.

A new 100 ton bunker was built at the works, fed by a conveyor from a 30 ton bunker in the pit, the latter loaded by direct methods. The plant was then able to dry 20 tons of sand per hour, continuously, which had been impossible with sand supplied by rail. A train of four wagons had brought only six tons at a time and little stock was held in the existing hoppers. The new conveyor was brought into use in May 1963, and the railway finished. The locomotives were sold, to Flettons Ltd, Kings Dike, Cambridgeshire, in August 1963 and the rest went for scrap.

By May 1988 the quarry was operated by Buckland Silica Sand Co., part of the ARC Group. The embankment to the former works tip remained, overgrown, behind the weighbridge.

Locomotives

For explanation of locomotive list see page 172.

Works No. Type	Ordered HP	Ex-Works Weight	Cost Gauge	Notes
MR 8588	21/5/40	14/1/41		New to War Office (1 of order of 54).
4wDM p	20/28 hp	2.5 ton	2 ft	To MR.
	3/3/47	9/4/47		To Chas T. Olley, Grove Farm Sand Pits, South Ockenden. Resold as 'slightly used War Surplus loco' with steel cab. To MR.
	8/1/48	6/2/48		To Bedford Silica Sand, Heath and Reach, Leighton Buzzard as 'slightly used War Surplus loco' with steel cab Loco overhauled by MR 6/61. To Flettons Ltd, Whittlesea, Cambs 8/63. s/s between 1970 and 1973.
MR 8592	3/12/40	6/12/40		New to DLH.
4wDM p	20/28 hp	2.5 ton	2 ft	Sold as Reconditioned loco.
	17/5/46	13/6/46		To Bedford Silica Sand, Heath & Reach, Leighton Buzzard. To Flettons Ltd, Whittlesea, Cambs 8/63. To Alan Keef Ltd, between 1970 and 1973. Sold to Sam Henry & Partners (contrs) Killingholme Jetty contract, Immingham Humberside c.77. Loco 'disappeared' said to have been sold to quarry after contractors went into liquidation. Never traced since.

Also had MR diesel dumpers Works Nos 8384 (ordered 30/3/48) and 9176 (ordered 5/5/58).

H.G. Brown, Kings Farm, Leighton Buzzard
(SP929246)

H.G. Brown, Kings Farm, Stanbridge Road, Leighton, was a timber and sand haulier. He cut the original sleepers for the LBLR in 1919. Around 1920 he began to dig sand from a pit between his farm and Page's Park. A sleeper road was laid into the pit so that carts could be loaded at the face. About 1926 this was replaced by a light 2 ft gauge railway.

The railway climbed out of the pit on to an embankment and terminated on a gantry of heavy timbers with a sleeper floor. The gantry was built beside the farm road and against a wall of the shed where Brown kept his steam wagons. (He had been the first to use steam wagons to haul sand in this district.) There was a large door in this wall so

Two views of the Leighton Buzzard Brick Company's Ledburn Road pit *c.* 1930.   *F.C. Rickard*

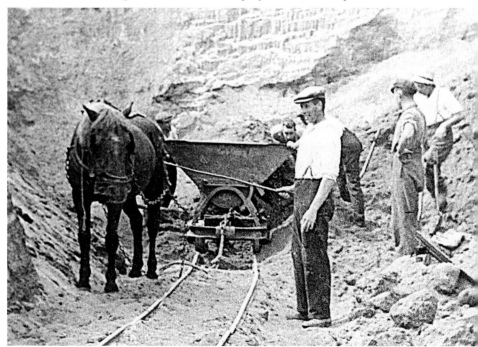

that sand could be tipped into the wagon while it stood in the shed in the dry. Other men's carts were loaded from the other side of the gantry in the open. The tip was about 170 yards from the end of the long (200 yard) narrow pit, making a probable total length of railway about 350 yards.

There were about 20 Hudson wagons of 1 cu. yd. capacity. They were hauled out of the pit one at a time by a horse. Sidings in the pit were mainly reached by turning plates instead of points. Six or eight men were employed digging sand and overburden, which was removed in barrows.

In 1935 or 1936 Brown wanted to run a line down to Grovebury sidings so he could load main line wagons direct. He made a gap about 20 ft long in the wall beside Billington Road (the houses opposite had not then been built) but the Council refused permission for the necessary level crossing. The gap in the wall was still visible in 1969.

One of his employees, 'Fatty' Orchard, is remembered for his ability to transfer 1½ cu. yd. (say 37 cwt) of sand from a cart to a railway wagon in 3½ minutes, using a No. 4 pan coke shovel!

In 1947 the quarry was let to Henry Winfield and the railway finished. Winfield laid a road of 'conks' (sand rejects from the screens) for his lorries which were loaded directly by a 10RB excavator through a ½ in. vibrating screen. This pit's sand had few rejects, so conks for the road were brought from Winfield's other pit at Heath and Reach. The pit closed in 1963.

H. Paul, Page's Park
(SP925245)

Paul started a small unauthorised breeze block making plant beside Page's Park in about 1950. A short 2 ft gauge railway was laid to take the blocks to concrete drying areas nearby. The wagons were tipping wagon frames with wooden floors, and were pushed by hand. However, as the plant had been built without planning permission, the Council ordered it to be closed in 1954 or 1955. The shed and a length of track set in concrete remained in the back of C. Nash's yard and could be seen from Page's Park in 1969.

Leighton Buzzard Brick Co. Ltd Ledburn Road Pit, Leighton Buzzard
(SP914236)

The Leighton Buzzard Brick Co. Ltd opened its pit at Ledburn Road, a mile south-west of Leighton, in 1923. At first the sand was barrowed to carts (or occasionally lorries), which carried it to the railway at Wing Sidings. Most customers were Luton firms and sand was sent by rail, via Bletchley and Bedford, to the MR sidings at Luton. Oh for the LB&HR!

A 2 ft gauge railway was introduced in 1927 as the pit became deeper. There were six or eight Hudson side tipping wagons, capacity 1 cu. yd. A steam winch hauled them one at a time up to the loading stage by the road under which the lorries backed for loading.

Later the steam winch was replaced by a more powerful petrol driven one capable of hauling three wagons at a time up to the tip. A pony was used to haul the trucks from the several faces to the foot of the incline, where they were coupled into trains of three and hooked to the cable. The incline eventually had a length of about 200 yards. There

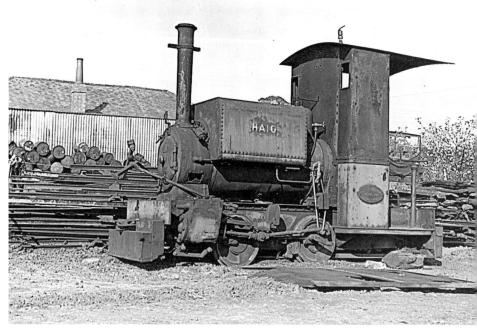

Leighton Buzzard Brick - Potsgrove: 0-4-0ST *Haig* KS 3105.   *G. Alliez*

Another view of *Haig* out of use at Leighton Buzzard Brick's Potsgrove pit, 18th November, 1945.   *A.G. Wells*

Leighton Buzzard Brick - Potsgrove: RH 172902 and RH 174545 in February 1952. *G.P. Roberts*

Leighton Buzzard Brick - Potsgrove: Wagons (note the end tipper), parts of *Haig*, and the ex-West Coast Joint Stock coach body used as a store. *G.P. Roberts*

were now about a dozen wagons in use, none brake fitted.

The sand was dug by hand, the men often standing on ledges cut in the pit face which averaged 35 ft high. When pockets of unclean sand were struck the sand was thrown through a nearly vertical screen, mounted either beside the wagon or on the ledge. In 1935 the company obtained its first excavator, a Priestman. A sleeper road was laid down and lorries loaded directly at the face. The railway was then used to remove overburden. It eventually fell out of use and most of the equipment was sent to the Watling Street (Potsgrove) pit when it opened in 1944. Ledburn Road pit continues to be worked. Sand is now pumped from workings across the road beside the BR main line into hoppers, and thence loaded into lorries directly.

Leighton Buzzard Brick Co. Ltd Potsgrove Pit
(SP939298)

The Leighton Buzzard Brick Co. opened its Potsgrove quarries in September 1944. These were situated on the south side of the Watling Street (A5), beside a garage and the junction with a lane leading to the hamlet of Potsgrove, and were adjoining Garside's Double Arches workings.

A 2 ft gauge railway was built to carry the sand up out of the pit. Some of the materials came from the Ledburn Road system. The track was laid in the concrete at the edge of a steep road leading into the pit. At the top of the gradient the line curved north across this road to run parallel with the A5. A trailing point gave access to a level siding which was laid on girders supported by brick pillars beside the steep road. Here lorries were loaded. There was no locomotive shed; locomotives not in use were just sheeted over.

The railway had a short life. Arthur Wells visited the quarry in November 1945 to see the steam locomotive *Haig* which stood on a short length of track just inside the entrance. He does not remember having seen any more track or railway equipment, so presumably the line was still being built. It operated for only about a year and closed in 1946. The haul was too short, the gradients too severe, and it was found more economical to lay a sleeper road into the pit thus enabling lorries to be loaded directly by the excavator.

Following the closure the track was lifted and all the equipment dumped on the waste ground near the A5, where most of it remained until 1952. The two Ruston & Hornsby diesel locomotives were sold. *Haig* and the wagons were scrapped. All that remained in 1961 was a short length of track embedded in the concrete road and a battered Hudson wagon frame with an oil drum chained to it.

Despite its small size and short life the railway had no less than four locomotives. The first was *Haig*, a Kerr, Stuart 'Wren' class 0-4-0ST, No. 3105, ordered in October 1917 and delivered on 27th April, 1918 for the construction of Kidbrooke Aerodrome, London. It was painted grey and was fitted with a steel firebox and tubes. The price was £659. *Haig* spent about 25 years at Kidbrooke (although spares were sent to the Air Ministry at Uxbridge in September 1929) before being sold to the Leighton Buzzard Brick Co. Ltd but did little work after the arrival of the diesel locomotives. In February 1952, G.P. Roberts found the boiler lying beside the frames while the tank, bunkers and other components lay in a pile nearby.

The 'Wren' class was the smallest in size yet the largest numerically of Kerr, Stuart's standard range of locomotives, and a total of 167 were built between 1905 and 1941 (the last four were constructed by Hunslet who had obtained Kerr, Stuart's goodwill). Two outside cylinders 6 in. by 9 in. drove the rear coupled wheels, 1 ft 8 in. in diameter. The boiler contained 35 1¾ in. tubes and generated steam at 140 psi. Heating surface was: firebox 13.9 sq. ft, tubes 72.1 sq. ft, total 86.0 sq. ft, and grate area 2.19 sq. ft. The water capacity was 87 gallons. In working order the locomotive weighed 4 tons 3 cwt and had a tractive effort at 75 per cent boiler pressure of 1700 lb. Overall measurements were approximately 9 ft 6 in. long, 4 ft 3 in. wide, 7 ft 8 in. high and wheel base 3 ft. The first 'Wrens' had inside Stephenson link motion, but most 'Wrens' built after 1915 including *Haig* and *Pixie* (LBNGR) were fitted with outside Hackworth valve gear.

A Motor Rail diesel locomotive was obtained and handled the majority of the traffic. One informant alleged it was new, but Motor Rail records do not show any sales to this company of either locomotives or spares. It was sold in 1949 after the closure. Another source said that this locomotive was hired from Diesel Loco Hirers, which would explain both the absence of records and its early disappearance.

Two second-hand cabless Ruston & Hornsby diesel locomotives were obtained from John Heaver Ltd, Chichester, who had bought them new. Following the line's closure they were sold to Frank Isaacson Ltd, West Drayton in 1952 and were observed still in their yard in 1953. Only one of them had done any work at Potsgrove.

Rolling stock comprised about a dozen Hudson side tipping wagons, at least one of which had a screw brake. There was also an iron end tipping wagon with a scoop shaped body and inside frames.

An interesting relic which lasted until about 1962 was the body of a West Coast Joint Stock 6-compartment corridor coach with coupé at one end. At each end was a lavatory, and the opaque glass of the windows had the coats of arms of the owning companies, WCJS in one and LNWR in the other. The coach was used as a store and shack for the quarrymen. Bodies such as this were sold (less bogies) by Wolverton Carriage Works at £1 per foot length.

Locomotives

Haig	KS3105/1918	0-4-0ST	ex-Kidbrooke Aerodrome *c.* 1944, scr. *c.* 2/52
	MR	4wDM	Hire from Diesel Loco Hirers? s/s/49
	RH172902/1935	4wDM	ex-John Heaver Ltd, Chichester, No 2. Class 16/20HP, Lister 18/2 engine rated 16 hp. Weight 2.75 tons. To Frank Isaacson Ltd, West Drayton 1952.
	RH174545/1937	4wDM	ex-John Heaver Ltd, Chichester, No 3. Class 18/21HP, Lister 18/2 engine rated 20 hp. Weight 2.75 tons. To Frank Isaacson Ltd, West Drayton 1952. (LBNGR 37 is similar).

Harry Sear, Manor Farm, Eggington
(SP959255)

For a few years in the 1930s, Harry Sear, farmer of Manor Farm, Eggington, worked a small sand pit on his land. It opened in 1931 or maybe 1930, and was still in production in 1936 when some Fourth century Roman British remains were excavated and examined by Mr R. G. Gurney.

The pit produced loamy sand for building. It was dug by hand and loaded into 2 ft gauge wagons, which were pushed to a staging by the gate opposite the spinney above Eggington House, where the sand was tipped into lorries. Much was collected by Luton firms. The staging remained up to about 1940. A horse may have been used to haul the iron side tipping wagons (1 cubic yard capacity) of which there were about six. They were probably built by Hudson. The sand was screened during loading by throwing it

Arnold - Stone: No. 8 MR 9409 by the screen in the yard, 12th August, 1969.   *Author*

Arnold - Stone: The fuel tank and skips in the yard, 12th August, 1969.   *Author*

through a portable framework mounted on the wagon.

In 1969 about 20 yards of track were exposed along the western lip of the quarry. The rail was 2⅛ in. high and the gauge, measured at several sleepers, was 24¼ in. - presumably 24 in. with worn rails.

Stone Hill Lane, Heath & Reach
Arnold (SP928290)

This was Joseph Arnold's original quarry and was on the opposite side of the hill from the later workings at Double Arches. Following his visit in April 1958, D. Clayton wrote: 'This shows signs of rail operation, but appears unconnected with the LBLR [wrong side of the hill. SAL] and no locos remain, only lines and impedimentia'. By 1958 serviceable equipment had been taken to the other quarries.

Although the large scale OS maps do not show a railway in this quarry, in view of Arnold's extensive use of railways in other quarries it would have been strange if this one had never had a system. In view of its small size and isolation it was probably always hand or horse operated, running from the face to a tip at the quarry entrance from the main road. In fact, in 1986 an old timber roadway, a length of heavy section rail and a pair of flanged wheels on an axle were uncovered some 65 ft below ground level. They were under clay overburden which had been used to backfill old 19th century workings.

Aylesbury Sand Co., Eythrope Road, Stone
Arnold (SP779127)

Albert and Ernest Arnold bought the Aylesbury Sand Co. at Stone, two miles west of Aylesbury, from a Mr C. Castle in 1908. This quarry produced a fine white sand and was operated until 1973. The site was later used for landfill and has now been returned to agriculture. The output was all dispatched by road - there was no main line railway nearby - although in earlier days some sand was carted to Aylesbury Wharf for dispatch by canal.

The railway ran westwards from a yard beside the road to the quarry. In 1969 the track layout was simple. A single track ran from the concrete yard by the office and stores up a short steep gradient to the tip for the screen and washer. Pipes from this plant fed the sand to two stockpiles in the yard. Opposite the tip was an elevated tank for locomotive fuel. Beyond the tip the line fell again to yard level, and threw off a trailing siding into the yard. A branch was thown off which went to a reversing neck and then into an old quarry, where the rails disappeared under the water. Continuing, there was a branch to a spoil tip and then the branch down to the active face, approached by a reversing neck long enough for a locomotive and three skips. All the sidings and branches were on the left when proceeding towards the quarry.

Motor Rail had sent the company information about their 20 hp and 40 hp locomotives on 31st October, 1919, so locomotive operation was probably introduced in the early 1920s. There was only one locomotive here at a time, always No. 8. Presumably it was easier to record a single locomotive than to record transfers between the Aylesbury Sand Co. and the parent company. Known locomotives here are:

8	*Louie*	4wPM MR	Recorded at Double Arches in 11/1945, but to Stone by 12/1946. s/s
8		4wDM MR9409	To Stone 29/11/66, returned to Leighton Buzzard /69, probably on 29/11/69 on the lorry that brought MR7217
8		4wDM MR7217	To Stone 29/11/69, returned to Leighton Buzzard *c.*/73

Locomotive details are given in Chapter 15.

In 1969 there were eight skips on site, with ordinary size wheels.

An unidentified locomotive at 21 Acre which does not appear to be a standard MR product, although it has strong MR characteristics *c.* 1935. Perhaps it is one of Arnold's unrecorded purchases (*see text*).   *F. Biley*

Chapter Fifteen

Quarry Locomotives

Horses used to be used for hauling wagons in the quarries, and in fact they lasted until about 1939 for taking wagons on to Billington Road gantry. However, once the LBLR opened it was not long before locomotives were introduced. The Motor Rail & Tramcar Co. of Bedford had sent a folder of information about their 20 hp and 40 hp locomotives to the Aylesbury Sand Co. (Albert and Ernest Arnold) on 31st October, 1919. In the light of future events this was obviously useful information. Although Arnold bought many Motor Rail locomotives over the next 50 years most were second-hand, unlike Garside who usually bought new until about 1940. The progressive replacement of horses in the sand trade resulted in the closure of three saddlers in Leighton Buzzard.

Arnold's first locomotive was bought for £265 on 6th January, 1920, apparently at the same time as one for the LBLR. Indeed, it seems that Arnold bought both and then resold one immediately to the LBLR. Arnold's first order to Motor Rail for spares was on 27th January, 1920, presumably to put this locomotive into order.

Garside's first Motor Rail locomotive was obtained around May 1920, and could well have been bought from the LBLR contractor Lamb & Phillips, as described in Chapter 9. Four more Simplex locomotives were bought in 1926 and by the mid-1930s the company had about a dozen at work. Possibly the delay between 1920 and 1926 was due to problems with the small Austro-Daimler locomotives used at Rackley Hill and Grovebury quarries which discouraged purchases for a time.

Arnold's subsequent locomotive purchases are less clear. According to Motor Rail records the firm had only about half a dozen locomotives by the early 1930s, which seems most unlikely. Peter Arnold wrote to me in early 1970 soon after the publication of the first edition of this book. His information, gleaned from Arnold's accounts, made interesting reading. According to the annual accounts, the company bought locomotives as shown in the left hand columns below.

Year	Loco. Purchases Number	Cost £	Repairs to Plant & Machinery £	Possible Locos Cost £	Number at £300 each
1920	1	265			
1921			2,879	2,179	7
1922			1,400	700	2
1923			1,603	903	3
1924			1,903	1,203	4
1925			1,269	569	2
1926			1,358	668	2
1927	2	495	760		
1928	2	400	952		
1929			1,127	427	1
1930	1	292	1,258		
1931	1	110			
1932	1	125			
1933	1	152			
1934	3	747 10s.			

Peter noticed a pencilled correction in the 1926 accounts, dividing the figure of £1358 into Repairs £690 and Locos £668. Such a value for Repairs is comparable for the amounts shown in 1927 and 1928. If the amounts for Repairs in the years 1921 to 1926

Garside No. 21 *Festoon* MR 4570 at Cedars School, Leighton Buzzard for the LBLR 50th Anniversary Exhibition. Note the re-railing ramp placed over the rail (a vital piece of equipment carried by quarry locomotives), and the sprag formerly fitted to the last wagon of Garside's trains when ascending Marley's Bank, 30th December, 1969. *Author*

Arnold No. 32 FH 2161 at Billington Road washing plant. Note the different buffer beam compared to *Festoon*, 13th April, 1957. *Author*

are assumed to be approximately £700 as well then subtraction gives the figures shown in the 'Possible Locos Cost' column. The number of possible locomotives bought was then calculated, using a price of £300. The result is about 20 locomotives purchased in the years 1921 to 1926! There is no obvious reason why the locomotive purchases were shown as repairs.

Peter also wrote, 'My father (Joseph (2) Arnold) says that more locos very quickly followed the 1st one in 1920' which supports the hypothesis above; if these figures are correct the firm would have owned eight to ten by the end of 1921. Against this is the fact that when MR3996 was bought in October 1933 it became No. 9 and the Loco Purchases No. column then totalled nine . . . .

If Arnold bought Simplex locomotives direct from army suplus dealers (possibly through his friend Fred Syme of the Ministry of Munitions) they might have been cheap but in relatively poor condition. Replacement might have been cheaper than repair, until the source dried up and he was forced to use other dealers or even go to Motor Rail. A new purchase could have taken the running number of a withdrawn one, so No. 9 could have been a coincidence.

Arnold also bought locomotives from F.C. Hibberd in the 1930s and may well have bought ex-WDLR Simplex locomotives from their predecessor Kent Construction. This would also account for the lack of purchases recorded by Motor Rail themselves. Some evidence for these additional locomotives (from army surplus or Kent Construction) arises from the names carried by some locomotives. In 1945 four were named, numbers 1, 4, 8 & 10. Were these perhaps the last examples of the early fleet, and had been numbered to bring them into line, possibly in the mid-1930s?

The first quarry locomotives, as well as many later additions, and the small ones on the LBLR, were 2½ ton 20 hp petrol-engined Simplex machines built by the Motor Rail and Tramcar Co. Ltd, Bedford. They were originally used on the 60 cm gauge War Department Light Railways which served the Western Front during World War I. The design proved ideal for use on lightly laid lines in forward areas, and about 675 were built from early 1916. The works regularly produced 20 to 25 per week. After the war many of these locomotives were sold and passed into the hands of contractors, quarry owners, dealers etc.

Simplex locomotives had a distinctive bowed channel under-frame in the shape of an elongated octagon, known by the makers as bent frame and to others as bent, bow or, (in the Leighton Buzzard area only) boat frame. As with the contemporary 40 hp locomotives the tapered ends of the frame may have been an attempt to enable the locomotive to move lineside obstructions. The frame had four stretchers, two at the ends which also supported small ballast weights, and two near the centre which carried the engine and gearbox. The axle boxes were carried on additional longitudinal girders between the end and central stretchers, thus leaving the centre section clear.

A Dorman 2-cylinder 20 hp petrol engine was mounted transversely on the left hand side of the locomotive. Originally 2JO engines with monoblock cylinders (i.e. the head and cylinder block were cast as one) were fitted. Later 2JOR engines were fitted, identical except that the cylinder head was removable. The engine drove a Dixon Abbot patent 2-speed gearbox mounted on the right hand side via an inverted cone clutch. The final drive was by roller chains to both axles. Nominal speeds were 3.5 and 7 mph in either direction. Haulage capacity was 36 tons at 3 mph or 18 tons at 6 mph on the level.

A distinctive sheet metal bonnet in two parts, hinged on the top, covered the engine, gearbox and the 14 gallon petrol tank mounted above the latter. Originally the petrol tanks were rectangular; from the mid-1920s cylindrical ones were fitted. The aluminium WDLR number plate was mounted on the bonnet sides. The figures were nailed on the

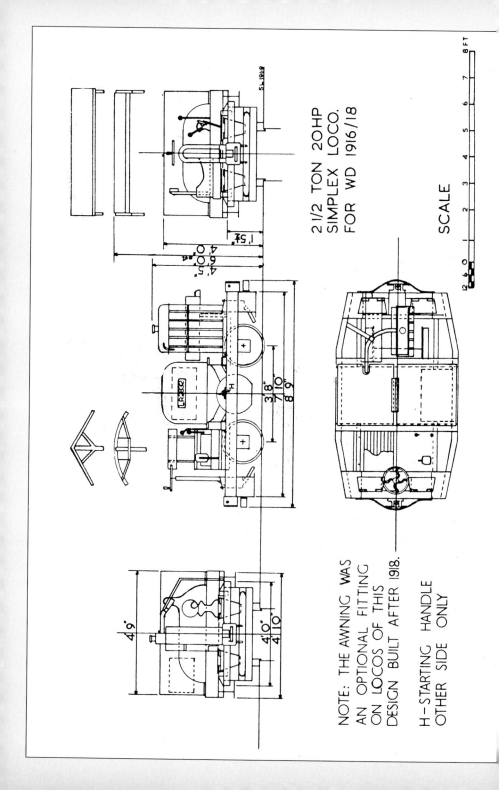

2 1/2 TON 20HP
SIMPLEX LOCO.
FOR WD 1916/18

SCALE

NOTE: THE AWNING WAS
AN OPTIONAL FITTING
ON LOCOS OF THIS
DESIGN BUILT AFTER 1918.

H — STARTING HANDLE
OTHER SIDE ONLY

20/28 bhp MR diesel

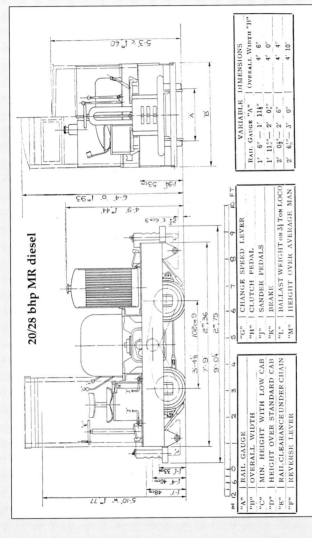

VARIABLE DIMENSIONS	
RAIL GAUGE "A"	OVERALL WIDTH "B"
1' 6" — 1' 11½"	4' 6"
1' 11½" — 2' 0"	4' 0"
2' 0½" — 2' 6"	4' 4"
2' 6½" — 3' 0"	4' 10"

"A"	RAIL GAUGE
"B"	OVERALL WIDTH
"C"	MIN. HEIGHT WITH LOW CAB
"D"	HEIGHT OVER STANDARD CAB
"E"	RAIL CLEARANCE UNDER CHAIN
"F"	REVERSE LEVER
"G"	CHANGE SPEED LEVER
"H"	CLUTCH PEDAL
"J"	SANDER PEDALS
"K"	BRAKE
"L"	BALLAST WEIGHT OR 3½ TON LOCO
"M"	HEIGHT OVER AVERAGE MAN

GUARANTEE.

In lieu of any warranty implied by law, we expressly guarantee to repair or supply new, any parts which, within a period not exceeding **twelve months** from delivery, may prove defective through bad material or workmanship, providing such parts are sent for inspection at our Works. All goods are supplied on condition that we shall not be liable for any loss incurred through stoppages, nor for any subsequential damages. The details of the illustrations are subject to modifications as improvements are introduced. The dimensions, weights, and other particulars are carefully stated, but must be taken as approximate only.

wooden pattern and the nail heads appeared as projections on the final casting.

The driver sat sideways (so he could see both ways with equal ease) at the rear. His simple slatted wooden seat covered a toolbox. Within easy reach were the gear levers, a foot pedal for the clutch, and a screw handbrake with a klaxon mounted in the pillar. No cab was fitted. At the front, slightly offset from the longitudinal axis of the locomotive, was a sideways-mounted radiator. Earlier locomotives had either cast aluminium Randle radiators or Reliance pressed steel ones (which were also fitted by Kent Construction and Hibberd). After 1926 Davies Patent radiators, with 'Simplex' cast in the top, were used. On one side of the radiator was the silencer and radiator fan. The other side was an empty space, which enabled a second man to ride on the locomotive. This space was also used to carry re-railing ramps, spare coupling chains etc. Handrails were fitted across the locomotive front, and often to the radiator top, for the benefit of the second man. At first the main handrails were an inverted 'V' but later they were rectangular.

Four sandboxes at the corners of the frame supplied sand to each wheel. Central buffer couplings with a sprung buffer bar beneath them completed the rugged locomotive. Its basic measurements were 7 ft 9 in. over frame, 8 ft 11 in. long over buffers, 4 ft 10 in. wide (centre) and 4 ft ends, 4 ft 4½ in. high, 1 ft 5¾ in. wheel diameter with 3 ft 6½ in. wheelbase. This design continued to be built by Motor Rail until about 1926.

While various improvements and modifications were made over the years, the basic layout and dimensions altered very little in subsequent designs of 20 hp to 50 hp locomotives. Straight channel side frames were introduced in 1918, but were replaced about 10 years later by deep plate side frames. A heavy casting with several slots for different coupling heights, large diameter single plate clutches, and a pressed steel driver's seat became standard in the 1920s.

The first diesel locomotives in the quarries were obtained in the mid-1930s and proved far more economical than the petrol ones, although Motor Rail continued to build them for some years. Arnold converted one petrol engine to TVO but it was not a success, and so the petrol-engined fleet lasted until after World War II. Some had diesel engines fitted into the original frames, but more often the withdrawal of a petrol locomotive followed the introduction of a second-hand diesel one.

In 1968 both companies had only one bent framed petrol engine locomotive left. The last of Arnold's petrol locomotives, No. 21, was converted in 1962 to an air compressor for rock drills, primarily for use in Chamberlain's Barn quarry. The compressor was mounted on the right-hand side, replacing the gearbox in the space normally occupied by the fuel tank which was moved to the rear. The air reservoir was mounted beside the radiator. The air plant appears to have been salvaged from a trailer compressor, formerly used in the quarries, whose 10 hp engine was insufficiently powerful. By 1969 Garside's last petrol locomotive, also No. 21, was stored in a shed at Churchways quarry. For some years it had been used as a mobile workshop for the fitters, for which purpose it was fitted with a vice and toolboxes on the frame.

The 2-cylinder Dorman diesel engine with cylinders 115 mm bore by 130 mm stroke (developing 20 hp at 1000 rpm or 28 hp at 1600 rpm) had about half the fuel consumption of the equivalent petrol engine. The first diesels were started by putting a smouldering wick into the top of the cylinder before cranking the engine. The alternative was to give them a push start with a petrol locomotive; latterly *Festoon* had been used for this at Grovebury. However, improved cylinder heads and other developments made diesel engines easier to start so this became unnecessary.

Cabs were optional on small Motor Rail locomotives. Wooden cabs with curved roofs were fitted to the earlier bent, channel, and plate frame locomotives. These developed into metal cabs with curved roofs, fitted until the late 1930s, and later replaced by the familiar metal cab with ridged roof. The standard cab in later years had the side facing the driver open and the side behind him closed by a steel door, opened for maintenance and emergencies. There were narrow horizontal windows back and front. Garside's locomotives usually had the standard Motor Rail cab if anything, although even in the 1960s some of Garside's locomotives had no protection for the driver at all. Most of Arnold's locomotives had home-made cabs very similar to the standard Motor Rail cab. Two of Garside's second-hand purchases had wooden cabs with semi-circular roofs which had been specified when Glasgow Corporation originally ordered these locomotives. Awnings, a simple roof on a light support, were once common. Extra protection could be obtained by hanging a tarpaulin sheet from the awning roof, with a square hole cut in the sheet to act as a window.

Flat cast iron weights could be bolted under the ends of the frame to increase the locomotive weight from the basic 2½ tons up to 3½ tons, and hence increase the maximum load that could be hauled. The ballasted locomotives tended to be those working over extra steep gradients, for example out of Pratt's Pit, and on the New Trees to Double Arches run.

The WDLR locomotives had been fitted with klaxon horns, fitted to the brake column. A sharp downwards push on the operating lever generated current which caused the horn to sound. Later locomotives had whistles. Petrol-engined ones had the whistle fitted to the cylinder head and worked off the compression. On diesels the whistle was mounted on a hollow box with a hole in one face. The box was pivoted so that the hole could be brought over the end of the exhaust pipe, thus causing the waste gases to pass through the whistle.

Although Motor Rail had abandoned bent frames from about 1926, such locomotives could be obtained from another manufacturer for another 15 years. Kent Construction & Engineering Co. Ltd, Ashford, Kent, bought a large number of ex-WDLR Simplex locomotives and spares soon after World War I. The locomotives were reconditioned and sold as 'reconditioned Simplex locomotives'. Some of the spares were used to build 'Planet' locomotives (designed by Kent Construction) but based very closely on the Motor Rail design. Kent Construction ceased to trade in 1926 and eventually their stock and drawings passed to F.C. Hibberd & Co. Ltd, formed about 1930. From 1932 their works were at Park Royal, London. Hibberd continued to sell reconditioned Simplexes and also Planets. Some were advertised as Planet-Simplex locomotives. Hibberd's 'Simplex' locomotives all had bow frames and were virtually undistinguishable from the Motor Rail 'Simplex'. The length, maximum width and height were all increased slightly to 9 ft, 5 ft and 4 ft 6 in. respectively. New sandbox lids were fitted as the Motor Rail ones had 'Simplex' cast on them. Hibberd locomotives had a different type of buffer, and a single deep buffer beam instead of the pair of angle sections used by Motor Rail. Other makes of engine, e.g. National, Paxman were often used instead of Dorman, which was the Motor Rail standard. Where the two types of locomotives have worked side by side, a complete interchange of parts has often occurred. Arnold had at least seven known Hibberd locomotives and may well have had more.

Although Motor Rail had a virtual monopoly a few locomotives from other manufacturers have worked in Arnold's and Garside's quarries. The Kent Construction and Hibberd versions of Simplex locomotives have already been described. Two Austro-Daimler petrol locomotives, one really a motorised skip, worked in the Grovebury area in the 1920s. One may have been transferred to Double Arches around 1930 but did not last long. The engine was later removed from the motorised skip and

A pair of cabless 20/28 hp locomotives parked at the far end of Garside's Billington Road washing plant on the former connection to Page's Park, just by the entrance to Arnold's plant. No. 14 *Devon Loch* MR 7145 and No. 18 *Honeylight* are seen on 9th January, 1962.

P.R. Arnold

A 10 hp Kent Construction petrol locomotive as may have been used by Parrot & Jones. This example was photographed at Ashton-under-Lyme sewage works in 1974. *Author*

it was converted to a 'bogie'. It may have been the inspiration for Garside's own locomotive. Around 1927 Garside built a locomotive round a Ford T engine mounted on 16 in. skip wheels. Only the first two gears were used as it was too fast. This locomotive was used for about 10 years on overburden removal before being scrapped. Arnold hired a Ruston Hornsby diesel in August 1933 but it evidently did not find favour. In the early 1950s Garside obtained a second-hand Jung diesel and also a second-hand Orenstein & Koppel one, but both were soon resold. Possibly they were available when required and bought as stopgaps.

A 10 hp Planet locomotive is said to have been used in Parrot & Jones' quarry at Shenley Hill. These were the first true Planet locomotives, built by Kent Construction in the mid-1920s. A 4-cylinder Dorman petrol engine mounted longitudinally drove a 2-speed gearbox with bevel reverse. The transmisssion continued with roller chain to a central countershaft and chains to each axle. The overall dimensions were: length 8 ft 5 in., width 4 ft, height 4 ft 4 in., wheelbase 4 ft and wheel 15 in. diameter. The locomotive weighed 1¾ tons and had a maximum tractive effort of 850 lb.

After 1945 both quarry companies tended to buy second-hand locomotives instead of new. In the late 1940s and early 1950s most locomotives purchased had petrol engines, but from the mid-1950s diesel-engined locomotives were obtained, replacing both petrol-engined locomotives and petrol-engined locomotives converted to diesel.

Arnold tended to scrap their withdrawn locomotives quite quickly, but Garside dumped withdrawals on a pair of sidings behind the Billington Road washer. This dump of derelicts (25 in May 1958, 14 in April 1961) existed throughout the 1950s and was not cleared until 1962. From time to time locomotives here were broken up, and useful spares were removed. Both firms kept the frames of two or three locomotives spare, in case of accidents. Garside took two old frames up to Double Arches on leaving Billington Road, and a new line of derelicts (8 in August 1968) formed on the embankment to the old tipping dock beside the later workshops. Parts of Arnold's locomotives, particularly cabs and bonnet covers, used to be dumped against the roadside hedge just south of Billington Road workshops. When the main line closed, Arnold's locomotives were taken to Billington Road workshops for repair by lorry. The locomotives were loaded and unloaded using a length of track supported on sleepers or blocks of wood.

Both companies also bought locomotives second-hand for spares, a practice which resulted in a number of locomotives being seen which did not in fact work in the quarries. Arnold especially did this when a replacement crankshaft was needed. Quarry locomotives averaged three to five years between heavy repairs. The tables show that locomotive allocations to the quarries were remarkably permanent.

While most of the locomotives used were 2 ft gauge, some were 60 cm (1 ft 11⅝ in.) gauge. They may have been re-gauged when new wheels were required, but in the meantime they probably ran without difficulty as manufacturers of light railway equipment tend to give their products wide wheel tyres to offset the variations of gauge often found on industrial and contractors' railways.

When the LBLR ceased to provide motive power its modern locomotives were shared between Arnold and Garside. Arnold took three large locomotives and one small, and Garside two large. However, with the closure of Billington Road depot in 1964, Garside no longer needed its two main line locomotives which were therefore sold to Hopkins-England Ltd of Woburn Sands in 1965. (This firm was periodically employed to scrap Garside's locomotives, for example breaking up 11 in October 1976.) After overhaul by Motor Rail, Garside's LBLR locomotives were resold to a firm in Singapore in August 1966. Arnold tended to use its largest locomotive, No. 43, for main line haulage in

Garside - Double Arches: Two 20/28 hp locomotives Nos. 13 *Arkle* MR 7152 with standard cab and 27 MR 5852 with curved roof cab, 14th August, 1968. Note re-railing ramps on the front footplate.   *Author*

Garside No. 13 *Arkle* MR 7108 20/28 hp locomotive now with curved roof cab outside Double Arches shops. The starting handle is in position, 27th July, 1977.   *Author*

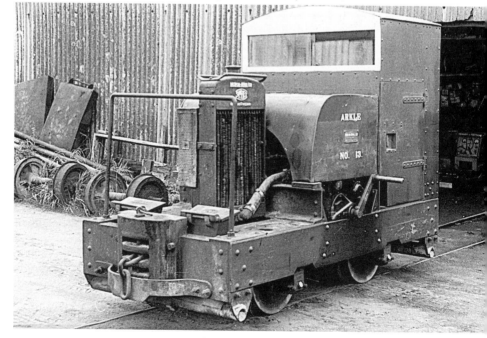

preference to the 5 ton Nos. 42 and 44.

All locomotives were well maintained and painted medium green with white round the cab windows. Numbers (and names) were painted in white on the bonnet sides, and Arnold's locomotives had the number in black above the cab windows too. Bonnet numbers were all prefixed by 'No.' It would appear that at first locomotives were numbered in the order of purchase, and any blanks existing through withdrawals were filled before creating new numbers. Positive locomotive identification was not easy. With running numbers on the easily removed bonnet covers and cab, it was possible for two locomotives to exchange identities if they passed through the workshop simultaneously.

The identification situation was further confused by the lack of works plates on many locomotives, especially the older ones. The plate on Simplex locomotives was usually rivetted to the rear engine bearer of the frame, but on petrol locomotives (20 & 20/26 hp) the works plate was fitted on the stretcher plate in front of the radiator (except in the case of very early WDLR 20 hp locomotives with the wide brake columns, which had it in the stretcher plate beneath the brake spindle). The works number was also usually stamped at the base of the brake column, but this was not generally known when there were large numbers of plateless locomotives in the quarries, so they were largely unidentified. Even some of the locomotives existing in 1969 were only positively identified around that time.

An example of the problem was the case of an ex-WDLR locomotive in Garside's dump which had no plate and carried a different name and number each side, with a third name visible beneath the paint on one side! Then there was the case of No. 34 *Kilmore* (Motor Rail 7105) - the Double Arches fitters' locomotive. This had the frame from No.35 *Doutelle*, the bonnets of No.34, the cab off No. 13 and a reconditioned spare engine! The frame of the original *Kilmore* lay outside, dumped, sporting the bonnet (and name) of *Doutelle*. Some locomotives apparently bought for spares may have assumed the identity of an existing locomotive by having identifiable parts (e.g. bonnet cover) put on for weather protection or storage.

Most of Garside's locomotives were named after racehorses which won important races. The names could be changed when the locomotive was shopped, the foreman asking Mr Delafield for his suggestions, but on the whole running numbers were not changed. Deliberate changes of names were more common in the later years. Not all Garside's locomotives were named, and some were not named all the time.

Arnold did not scrap all their old locomotives when replacements were obtained, and since about 1951 managed to build up a small reserve of serviceable locomotives kept at the workshops. Thus in the 1950s and 1960s, when a quarry locomotive came in for repair, an unnumbered spare was sometimes given its number and sent out straight away. In this case, after the repairs were completed, the old number was painted out, and the locomotive went into reserve until it was sent out as a replacement for another locomotive whose number it then took. This accounts for much of the renumbering that took place.

The locomotive fleet lists that follow have been compiled from various sources. A locomotive list compiled by F. Jux in 1962 was combined with observations from other enthusiasts who visited the area (A.G. Wells 11/45, E.S. Tonks 12/46, D.Clayton 5/58) and with Ian Jolly's detailed Motor Rail information (the first tables) to give a basic picture. A few locomotive identities were assumed, for example to allocate known locomotives into gaps in the numbering sequence. Observations published in the *Bulletin* (Industrial Railway Society) and in *Narrow Gauge News* (Narrow Gauge Railway

Society), plus my own observations were used for the post-1960 period. This gave the following locomotive lists based on works numbers.

The information was then reorganised into running number order, assuming that two different locomotives with the same number did not usually exist at the same time, and inconsistencies removed as far as possible. The final fleet allocation lists were then checked against the original sources.

Key for Locomotive Fleet & Allocation Lists

D	Diesel
DxP	Diesel converted from petrol
P	Petrol
( )	Previous running number
CB etc	At this quarry on date shown. If in italics then at quarry soon after date shown, i.e. an entry CB in 11/45 column means present, but if seen in 12/46 then entry is *CB*.
New	Delivered direct from MR. Includes reconditioned locomotives allocated a new works number.
DLH	Obtained from Diesel Loco Hirers, often after reconditioning.
LBLR	Obtained from LBLR.
PLH	Obtained from Petrol Loco Hirers, often after reconditioning
pres	Preserved
reb	Rebuilt
ret	Returned to manufacturer
scr	Scrapped
see	Subsequent number, see for later history
sold	Sold to a commercial user
s/s	Scrapped or sold, disposal not known
was	Previous number, see for earlier history
me	Manuscript entry in Maker's records
b	Bent Frame
c	Channel Frame
p	Plate frame
IJ	Ian Jolly comment

Locomotives of Joseph Arnold & Sons Ltd, Leighton Buzzard

Compiled from the Maker's Contract Sheets, Material Sheets and Spares Sheets and other sources by Ian B Jolly.

First spares order was on 27/1/20 for 12 cup washers, followed by several orders, probably for a single locomotive until the first identifiable spares on 5/7/20 for chain for 20 hp locomotive. By the end of 1920 spares were being ordered several times a month.

Locomotives of Joseph Arnold & Sons Ltd, Leighton Buzzard

Running Number	Works No. Type	Ordered HP	Ex-Works Weight	Cost	Gauge	Notes
11	MRTC 342 4wPM b	31/1/17 20 hp	27/4/17 2.5 ton		60 cm	New to WDLR as LR1742. *me* MacCreadie, Cochrane & McTaggart (Macreadie Cochrane & Co. 180 West Regent St Glasgow who had several locomotives from PLH - spares 4/24 until 9/27. Ordered on one occasion by MacCreadie Cochrane & Co. for despatch to J.A. McTaggart & Co. Ltd (Contractors) of Corkerhill, Glasgow). *me* 1/11/26 J. Somerville (40 Carston Road, Dumfermline ordered spares from 1/11/26 for 20 hp locomotive - until 5/11/40) To J. Arnold by 11/45 (between 11/40 and 11/45 ? - II). Scr. /63.
	MRTC 916 4wPM b		6/18 2.5 ton		60 cm	New to WDLR France as LR2637. To J. Arnold by ? s/s by /60 - rebuilt as compressor (21) ? but see notes below.
21	MRTC ???? 4wPM b	20 hp	2.5 ton		60 cm	Ex ? This loco was constructed such that it could never have had sandboxes, suggesting that it was built for the 'sandlines' where sandboxes were of little use, unless both cross members at each end were renewed after collision(s)! (Unlikely.) Axleboxes dated 1918 and 1920. Converted to mobile compressor 1962 by replacing gearbox with compressor. Note remained as petrol, NOT converted to diesel. PRESERVED by Ian Jolly, Mold, Clwyd 30/3/78 .
20	MRTC 999 4wPM b	20 hp	8/18 2.5 ton		60 cm	New to WDLR France as LR2720. *me* 17/2/26 Establishment Decauville Aisne Paris, to J. Arnold by 11/45 (c./38?); Scr. c./60.
2	MRTC 1169 4wPM b	20 hp	10/18 2.5 ton		60 cm	New to WDLR France as LR2890. *me* 11/2/20 Group des Houilleres Enhavier. To J. Arnold by 11/45 (c./28?); Scr. c./60.
14	MRTC 1704 4wPM b	20 hp	7/18 2.5 ton		60 cm	New to WDLR France as LR2425. To J. Arnold by 11/45 (c.36?); Scr. c./60.
12 (1, 21)	MRTC 1757 4wPM b Conv 4wDM	23/1/18 20 hp	8/18 2.5 ton		60 cm	New to WDLR France as LR2478. To LBLR. To J. Arnold c./23; Scr. c./60.
7	MRTC 3862 4wPM b	21/6/28 20 hp	2.5 ton		60 cm	'Examine & overhaul Loco 371'. PLH purchased five locomotives from contractors William Moss of Leicester - all were overhauled and given new numbers. Several of them had water tanks (to wash the rails clean) in lieu of sanding gear. MRTC 3862 says 'Water tanks to be removed and sanding gear fitted'. Overhauled 3/9/28, 28/11/28, 5/2/29.
		5/2/29	14/2/29	£290 delvd		Reconditioned locomotive ex-MR to Chittenden & Simmonds Ltd (later British Quarrying Co and eventually taken over by Amalgamated Roadstone Corporation Ltd), Allington Quarry, Maidstone, Kent.

Running Number	Works No. Type	Ordered HP	Ex-Works Weight	Cost Gauge	Notes
7	Conv 4wDM				To J. Arnold by early /30s? Scr. c.5/61.
9	MRTC 3996 4wPM6	19/10/33 20 hp	20/10/33 2.5 ton	£152 delvd 60 cm	To J. Arnold. Recond. loco. (Old No. not known). Purchased on HP Scr. c./63.
26(19)	MR 4701 4wPM p Conv 4w DM	23/1/35 20/26 hp 19/2/36	23/11/34 2.5 ton	2 ft	New to PLH; reconditioned for PLH 20/3/35 & 26/8/35. Resold to MR to J. Arnold (NO ex-works date - possibly already there ex-hire - IJ). Frame only at Billington Road by 1/79. Last loco,(frame only) at Billington Road 6/82, Scr. c. 5/83.
	MR 4705 4wPM p	4/3/35 20/26 hp 20/11/36 (19/12/36 on spares sheet!)	4/3/35 2.5 ton 24/11/36	2 ft £180	New to PLH; Overhauled for PLH 20/8/35, 9/1/36, 20/3/36, 16/4/36 & 21/10/36. Resold by MR to J.C. Oliver Ltd, Airedale Works, Leeds. (Oliver ordered spares from 9/25 regularly until 9/48 then on a couple of occasions until 1/52. They had 15 locos from MRTC/MR. Contracts Journal 15/4/53 advertised 'for sale Simplex Petrol Loco 2 ft gauge' - IJ). me sold to J. Arnold & Sons by ? Scr c. 5/83 .
14 (2, 17)	MR 4707 4wPM p Conv. 4wDM	18/1/36 20/26 hp 31/10/36	18/1/36 2.5 ton 19/10/36	2 ft £200	New to PLH. Overhauled on 24/6/36 & 5/10/36. To MR. To MR. To J. Arnold & Sons Reconditioned Loco, to Billington Road. Note that the ex-Works date preceeds the Order Date.) Frame only at Billington Road by 1/79. Scr c. 5/83.
	MR 4708 4wPM p Conv4wDM p	18/1/36 20/26 hp 5/1/45 20/28 hp	18/1/36 2.5 ton 10/3/45 2.5 ton	2 ft 2 ft	New to PLH; overhauled for PLH 24/6/36, 1/12/36, 22/12/37,15/6/38, 15/7/38, 29/4/38 & 19/12/39; 5/1/45 overhaul and convert to diesel. Transferred to DLH stock. 11/46 Fit exhaust quencher. No subsequent overhauls for DLH.
33					To J. Arnold late 40s? s/s.
16	MR 4709 4wPM p	5/2/36 20/26 hp 31/10/36	5/2/36 2.5 ton 10/9/36	2 ft £200	New to PLH (no overhauls recorded). To MR. Resold to J. Arnold (Note the ex-Works date precedes the Order Date - possibly on hire prior to purchase, as loco not sent back for overhaul before sale - IJ). PRESERVED by J. Butler, Ripley, Surrey 27/1/79.
15	MR 4803 4wPM p Conv 4wDM	3/12/34 20/26 hp	3/12/34 2.5 ton	2 ft	New to PLH (PLH records - 11/1/35 examine damaged loco!) Recondition loco 20/8/35, 30/9/36, 5/1/37, 30/6/37 & 11/10/37. me Sold (by PLH - IJ) to J. Arnold & Sons. (c.11/10/37 - IJ) PRESERVED Runcorn Transport Collection 10/3/79. To West Denbighshire Light Railway, Mold, Clwyd 31/8/80.

No.	Maker/Type				Notes
24 (18,19)	MR 4805 4wPM p Conv 4wDM	23/1/35 20/26 hp	23/1/35 2.5 ton	2 ft	New to PLH; overhauled for PLH 20/8/35, 29/1/36,19/6/36, 30/9/36,13/5/37,16/8/37, 23/7/37. ('11/10/37 Overhaul to PLH standard'.) me 11/10/37 Sold to J. Arnold & Sons £200. Preserved LBNGR 2/5/83 ex-Double Arches shed (last loco there).
See Notes	MRTC 5073 4wPM c Conv 4wDM	2/5/30 20 hp	6/5/30 2.5 ton	£292 2 ft	New to J. Arnold (probably No. 3,4,5 or 6). s/s by /68.
41	MR 5839 4wDM	28/5/34 20/28 hp	29/5/34 3.5 ton	2 ft	New to PLH (No record of overhaul for PLH - already at Ham River Grit ? II). me 13/7/34 sold to Ham River Grit Ltd for £370.10.0. To J. Arnold c. 1/65 ex-Bletchingley Pits, Surrey via HRG's Washington Depot, Sussex as HRG 107. PRESERVED Ian Jolly, Mold, Clwyd 1/12/79. To Abbey Light Railway, Leeds 29/11/80.
27?	MR 5854 4wDM p	20/1/34 20/28 hp 31/5/34	(20/1/34) 3.5 ton ex-stock	ex-stock 2 ft	New to PLH with PLH plates. Overhauled 14/3/34, 25/4/34. me 31/5/34 Converted to 2.5 ton and sold to J. Arnold, Leighton Buzzard for £75 down and 12 monthly payments of £22.10.0 (£330 gross) - This loco has been sold through PLH with MR plates. 28/8/34 This loco returned with engine troubles and loco 5863 sent in its place. J. Arnold & Sons Ltd have agreed to retain it. To PLH with PLH plates. Overhauled 18/1/35, 16/2/35 convert to 3.5 tons, 12/4/35, 24/5/35. To DLH Overhauled 24/8/36. To Greenham Plant Hiring Co. Reconditioned loco with MR plate s/s.
27	MR 5863 4wDM p	27/8/34 20/28 hp	24/8/36 2.5 ton	£250 delvd 2 ft	New to J. Arnold, Billington Road. 'Note this loco sent in exchange for loco 5854 supplied on 31/5/34 which was returned to these works with engine troubles, Arnold's having agreed to retain 5863 in its place.' *HP: £75 deposit and 12 monthly payments of £21-5-0. PRESERVED R. Marner, Surrey 18/8/79. To Chalk Pits Museum, Amberley, Sussex.
			Already delvd £330* 2.5 ton	Already delvd £330* 2 ft	
3	MR 5881 4wDM p	16/5/35 20/28 hp	16/5/35 2.5 ton	2 ft £360	New to PLH delivered to Ham River Grit, new works, Bath Road, Harlington, Middlesex. (No record of overhauls for PLH before sold). me 27/5/35 Sold to Ham River Grit Co. Ltd (Was on hire and has been purchased). To J. Arnold c.1/65 ex-HRG Bletchingley Pits via Washington Depot Sussex, as HRG 108. To Thos. E. Gray, Burton Latimer, Northants 13/8/69; PRESERVED North Warwickshire Rly Society 2/5/82 to store in Leamington Spa.
33	MR 7037 4wPM p Conv 4wDM	16/12/36 20/26 hp	(16/12/36) 2.5 ton	2 ft	New to PLH (No record of overhauls) me Sir Robert McAlpine, Loco was on hire but has been purchased £198.3.0 me 7037 conv. diesel. To J. Arnold c.1960. To Scottish Agricultural Industries Ltd, Bolton Fellend Peat Works, Cumbria 18/10/79.

Running Number	Works No. Type	Ordered HP	Ex-Works Weight	Cost Gauge	Notes
35	MR 7126 4wDM p	8/4/36 20/28 hp	30/4/36 3.5 ton	£380 delivd 2 ft	New to Richard Briggs & Sons Ltd, Bankfield Lime & Roadstone Works, Clitheroe, Lancs. To J. Arnold by 1950s (first observation 5/58. PRESERVED Vale of Teifi NG Rly 2/6/79 (frame only).
23	MR 7128 4wDM p	20/5/36 20/28 hp 10/6/38	(21/5/36) 3.5 ton	2 ft £310 less hire	New to DLH. Overhauled 27/5/37, 7/10/37, 31/12/37, 5/5/58.me 31/5/37 DLH Plates replaced by MR plates when loco sent on hire to Pollock Brown & Co. Sold to Land Reclamation Co Ltd. 'Was on hire but sold' (LR's last spares order 27/1/56). To J. Arnold 2/56. Frame only by 1/79 PRESERVED Surrey & Hampshire Industrial Tramway Surrey 25/7/81. To Light Railway Association, Bedfordshire late 1985.
40	MR 7153 4wDM p	22/12/36 20/28 hp	1/1/37 2.5 ton	£345 2 ft	New to River Ouse (Yorks) Catchment Board, Tower House, Riccall, Yorks. (See below for RO(Y)CB disposals). To J. Arnold by 5/58 Double Arches. PRESERVED J. Butler, Ripley, Surrey after 26/2/79, by 7/79. To E. Ingram, Surrey c. 10/81.
18(1)	MR 7188 4wDM p	26/6/37 20/28 hp	ex-stock 2.5 ton	2 ft	New to Ham River Grit Co. Ltd, New Pit, Woodley, Reading, Berks. 30/6/37 'To be fitted with driver's cab'. To J. Arnold from HRG Bletchingley Pits via Washington Depot, Sussex c./65 as HRG R110. 3.5 tons for a while at Arnold. To Scottish Agricultural Industries, Bolton Fell End Peat Works, Cumbria 18/10/79.
4(3)	MR 7201 4wDM p	20/10/37 20/28 hp	ex-stock 2.5 ton	2 ft	New to Sir Lindsey Parkinson & Co. Ltd Royal Ordnance Factory near Chorley. To Cementation Ltd. To J. Arnold 8/59 ex-Kennel, Hayes, Middsx. PRESERVED Runcorn Transport Collection 10/3/79. To West Denbighshire Light Railway, Mold, Clwyd 31/8/80.
36 (25,24)	MR 7214 4wDM p	28/2/38 20/28 hp 14/10/38 20/28 hp	(28/2/38) 2.5 ton 18/10/38 3.5 ton	2 ft £310 2 ft	New to DLH (Only overhaul 10/10/38).
36(25,24)					Resold by MR to Land Reclamation Ltd as 3.5 ton 20/28 hp 2 ft gauge loco. (24/11/55 LR Ltd offered 6 Simplex 2 ft gauge diesel locos for sale.) To Wakeley Bros & Co Ltd, Honduras Wharf, Bankside, London (No spares records for Wakeley Bros.) To J. Arnold 2/56. PRESERVED LBNGR 5/81.
21(8)	MR 7215 4wDM p	7/3/38 20/28 hp	9/3/38 3.5 ton	£398 2 ft	New to Ham River Grit Co. Ltd Lock Road, Ham, Surrey. me 'Bungey'. (17/10/51 HRG offered several Simplex diesels for sale) (Last spares order 11/9/63). To J. Arnold ex-HRG Bletchingley Pits Surrey via Washington Depot Sussex. c./65 HRG No 111. To J. Arnold's Stone Pits, Aylesbury, Bucks 29/11/69. To Double Arches by 6/73. Frame only by 1/79). PRESERVED Vale of Teifi NG Rly, Dyfed 20/3/82.

No.	Works No. & Type	Dates	HP	Weight	Gauge	Price	History
6	MR 7403 4wDM p	17/8/39 (17/8/39) 7/7/48	20/28 hp	2.5 ton Already on hire	2 ft		New to DLH (Overhauled for PLH on 31/8/39, 7/9/40, 16/7/43, 4/4/46 Fit Exhaust Washer, 6/12/46, 6/3/47 - convert loco 7403 to 3.5 ton, 30/6/47, 20/11/47). To Land Reclamation Ltd from hire. (LR Ltd offered 6 Simplex diesels for sale 24/11/55). To J. Arnold 2/56. PRESERVED D. Billmore, Sheffield 18/1/80. To T. Hall, Ruskington, Lincs 16/2/81.
42	MR 7710 4wDM c	8/6/39 9/6/39	32/42 hp	5 ton	2 ft	£536 less 5%	New to Sir Robert McAlpine (Midlands) Ltd., Pant Farm Gravel Pits, Gresford, Near Wrexham. me 'Derbyshire Stone'. Hopton Quarry then Hartington Quarry. To LBLR 10/56, No. 14. To J. Arnold 12/58. PRESERVED Cadeby Light Railway, Leics. 12/5/79.
44	MR 7933 4wDM c	7/10/41 31/10/41 3 speed	32/42 hp	5 ton		£688 less 5%	New to Sir Alfred McAlpine & Sons Ltd, Pant Farm Gravel Pits, Gresford, Wrexham. me '22/10/56 Now owned by LBLR as phoned Mr Gaskin'. To LBLR 10/56, No. 13. To J. Arnold 12/58. PRESERVED LBNGR c. 3/75.
38(39)	MR 8540 4wDM p	21/5/40 25/7/40	20/28 hp	2.5 ton	60 cm		New to War Office, order of 54 . To Geo Bungey, Hayes, Middlesex. To Docks & Inland, Waterways, Southall (latterly British Waterways). To J. Arnold /58 PRESERVED J. Butler, Ripley, Surrey 13/1/79.
	MR 8597 4wDM p	3/12/40 12/12/40	20/28 hp	2.5 ton	2 ft		New to DLH; overhauled for DLH 23/2/42, 12/10/42, 22/1/43, 5/4/44, 16/10/47 fit radiator guard, 23/7/47, 5/3/48, 29/4/53, 4/7/56, 22/12/56, 11/4/58, 19/1/59, 28/4/60, 3/8/60 convert to 3.5 ton, 5/12/60, 23/5/61. To J. Arnold c./66, for spares? Scr c./78.
1 (13,33)	MR 8683 4wDM p	11/11/41 14/11/41	20/28 hp	2.5 ton	2 ft		New to Slindon Gravel Ltd, Slindon Common, near Arundel. 19/4/56 SG Ltd offered for sale 3 Simplex diesel locos. Locos to Bungey. To J. Arnold c.9/56. PRESERVED Vale of Teifi NG Rly, Dyfed 2/6/79.
30	MR 8695 4wDM p	15/12/41 26/12/41	20/28 hp	2.5 ton	2 ft		New to Sir Alfred McAlpine & Sons Ltd Hawthorn, Wilts with exhaust conditioner. To River Ouse (Yorks) Catchment Board (26/11/59 5:MR diesel locos for sale). To J. Arnold 1/60. PRESERVED Dovery Down School, Leighton Buzzard c. 1972. To LBNGRS'? To Light Railway Association, Bedfordshire /88 (after 1/87).
2	MR 8700 4wDM p	15/12/41 22/12/41	20/28 hp	2.5 ton	2 ft		New to Sir Alfred McAlpine & Sons Ltd, Hawthorn, Wilts. Exhaust washer. To River Ouse (Yorks) Catchment Board (26/11/59: 5 MR diesel locos for sale). To J. Arnold 1/60. To Sir William Lithgow, Hardridge Railway, Renfrewshire 9/69.
26(18)	MR 8720 4wDM p	3/2/41 21/3/41	20/28 hp	2.5 ton	2 ft		New to Sir Robert McAlpine & Sons Ltd, Royal Ordnance Factory, Burghfield, Reading with Motor Rail and Customer's numberplates (5032). To J. Arnold /60 Ex-McAlpine. PRESERVED Runcorn Transport Collection, Runcorn, Cheshire 10/3/79. To Chwarel Wynne, Glyn Ceiriog, Clwyd 31/8/80.

Running Number	Works No. Type	Ordered HP	Ex-Works Weight	Cost Gauge	Notes
14(7)	MR 8723 4wDM p	3/2/41 20/29 hp	3/4/41 2.5 ton	2 ft	New to Sir Robert McAlpine & Sons Ltd, Hayes Depot, Middlesex with Motor Rail and Customer's numberplates (5035). To J. Arnold c./60 ex-McAlpine. Used to haul trains on first day of operation by Iron Horse Society. PRESERVED Ian Jolly, Mold, Clwyd 2/6/79.
	MR 8724 4wDM p	3/2/41 20/28 hp	3/4/41 2.5 ton	2 ft	New to Sir Robert McAlpine & Sons Ltd, Hayes Depot, Middlesex with Motor Rail and Customer's numberplates (5036). To G Bungey. To DLH 'Examine & test locos ex-Bungey' 9/7/56, Convert 2.5 ton locos 8724 and 8994 to 3.5 ton (see MR 8994). Overhauled for DLH 21/3/57, 6/11/57, 13/5/58, 10/6/58 convert to 2.5 ton, 16/10/58, 25/6/59, 22/4/60, 13/6/60, 18/7/61, 20/12/61 (rebuilt to standard list 12428/38 and Dorman engine replaced by Perkins 3/152 engine ex-works 24/1/62), 8/2/62. To J. Arnold c./64, for spares? Scr./66.
22	MR 8727 4wDM p	24/4/41 20/28 hp	22/5/41 2.5 ton	£458 2ft	New to River Ouse (Yorks) Catchment Board, Riccall, Yorks (26/11/59: five MR diesel locos for sale). To J. Arnold 1/60. To Overstone Solarium Light Railway Sywell nr Northampton 7/70; still present 1988 with steam outline.
	MR 8732 4wDM p	5/6/41 20/28 hp	7/6/41 2.5 ton	2 ft	Ministry of Supply, Forestry Unit, Carrbridge, Inverness-shire. To DLH Ltd Overhauled 23/5/57, 24/2/58. (Note latter date is after sale to McLean - IJ.) To MR Ltd.
		25/11/57	23/11/57	2 ft	Resold to M McLean Ltd Cromer '1 Reconditioned 2.5 ton loco' (McLeans spares until 7/59) To J. Arnold early 60's, for spares? Scr. by /68.
20	MR 8748 4wDM p	20/1/42 20/28 hp	18/2/42 2.5 ton	£478 2 ft	New to Sir Alfred McAlpine & Sons Ltd, Hawthorn, Wilts with Exhaust Washer. To River Ouse (Yorks) Catchment Board (26/11/59: 5 MR diesel locos for sale). To J. Arnold 1/60. PRESERVED Cadeby Light Railway, Leics 4/5/79.
36	MR 8756 4wDM p	19/2/42 20/28 hp	24/2/42 2.5 ton	2 ft	New to Sanstone Ltd, Setch near Kings Lynn. me 14/10/46 in service Cromhall Qys, Charfield, Glos. (Spares 21/11/46 until 10/10/49). To G. Bungey. To J. Arnold c./55. PRESERVED Northants Ironstone Trust, 10/2/79.
17(13)	MR 8994 4wDM p	10/1/46 20/28hp	3/4/46 2.5 ton	2 ft	New to Sir Robert McAlpine & Sons Ltd Hayes Depot, Rebuild of MR 8618 (New to War Office). To Bungey. To DLH (See note MR 8724); 13/7/56 Convert to 3.5 ton; Overhauled for DLH 9/9/60, 14/9/61, 2/3/62. To J. Arnold c./63. PRESERVED J. Butler, Ripley, Surrey 17/2/79.
8	MR 9409 4wDM p	21/4/48 20/28 hp	7/12/48 3.5 ton	2 ft	New to Holloway Bros. (London) Ltd, contractors, Depot, Stewarts Road, Battersea, London (Spares until 6/62). To J. Arnold c./64, to Arnold's Stone Pits, Aylesbury 29/11/66 returned by 6/73. To Drusilla's Zoo Park, Berwick, East Sussex 2/81 (Bill).

No.	Builder / Type	Date / hp	Date / Weight	Price	Gauge	Notes
34	MR 9415 4wDM p	21/4/48 20/28 hp	27/4/49 3.5 ton		2 ft	New to Holloway Bros. (London) Ltd, contractors, Depot, Stewarts Road, Battersea, London (Spares until 6/62). To J. Arnold c./64. Scr. following collision mid-1965.
	MR 9418 4wDM p	21/4/48 20/28 hp	14/6/49 3.5 ton		2 ft	New to Holloway Bros. (London) Ltd, contractors, Depot, Stewarts Road, Battersea, London (Spares until 6/62). To J. Arnold c./64. Frame only by /68. Scr. c./73.
34(41)	MR 9547 4wDM p	4/8/50 20/28 hp	28/11/50 2.5 ton	£484	60 cm	New to Leighton Buzzard Light Railway Co Ltd, No. 9. Fitted with cab 'Deliver loco and collect loco on loan (see MR8682). Fitted with cab and batteryless electric lighting.' Ran as 3.5 ton for a period. To J. Arnold, 3/12/58. PRESERVED by Ian Jolly, Mold, Clwyd 15/1/79. To Welsh Highland Railway, Porthmadog (on loan) 31/5/80 to 5/5/86.
43	MR 10409 4wDM c	6/10/53 32/42 hp	14/1/54 6 ton		60 cm	New to Leighton Buzzard Light Railway Co.Ltd No. 11. Fitted steel cab and batteryless electric lighting. To J. Arnold, 3/12/58. PRESERVED LBNGR c. 3/72.
	MR 20558 4wDM p	21/10/54 20/28hp	11/1/55 2.5ton 25/7/60 26/8/60		60 cm	New to DLH - Overhauled for DLH 9/8/55, 7/8/56, 18/9/56. 'Convert loco 20558' (to 3.5 ton? - II). Overhauled 21/4/58. To MR Ltd. Overhauled fitted with cab and resold as reconditioned loco. To British Transport Waterways, Brimsdown, Enfield, Middlesex. To Ham & Hall Ltd, Woodside Brickworks, Croydon. To J. Arnold c./67. PRESERVED Ian Jolly, Mold, Clwyd 8/12/78.
11?	FH 1851 4wPM	20 hp		£155		Bought 2/34 'Simplex petrol' s/s.
12?	FH 1893 4wDM	20 hp		£290		Bought 10/34 'Rebuilt Simplex diesel' s/s.
26(13)	FH 1917 4wDM	20 hp		£310	2 ft	New to J. Arnold 1/5/35 'Simplex diesel'. National 2D engine s/s c./63.
30	FH 1922 4wDM	20 hp			2 ft	New 11/5/35 to Holloway Bros, Millbank, London. Dorman 2JO engine ' Simplex diesel'. To J. Arnold in 1950s, scr. by /58.
14?	FH 1960 4wDM	20 hp				Bought 12/35 'Simplex rebuilt petrol' s/s.
14(32)	FH 2161 4wDM	25 hp			2 ft	New 30/11/38 to Royal Naval Armaments Depot, Ernesettle, Plymouth. Paxman 2RQT engine ('Simplex diesel'). To J. Arnold c. 1958 s/s c./65.

Running Number	Works No. Type	Ordered HP	Ex-Works Weight	Cost Gauge	Notes
12	FH 2289 4wDM b			2 ft	New 30/7/40 to Royal Ordnance Factory No 7, Kirby, Liverpool, National 2 D engine purchased from Holloway Bros (Contrs) Ltd, London. *c.*/41? 'Simplex diesel'. Scr. *c.*/46.

Arnold hired a locomotive from Petrol Loco Hirers in June and July 1933 at £14 per month, and one from Ruston & Hornsby in August 1933 at £13 5s. 0d. Possibly this was to compare the new design of locomotive from Lincoln (Ruston & Hornsby began production of narrow gauge diesel locomotives in 1931) with the familiar product from Bedford. The hirings may be linked to the purchase of MR 3996 in October 1933.

Notes on River Ouse (Yorks) Catchment Board

Spares included (10/47) 6 sets of cab equipment (cabs? - IJ) and (12/50) 2 drivers cabs. Spares were maintained until at least 10/63 regularly but tailing off in the early 1960s.

Sales: 6/48 six 20/28hp new in 34/37 (6 of MR 5858, 5874, 7102, 7116, 7119, 7124, 7131, 7132).

9/49 three MR locos new in 35/36 (MR 7133?, 7134? and 7153? - IJ).

26/11/59 five MR diesel locos (MR 8695, 8700, 8727, 8748, plus one other).

This assumes locomotives disposed of in order of acquisition.

Arnold Locomotive Fleet & Allocations

No	MR	Type	Name	Delivd	11/45	5/58	4/61	8/68	6/73	2/77	Disp.	Notes
1?	1757	P	Winnie	/20							s/s	
1		P		LBLR/23	BR	see 21					s/s by /61	
1	7188	D		by /58				DA	see 18	DA		
2	8683	D		/65					DA		pres./79	
2	1169	P		was 33	9A	DA	DA				scr. c./60	
2	8700	D		c./28?				BR			sold /69	
2	4707	DxP		/60	DA	DA	DA	DA	see 14		scr. c./62	
3	5881	DxP		was 17	DA	DA	DA	DA			sold /69	
3	7201	D		by /45	DA	DA	DA	see 4				
3		D	Gertie	/65							s/s /59	
4	7201	P		/59	BR	BR	BR	BR	BR	BR	pres./79	
4		D		was 3	DA	DA	BR	BR	BR		s/s by /63	
5		P		by /45	DA						s/s by /59 (by /55?)	
6	7403	P		by /45	CB		9A		CB		pres./80	
6	3862	D		by /56	DA	CB		CB		CB	scr./61	
7	8723	DxP /58		c./31?		BR			BR	see 14	s/s c./64	
7		D		/60	DA		S?	see 4				
8	7215	P	Louie	by /45	DA	S		BR	DA	see 21	to Stone /69, ret c./73	
8	9409	D		/65				S	DA	DA	sold /81	
8	3996	D		c./64	DA				9A		scr. c./63	
9	FH1851	P		New /33	9A	DA	BR				s/s c./62	
10	342	DxP	Bertha	by /45	DA	9A	9A				s/s by /40	
11	FH1893	P		c./34?	BR	BR	BR				s/s c./40	identity assumed
11	FH2289	P		c./43?							scr. c./46	
12	1757	D		c./34?	DA						scr. c./60	
12	FH1917	P		c./41		CB			see 33			
12	8683	D		was 21	DA	see 26		DA				
13	8994	D		New /35		DA	9A	see 17			scr./60	
13	1704	D		c./56		DA		DA	DA		s/s	
13	FH1960	P		c./63	DA				br	br	s/s c./65	
14	FH2161	D		c./36			BR	CB	CB	br	pres./79	
14	8723	D		/35				DA	DA	BR	scr./83	at DA 10/69
14	4707	D		was 32				DA	DA	DA	pres./79	
14	4803	D		was 7		CB	9A	see 2			pres./79	
14	4709	DxP		was 2		DA	DA	CB	CB	NT	pres./79	
15	4707	DxP		PLH/37	BR	CB	CB					
16		DxP		PLH/36	DA	DA	DA	DA				
17	8994	DxP		PLH/36	CB	CB	CB	CB	CB			
17		D		was 13								

No	MR	Type	Name	Delt'd	11/45	5/58	4/61	8/68	6/73	2/77	Disp.	Notes
18	4805	DxP		PLH/37	DA	DA	DA	see 19	DA	DA	sold /79	
18	7188	D		was 1 /60				DA	DA			whistle & headlight, for DA to S'henge
18	8720	D					see 26			see 26		
19	4701	DxP		PLH /36	DA	DA		DA	DA	DA		to S'henge
19		DxP		was 18	BR	DA	DA	9A	see 24		scr. c./60	
20	999	P		c./38?		DA	DA	DA	DA	DA	pres./79	
20	8748	D		/60	9A	DA	CB	CB	DA	DA	s/s	rebuilt to compressor?221
21	1757	P		by /45		DA			NT		pres./78	
21	7215	P	compressor	was 1, c/46	reb /62	see 12				br		
21		P		was 8							pres./82	
22	8727	D		by /45	DA	DA	DA	DA	DA		s/s /59	
22		P		/60							sold /70	
23	7128	D		/46	CB		CB				s/s by /58	
23		P		by /56		DA	DA	BR	DA	BR	pres. 81	
24	4805	DxP		by /58		CB	CB	DA	DA	DA	s/s c./63	
24	7214	D		was 19					see 36		pres./83	last loco to leave DA at DA 10/69
24		P		was 25	DA	DA		DA				
25	7214	P		/46		BR	CB	BR	see 24	BR	s/s /59	
25		D		c./56	CB	CB						
26		P		/46	DA	DA	DA					
26	FH1917	D		was 13		DA		DA	DA	br	s/s by /58	whistle & headlight for DA to S'henge
26	4701	DxP		was 19				DA	BR	DA	scr. /83	last loco frame at BR
26	8720	D		was 18		9A	9A	9A	DA	BR	pres./79	
27	5863	DxP		New /34					DA		s/s c./74	was originally 10, 11 or 12?
27		D		c./48?		DA					pres./79	
28		P		c./48?		DA					s/s c./60	
29		P		c./51							s/s c./60	
30	FH1922	D		c./48?		DA	DA	DA			scr. by /58	
30		P		/60							s/s c./60	
30	8695	D					DA	DA			pres./72	
31				always blank, reason not known, error made when 32 bought and then perpetuated?									
32	FH2161	D		c./57			see 14				scr. c./56	
32		D		c./49?	BR		BR					
33	4708	DxP		c./60				9A	9A	DA	s/s	
33	7037	DxP		was 13					9A	9A	sold /79	
33	8683	D		by /58	9A	9A	9A			see 1	s/s	
34		D										

No	MR	Type	Name	Del'd	11/45	5/58	4/61	8/68	6/73	2/77	Disp.	Notes
34	9547	D	was 41			DA	DA	DA	NT	BR	pres./79	headlight for DA to NT
35	7126	D		c./55		DA	DA	DA	9A	DA	pres./79	
36	8756	D		c./55		CB	BR	CB	DA	NT	pres./79	
36	7214	D	was 24						CB	DA	s/s c./62	
37		P		by/58		CB	BR				s/s	
37		D							NT	NT	s/s c./61	
38		P		by/58		DA	DA	DA	DA	BR	pres./79	last loco in use 11/78, at DA
38	8540	D	was 39			DA	see 38	DA	DA		pres./79	
39	8540	D		/58		DA	DA					
40	7153	D		by/58		CB	see 34	DA	DA		pres./79	
41	9547	D		LBLR/58				DA	NT	NT	pres./79	headlight for DA to NT
41	5839	D		c./65		BR	BR	BR	BR		pres./79	
42	7710	D		LBLR/58		BR	BR	BR			pres./79	
43	10409	D		LBLR/58		BR	BR				pres./72	
44	7933	D		LBLR/58		BR	BR				pres./75	

Locomotives known to have been here but not identified in the above list:

No	MR	Type	Name	Del'd	11/45	5/58	4/61	8/68	6/73	2/77	Disp.	Notes
916		P									s/s c./60	
4705		P		c./54							s/s by/68	24 or 25?
5073		DxP		New/30							s/s by/68	3, 4, 5 or 6?
5854				PLH/34							ret. to MR	
8597		D		c./66				br	br	br	scr. c./78	spares
8724		D		c./64							scr./66	spares
8732		D		c./63					br	br	scr. by/68	spares
9418		D		c./64					br	br	scr. c./73	spares
20558		D		c./67				br	br	br	pres./78	spares

Note: In later days spare locomotives at Billington Road were not numbered. When a locomotive came in for repairs the replacement took the number of the locomotive being sent in for repairs. Following repairs the running number was painted out. The unnumbered state has been ignored. Locomotives are shown with the last recorded running number, even if there was then another locomotive with the same number, or if it was then in use at a quarry but without a number (which happened several times in the last years of the quarry railways).

Names seem to have been discontinued in the late 1940s or early 1950s. Only one was still named in 1958. A possibility is that originally all locomotives were named and numbers came later, in which case there may have been about six additional petrol locomotives (Kent Construction and/or Hibberd - see text) in the 1920s and 1930s. It is also probable that there were about 20 Simplex petrol locomotives bought in the 1920s and subsequently replaced, which could include this half dozen (see text). It is also probable that in the period from 1945 to about 1960 there were other, short-lived, second-hand petrol locomotives.

Code	Location	Allocation	11/45	5/58	4/61	8/68	6/73	2/77
BR	Billington Road incl. works		5	5	8	10	7	4
br	Billington Road derelict			1		3	5	6
CB	Chamberlains Barn		2	7	4	5	4	
DA	Double Arches		12	20	17	16	12	12
NT	New Trees					*	3	3
9A	Nine Acre		3	3	3	3	3	3
S	Stone, Aylesbury						2	
	Total (excluding derelicts)		22	36	33	35	28	19

* Served by Double Arches (2)

Locomotives 1 to 22 inclusive (except 2, 9, & 21) were noted in November 1945. When A.G. Wells had asked 'Were there any locomotives at Stonehenge?', which was the obvious name of the site, he had received the answer 'No' so had not visited it. However, these were seen a year later at Nine Acre, so have been assumed present in 1945.

In May 1958 running numbers reached 40, although Nos. 31 & 32 were not in use and No. 8 was at Stone.

George Garside & Co Locomotives

George Garside (Sand) Ltd from 1/1/1960

Compiled from the Maker's Contract Sheets, Material Sheets and Spares Sheets and other sources by Ian B.Jolly.

The first spares ordered by Messrs George Garside & Co. on 13/10/20 was Fan bracket W528A. On 11/2/21 a 'Brake Spindle old type' was ordered i.e. the type for a locomotive with the wide type brake column - this would have been for MRTC 374 (or possibly one of the unidentified locomotives) as later locomotives would have had the narrow type. It is interesting to note the number of ex-PLH hire locomotives acquired as 'reconditioned' locomotives from MRTC (i.e. with second contract sheet) or from PLH (possibly straight from hire).

Running Number	Works No. Type	Ordered HP	Ex-Works Weight	Cost Gauge	Notes
1	MRTC 374 4wPM b	23/12/16 20 hp	25/5/17 2.5 ton	60 cm	New to WDLR as 1775; spares supplied Garsides 15/11/21. Would have had early 'wide type' brake column. Scr. *c.*/61.
2(4)	MRTC 1044 4wPM b	1/1/18 20 hp	8/18 2.5 ton	60 cm	New to WDLR France as LR 2765. To Garside /26? Scr. *c.*/60.
9	MRTC 1107 4wPM b	1/1/18 20 hp	11/18 2.5 ton	60 cm	New to WDLR as LR 2828. *me* (Spares to Wilson Kinmond & Marr Ltd 25/2/20, 16/3/26 - WKM of Glasgow ordered spares - for 1 loco? - from 2/2/20 (Steel Cab to fit 20 hp loco) until 29/12/31 when they ordered the first loco. of a number that they bought over the years-IJ); to Garside by /46.
	MRTC 1856	1/8/19 20 hp	Not shown		New to Lamb & Phillips LBLR contract. To Garside 5/20? s/s.
2	MRTC 3789 4wPM b	13/1/26 20 hp	24/2/26 2.5 ton	£365 delvd 60 cm	New to Garside, reconditioned from MRTC 369 (new to WDLR/1917). Scr. *c.*/60.
5	MRTC 3795 4wPM b Conv 4wDM	8/7/26 20 hp	13/7/26 2.5 ton	£365 delvd 60 cm	New to Garside, rebuilt from MRTC 219/1916 (new to WDLR). Scr. *c.*/61.
10(3)	MRTC 3828 4wPM b Conv 4wDM as 3795 above	20/3/26 20 hp	22/3/26 2.5 ton	60 cm	New to Garside, Grovebury. Recond from LR 2542. (This should be MR 1821 but MRTC 3735 is shown as being rebuilt from 'MRTC 1751 LR 2542 & LR 2532' - heaven knows which loco. it really was rebuilt from! IJ.) Scr. *c.*/61.
6	MRTC 3841 4wPM b	9/11/26 20 hp	13/11/26 2.5 ton	60 cm	New to Garside, reconditioned from MRTC 3684 with canopy (but with engine from 3865) both supplied new to Dolberg-Jones, Durban, SouthAfrica. 3684 was rebuilt from MRTC 1998. Disposal unknown - probably scrapped by /59.
7	MRTC 3850 4wPM b	15/5/27 20 hp	2/6/27 2.5 ton	2 ft	Recondition for Petrol Loco Hirers Ltd Loco. No. 14 ex-Heaton Park Reservoir. Old No. not known. (PLH's record sheet shows for 17/5/27 'Overhaul loco 3850' which indicates to IJ that they already owned the loco. i.e. PLH had purchased the loco and were asking MRTC to overhaul it - having no number it was allocated 3850! He can find no trace of the loco ever being overhauled subsequently for PLH and so would come to the conclusion that it went - on hire? - to Garside and was sold without ever returning from hire). *me* Sold to Garside (by PLH). Scr. *c.*/61.

Running Number	Works No. Type	Ordered HP	Ex-Works Weight	Cost Gauge	Notes
8	MRTC 4019 4wPM b	25/1/26 20 hp 28/4/28 20 hp	25/1/26 2.5 ton 7/5/28 2.5 ton	£360 delvd 60 cm £315 delvd	New to PLH - & resold to MRTC. Resold to Garside as Record loco. Scr. c./60.
9	MRTC 4568 4wPM b	21/3/29 20 hp	21/3/29 2.5 ton	60 cm	New to PLH. Sold by PLH to Garside 13/7/29 (Not overhauled for PLH in this period - probably new on hire to Garside - IJ) me Converted to diesel 12/11/35 by MR Ltd. Scr. /65.
21(10, 12)	MRTC 4570 4wPM b	15/4/29 20 hp	15/4/29 2.5 ton	60 cm	New to PLH - overhauled for PLH 14/10/29. Sold by PLH to Garside 16/2/31. PRESERVED LBNGRS 21/6/81.
	MR 4808 4wPM p	2/12/36 20/26 hp (No date)	2/12/36 2.5 ton (No date)	2 ft	New to PLH; (PLH records show no overhauls - Sold to Sir R. McAlpine & Sons Ltd whilst on hire) - 'was on hire and has been purchased'. To Garside, Leighton Buzzard by 5/58, for spares. Scr. c./65.
	MR 4809 4wPM p	9/12/36 20/26 hp	9/12/36 2.5 ton	2 ft	New to PLH. Sold to Sir R. McAlpine & Sons direct from hire. To Garside, Leighton Buzzard by 5/58, for spares. Scr. c./65.
11	MRTC 5002 4wPM c	19/4/29 20 hp	20/4/29 60 cm	£340	New to PLH, 21/6/29 convert clutch, 21/8/29 overhaul loco. me Sold to Garside 16/2/31 by PLH. Scr. by /58.
12	MRTC 5008 4wPM c	16/5/29 22/7/31 20 hp	16/5/29 22/7/31 2.5 ton	£340 £200 2 ft	New to PLH, Overhauled 15/3/31. To MRTC & resold as Recond. Loco. To Garside, Grovebury Road, Leighton Buzzard as Recond Loco. Scr. by /58.
26	MRTC 5011 4wPM c	22/5/29 20 hp	22/5/29 2.5 ton	£340 60 cm	New to PLH, 21/6/29 convert clutch, 4/3/31 overhauled. me Sold by PLH to Peter Lind & Co.Ltd for £209'. To George Cohen & Co by 29/9/54. To Garside, Leighton Buzzard. Scr. /60.
27(36)	MR 5852 4wDM p	4/10/33 20/28 hp	18/10/33 2.5 ton	£363.5.0 delvd 2 ft	New to A.H. Worth, Fleet Station, Lincs. One of first pair of plate frame locos made. Not shown as having cab originally. With Garside by 5/58 (Worth ordered spares until 12/2/52- IJ). To Ian Jolly, Mold, Clwyd 24/11/79. Curved top metal cab.
	MR 5864 4wDM p	20/28 hp	16/8/34 3.5 ton	£380 2 ft	New to Sir R. McAlpine & Sons Ltd Kendoon Reservoir Contract, New Galloway. To Garside, Leighton Buzzard by 5/58, for spares, s/s c. 1968.

No.	Loco				Notes
18(13)	MR 5870 4wDM p	15/1/35 20/28 hp 18/7/35	16/1/35 2.5 ton 19/7/35	£332 delvd 2 ft £332 delvd	New to PLH ex-stock with PLH plates. The ONLY Overhaul for PLH. 18/7/35 *me* George Garside letter (on Contract Sheet for 5870). 19/7/35 5870 Sold to G. Garside Grovebury Road, £332 delivered. (Both Contract Sheet for loco, and Garsides spares sheet give 1935 as date not 1936. Note that this loco appears to have been sold from hire as despatch instructions say 'Already delivered', a case IJ suspects happened with a number of Garsides locos). s/s *c.*/78.
17	MR 7036 4wPM p	16/12/36 20/26 hp	16/2/36 2.5 ton	ex stock 2 ft	New to PLH - 1 of 3 - no record of overhaul for PLH by MR. 'All (three - IJ) sold Sir R. McAlpine £198.00 each were on hire & have been purchased'. To Garside, Leighton Buzzard by /58. PRESERVED LBNGR 9/11/81.
34(35)	MR 7105 4wDM p	21/1/36 20/28 hp 5/10/36	ex-stock 2.5 tons 17/10/36 (promised 13 Oct!)	£300 less 5% 2 ft	New to PLH. Sold Gloucester Tile & Sand Co Ltd Shurdington, Chelmsford (3 m. SW Gloucester - MR records give Chelmsford obviously a mistake as there is no Shurdington near Chelmsford). Painted Signal Red and lettered GTS in white on the bonnets. *me* 18/6/40 in svce H. Covington & Son Ltd, Cremorne Wharf, 27 Lots Road, Chelsea SW10 (rubbish tip contractor). To English China Clay Ltd, Drinnick Mill, Nanpean, Cornwall. To Bungey (dealer) Middlesex. To Garside by 5/58. PRESERVED West Lancs Light Rly, 13/11/81.
13 (37,34)	MR 7108 4wDM p	25/1/36 20/28 hp 23/4/37	28/1/36 3.5 ton 7/5/37	2 ft £300 less 5%	New to DLH. Returned to MR Ltd. Re-sold by MR to St Albans Sand & Gravel Ltd despatched to c/o A. Grub & Sons Ltd Waterhall Farm, Hertford. To Garside, Leighton Buzzard by 5/58. PRESERVED West Lancs Light Railway 13/11/81. Curved top cab.
	MR 7115 4wDM p	20/2/36 20/28 hp	27/2/36 2.5 ton	£348.7.6d. 2 ft	New to Glasgow Housing Dept, Household Wood Farm, Glasgow. *me* First loco with Volkes filter. To James N Connell, Coatbridge /49. To Garside by 5/58 ex-Connell (via Bungey?), for spares. Dsm by 1970: Scr. *c.*/76.
33	MR 7140 4wDM p	11/11/36 20/28 hp 4/5/37	12/11/36 2.5 ton Promised 14/5/37	2 ft £300 delvd	New to DLH (Loco overhauled for DLH 17/4/37, 8/5/37). Sold to Sir Lindsey Parkinson & Co Ltd delivered Rhyll [*sic*] N. Wales. To Garside by 5/58 ex-Sir Lindsey Parkinson & Co. The running number of this loco (33) was taken by MR 8587 sometime prior to 2/1979 and MR7140 scrapped after the interchange. Scr. by 1/79 assuming that 7140 was correctly identified in the first place!

Running Number	Works No. Type	Ordered HP	Ex-Works Weight	Cost Gauge	Notes
36(14)	MR 7145 4wDM p	18/11/36 20/28hp	19/11/36 2.5 ton	£348 2 ft	New to Garside. Scr. c./76.
15	MR 7148 4wDM p	25/11/36 20/28 hp	8/12/36 2.5 ton	£348 2 ft	New to Garside, Grovebury, Leighton Buzzard. Scr. c./76.
16	MR 7149 4wDM p	25/11/36 20/28 hp	8/12/36 2.5 ton	£348 2 ft	New to Garside, Grovebury, Leighton Buzzard. Scr. 8/80 Double Arches.
13(17)	MR 7152 4wDM p	17/12/36 20/28 hp	31/12/26 2.5 ton	£348 2 ft	New to Garside, Double Arches, Leighton Buzzard. Scr. c./79.
	MR 7154 4wDM p	18/1/37 20/28 hp 16/3/37	22/1/37 2.5 ton	2 ft £360 delvd	New to DLH - (no record of overhaul probably sent direct to Sir R. McAlpine - IJ). 'Sold to Sir R. McAlpine Glasgow Sewerage contract was on hire but has been sold'. To Garside between 1/70 and 1/73, spares. Scr. c./76.
30(10)	MR 7195 4wDM p	31/8/37 20/28 hp	30/9/37 2.5 ton	2 ft	New to Glasgow Corpn, Pollock Housing Scheme. Wooden cab. To James N Connell, Coatbridge /49. To Garside between /73 and /76. Dsm between /73 and /76. Scr. c./76.
31	MR 7371 4wDM p	31/12/38 20/28 hp	13/2/39 2.5 ton	£369.10.0 2 ft	New with cab to Glasgow Corpn, Robroyston Housing Contract. To James N Connell, Coatbridge /49. To Garside by 5/58 via Bungey. PRESERVED West Lancs Light Rly 13/11/81.
32	MR 7372 4wDM p	31/12/38 20/28hp	13/2/39 2.5 ton	£367.10.0 2ft	New to Glasgow Corpn, Robroyston Housing Contract. To James N.Connell, Coatbridge /49. To Garside by 5/58 ex-James N. Connell, Coatbridge via Bungey. Dsm by 1/70.
29	MR 7374 4wDM p	31/12/38 20/28 hp	22/2/39 2.5 ton	£367.10.0 2 ft	New with cab to Glasgow Corpn,Robroyston Housing Contract. To James N.Connell, Coatbridge /49. To Garside by 5/58 via Bungey. PRESERVED Wickford NG Railway Group, Wickford, Essex 10/11/81.
	MR 7414 4wDM p	5/7/39 20/28 hp	31/7/39 2.5 ton	£377.10.0 2 ft	New with cab to Glasgow Corpn, Penilee Housing Contract, Hillington Rd, Dryburn Avenue, Glasgow West. To James N Connell, Coatbridge /49. To Garside by 5/58 via Bungey, for spares. Dsm by 1/70, Scr? between /76 and /79.

No.	Builder/Type				Notes
14	MR 7492 4wDM p	27/9/40 20/28 hp	4/10/40 3.5 ton	£467 2 ft	New to Shelton Iron, Steel & Coal Co Ltd, Etruria Rd, Hanley, Stoke on Trent. To Garside by /68 (derelict) for spares? Dsm between /70 and /73. Scr. c./77.
12	MR 7932 4wDM c	3/10/41 32/42 hp	29/10/41 5 ton 3 speed	£688 less 5% 2 ft	Sir A. McAlpine & Sons Ltd, Pant Farm Gravel Pits, Gresford. me 22/10/56 now owned by Leighton Buzzard Light Railway, 12. To Garside 12/58 sold to Hopkins, England, Woburn Sands 2nd half /65 - resold to Jonallen, Singapore 8/66 as No 1.
33	MR 8587 4wDM p	21/5/40 20/28	14/12/40 2.5 ton	60 cm	New to War Office. me 'Merer' (Merer Ltd ordered spares 23/6/48 until 9/52 on 10 occasions, address unknown - IJ) To Garside (ex-Merer Ltd ?) by /77. (The loco carrying the identity '33 Utrillo' and thought to be MR 7140, was identified as MR 8587 from the number stamped at the foot of the brake column. When MR 7140 was disposed of is not known (by 1/79 for certain) and when MR 8587 was acquired is also a mystery. - IJ) Scr. 7/1/80 at Double Arches fitters shed.
35	MR 8713 4wDM p	3/2/41 20/28 hp	25/3/41 2.5 ton	£436 delvd 2 ft	New to Sir R. McAlpine Ltd (1 of order of 15) to Royal Ordnance factory, Burghfield Rd, Reading with MR nameplate and customer's numberplate 5025. To Garside, by 8/68 (derelict) for spares? Scr? c./76.
28	MR 8725 4wDM p	3/2/41 20/28 hp	4/4/41 2.5 ton	£436 delvd	New to Sir R. McAlpine & Sons Ltd (1 of order for 15) to Hayes depot with MR nameplate and customer's numberplate 5037. To Garside 8/68, for spares. Dsm by /73. Scr? by 1976.
28	MR 8917 4wDM p	9/9/43 20/28 hp	19/9/44 2.5 ton	60 cm	New to War Office 1 of 57. Later Geo Bungey. To Garside by 5/58. Withdrawn early /69. Scr. c./76.
10	MR 10272 4wDM c	2/5/51 32/42 hp	27/11/51 6 ton	2 ft	New to LBLR, Cab Batteryless Electric Lighting, No. 10. To Garside 12/58. To Hopkins England, Woburn Sands 2nd half 1965. To Jonallen, Singapore 8/66 as No. 2.
	Jung 1539 4wDM				Presumed obtained second-hand in 1950s. Soon sold to Bungey.
69	OK 5215 4wDM				Presumed obtained second-hand in 1950s. Soon sold to Bungey. Later to Lancashire Moss Litter, Horwich.

Notes on Glasgow Corporation

They had a number of MR locos (new with wooden cabs) and ordered spares until after 1963 - however they also had MR dumpers, Works Nos. 8256-8276 being the first batch ordered 30/5/45. The last recognizable locomotive spares are 'brake nut and spindle' ordered on 8/11/46. James Connell of Coatbridge offered locos for sale as follows:

12/7/44	20 Simplex petrol locos
6/8/47	'also narrow gauge steam and diesel'
18/8/50	Seven 20 hp Motor Rail diesel locos (Likely candidates for Garsides locos as we know they went to Connell in 1949 - IJ))
6/12/50	Ruston Hornsby and Simplex 2 ft gauge locos
7/9/59	One Simplex diesel loco
20/4/61	One Simplex diesel loco

Thos Dunlop (Machinery) Ltd, Glasgow offered six 20/28 hp Simplex 2 ton locomotives on 16/2/51 and three 20/28 hp plus one 12 hp locomotive on 6/2/58 for sale.

Hugh Leggatt Ltd Glasgow offered plant including Ruston Hornsby and Simplex diesel locomotives 18/6/59.

McNiell Industries, Glasgow offered 11 Simplex diesel locomotives for sale on 23/11/61.

Garsdale Locomotive Fleet & Allocations

Note: If the number column is blank the locomotive had two (or more names) in the order shown. For example, 16 (MR 7149) was first called *Pasch* but by 1958 the name had changed to *Ribot*, and by 1968 it was called *Anglo*.

No.	MR No.	Type	Name	Delivd	11/45	5/58	4/61	8/68	1/73	2/77	Disp.	Notes
1	374	P	*Benghazi*	/21	DA	br					scr. c./61	carried plate reading 79 Lombard Street, London EC1, not Bedford
1		P	*Steady Aim*	was 21	DA						scr. c./59	
2	3789	P	*Nickel Coin*	New /26	BR	br					scr. c./60	
2	1044	P	*Monty*	was 4	DA	DA					scr. c./61	new to Grovebury
3	3828	DxP	*Migoli*	New /26	DA	see 10					s/s c./60	
3	FH?	P	*Nickel Coin*	/26?	G	see 2						
4	1044	P	*Airborne*	/26	DA	br					scr. c./61	
5	3795	DxP	*My Love*	New /26		br					s/s by /59	
6	3841	P	*Brendan's Cottage*	New /26	DA	br					scr. c./61	
7	3850	P	*Hellenique*	PLH /27	DA	br					scr. c./60	with *Steady Aim* bonnet?
7		P	*Monsieur L'Amiral*			br						
8	4019	P	*Golden Miller*	New /28	DA	br						
9	4568	D	*Brown Jack*	PLH /29	G	see 10						
9	1107	D	*Supertelo*	by /46	BR	br					s/s	
10	4570	DxP	*Uncle Joe*	PLH /31	DA	see 12					scr. c./61	
10	4568	P	*Foxtrot*	was 9	DA	see 19						
10	3828	DxP	*Cider Apple*	was 3	br	br					scr. c./,61	
10	7195	D	*Tearaway*	by /58	G		G	see 30			sold /66	
10	10272	D	*El Alamein*	LBLR /58			BR				scr. by /58	
11	5002	D	*Black Speck*	PLH /31	BR		BR				scr. by /58	delivered to Grovebury
12	5008	D	*Festoon*	PLH /31	G		G	see 21				
12	4570	P	*Lemon Cheese*	was 10			BR				sold /66	
12	7932	D	*Retrial*	LBLR /58	G							
13	5870	D	*Arkle*	PLH /35		DA	DA	see 18	DA	DA	scr. c./79	
13	7152	D	*Arkle*	was 17				DA	DA	DA	pres. /81	
13	7108	D	*Sun Chariot*	was 34		DA						
14	7145	D	*Devon Loch*	New /36		BR	DA	da	see 36		scr. c./77	
14	7492	D	*Devon Loch*	by /68				da	da			spares
15	7148	D	*Much Obliged*	New /36		BR	DA	DA			scr. c./76	new to Grovebury
15		D	*Brown Jack*									

No.	MR No.	Type	Name	Delivd	11/45	5/58	4/61	8/68	1/73	2/77	Disp.	Notes
16	7149	D	Pasch	New /36	BR							new to Grovebury
			Ribot			BR						
			Anglo				BR	G	DA	da	scr./80	
17	7152	D	Alexander	New /36	DA		see 13					
17	7036	D	French Design	by /58		br	G	G	DA	DA	pres./81	
			Damredub	c./63							scr. by /59	
18		P	Langton Abbott	by /58		br					scr. c./66	
18		D	Honeylight	by /58		BR	BR				s/s	
18	5870	D	Honeylight	was 13			BR	BR	BR	da	scr. c./61	
19		P	Lovely Lady	by /58		BR	BR				scr./65	
19	4568	P		was 10		BR	BR				scr. by /58	
20		P		by /58							s/s c./65	
21		P		by /58		see 1					pres./81	
21		P	Tosca	was 12, c./65		DA	DA				scr. by /58	
21	4570	P	Festoon	by /58			DA	DA	DA		s/s c./60	
22		P		by /58							s/s c./60	
23		P	Monty	by /58		br					scr. c./62	
24		P	Sheila's Cottage			br					scr./60	
25		P	Alycidon	by /58		DA					s/s by /61	
26	5011	P	Scratch II	by /54		br					s/s	
26		P				BR						
27		D	Torch Singer	was 36		DA	DA	DA	DA	DA	pres./79	
27	5852	D	Flush Royal	by /58		G	G	DA	DA	DA	scr. c./76	
28	8917	D	Supreme Court			G	G	DA	DA		scr. c./65	
29		D	Quare Times				G	G			pres./81	
29	7374	D	Ayala	by /68		DA	DA	DA	DA	DA	s/s	
30		D	Fleeting Moment			DA	DA	DA	DA	DA	scr. c./76	
30	7195	D	Larkspur	was 10		G		DA				
31	7371	D	Good Taste	by /58		DA	DA					
			Oxo				DA					
			Team Spirit					G				
			Mill Reef						DA	DA	pres./81	
32	7372	D	Teal	by /58		see 37						
32		D	Gay Donald	by /58		DA	DA					
			Hard Ridden				DA		DA	da		
			Gay Donald								scr. c./73	

No.	MR No.	Type		Delivd	11/45	5/58	4/61	8/68	1/73	2/77	Disp.	Notes
33	7140	D	*Royal Tan*	by /58								
33			*Crepello*				DA	DA				
33	8587	D	*Utrillo*	c./64			DA	DA	da		scr. c./78	
34	7108	D	*Utrillo*	by /77					DA		scr./80	
34			*Darius*	by /58			DA	DA	see 37			
34	7105	D	*Sundew*	was 35, c/65			DA					
			Kilmore					DA	DA		pres./81	
			Red Rum									
35	7105	D	*Doutelle*	by /58		BR	BR	see 34			scr. c./76	spares
35	8713	D	*Doutelle*	by /68				da	da			
36	5852	D	*Relko*	c./55		DA	DA	see 27			scr. c./76	
36	7145	D	*Gay Donald*	was 14				da			see 13	
37	7108	D	*Gay Donald*	was 34		DA	DA	DA			s/s c./76	
37	7372	D	*Gay Donald*	was 32		DA						

Locomotives known to have been here but not identified in the above list:

No.	MR No.	Type	Delivd	11/45	5/58	4/61	8/68	1/73	2/77	Disp.	Notes
Austro-Daimler	1856	P	5/20?							s/s	
Austro-Daimler		P	c./22?							s/s	
Garside		P	c./22?							s/s	at Grovebury motorised skip, reb as 'bogie'
		P	c./30							s/s c./40	
4808		P	by /58		br	br				scr. c./65	spares
4809		P	by /58		br	br				scr. c./65	spares
5864		D	by /58		br	br	da			scr. c./68	spares
7115		D	by /58		br	br	da	da		scr. c./.76	spares
7154		D	c./71					da		scr. c./76	spares
7414		D	by /58		br	br	da	da		scr. c./76	spares
8725		D	/68			br	br	da		scr. c./76	spares
Jung	1539	D	c./50							sold c./51?	
OK	5215	D	c./50							sold c./55?	

Code	Location	Allocation	11/45	5/58	4/61	8/68	1/73	2/77
BR	Billington Road incl. works		5	7	7			
br	Billington Road derelict			27	15			
DA	Double Arches		9	13	11	9	11	6
da	Double Arches derelict					8	10	3
G	Grovebury		3	5	5	4		
	Totals (excluding derelicts)		17	25	23	13	11	6

Locomotives 1 to 17 inclusive were noted in November 1945. In May 1958 running numbers reached 36, but there were a number of blanks, mainly in the numbers below 10.

Chapter Sixteen

Quarry Rolling Stock

The LBLR owned no rolling stock, except perhaps one or two wagon underframes used to carry permanent way materials. All traffic was carried in wagons supplied by the quarries. In December 1920 the LBLR accountants wrote a note concerning an item in the accounts headed Locomotives, Machinery & Trucks: 'we do not find the company owns any machinery or trucks'.

Arnold owned about 400 tipping wagons in 1961 and Garside about 250. Wagons were painted brown and grey respectively. They were numbered, Arnold favouring the stand and Garside the body end. Arnold also painted in white figures on the frame the date of the last overhaul.

An article about Arnold's quarries in the May 1934 issue of *Cement, Lime & Gravel* included this paragraph:

It is worthy of note, throughout the quarries the locos and wagons have been, as nearly as possible, standardised. The locos employed are all Simplex petrol machines, and the wagons are 1 yd Hudson tipping wagons, with special large wheels and axle boxes. By experience, the ordinary small wheels and roller bearings were found to be too troublesome for the long runs they were called upon to do. A few large eight-wheeled bogey wagons are employed, chiefly for bagged materials.

The commonest type of wagon used in the quarries and over the main line was an all-steel side-tipper with a capacity of 1 cubic yard (25 cwt. of sand) and a tare weight of about 9 cwt. The majority of these wagons were made by Robert Hudson & Co. Ltd, Leeds, although other manufacturers have also been represented. Two 'Excelsior' wagons by William Jones, London, were to be seen at Billington Road in 1968, while between the wars some Belgian wagons, and others with a rising sun embossed in the body ends, were used. Even amongst the Hudson wagons a number of varieties existed, but the general construction of all was very similar. The measurements given refer to a standard Hudson 'Rugga' wagon but the figures are typical.

The underframe of 4 in. by 2 in. steel channel was oval, 6 ft 2 in. long by 2 ft 10 in. wide with almost semi-circular ends; a 5 in. straight section covered by a steel buffing plate connected two quadrants. Modern wagons had the frame made of a single piece of channel whose flanges faced inwards. Earlier wagons had the frame constructed from four pieces of channel. Two straight pieces with the flange facing outwards were rivetted to curved end pieces with inward facing flanges. The sides were kept apart by a central crossbar of light angle. The manufacturers recommended that where locomotive haulage was employed the wagons should have underframes with a central longitudinal channel to take heavier buffing and drawbar stresses, but wagons with and without this longitudinal were used, both within the quarries and over the LBLR. These bars were sometimes added to earlier horse-drawn wagons.

The wheelbase was 22 in. or 27 in. Early axle boxes had plain bearings; later ball or roller bearings were the rule. Springing was by rubber blocks. The 4- or 6-hole disc wheels were mainly of 12 in. diameter, but most of Arnold's wagons used for main line traffic were fitted with 16 in. wheels for improved riding. (Garside once had a few large-wheeled wagons for the main line but later standardised on small-wheel wagons.) Large- and small- wheeled wagons were not usually marshalled together due to different buffer heights. Some of Arnold's small-wheel wagons with good bearings

Hudson Side Tipping Wagon

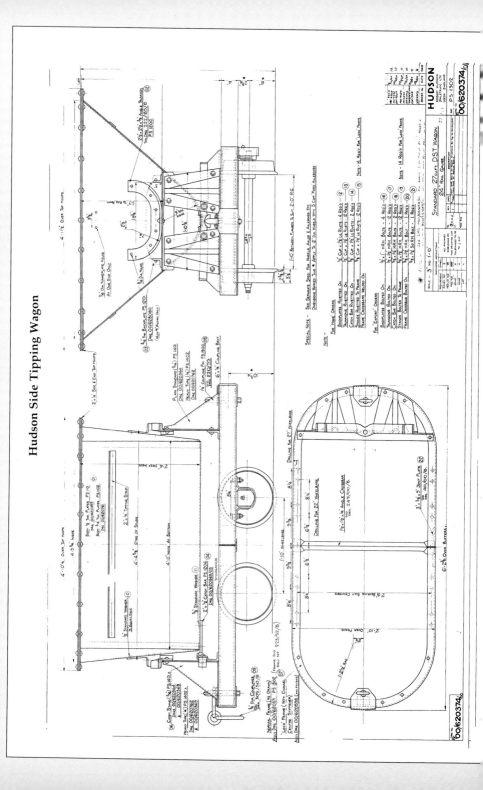

Hudson End Tipping Wagon

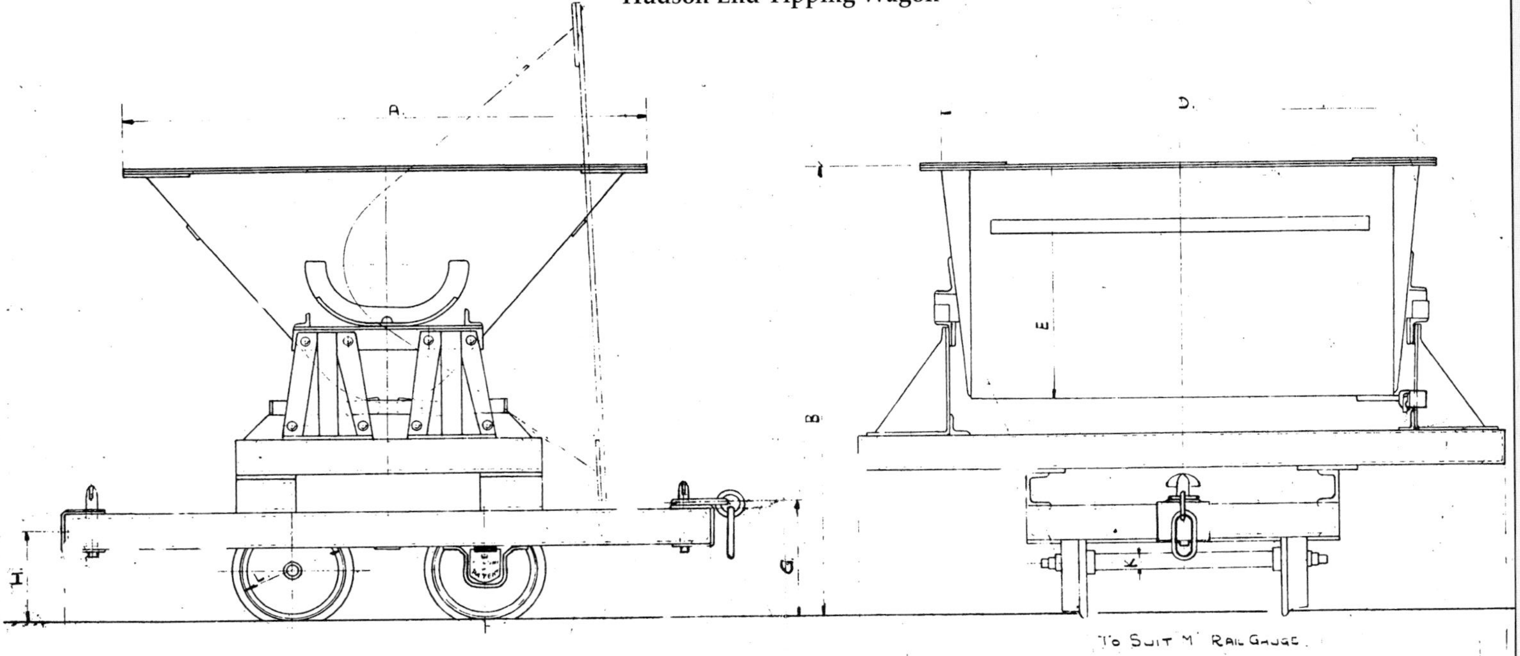

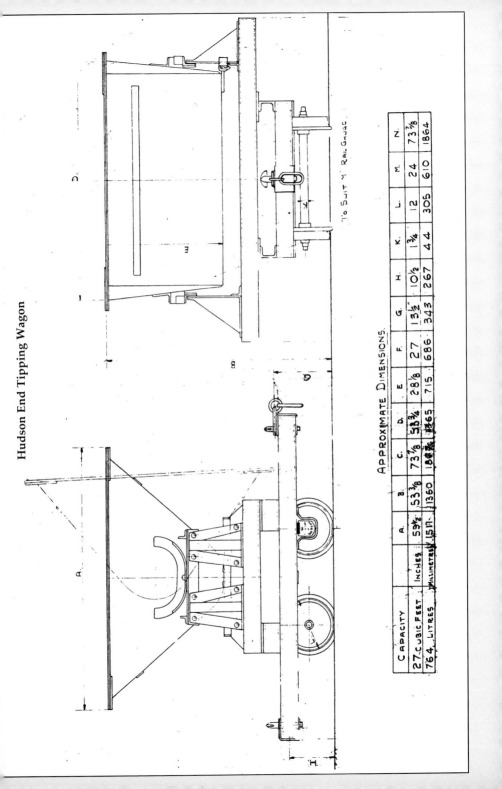

A.
D.
B.
E
G
I
L
K
To Suit 'M' Rail Gauge

APPROXIMATE DIMENSIONS.

Capacity		A.	B.	C.	D.	E.	F.	G.	H.	K.	L.	M.	N.
27 Cubic Feet	Inches	59½	53⅜	73⅞	53¾	28⅛	27	13½"	10½	1¾	12	24	73⅜
764 Litres	Millimetres	1511	1360	18[illegible]	1365	715	686	343	267	44	305	610	1864

Arnold's WDLR class 'D' 10 ton bogie open wagon for dried bagged sand. Note the vertical brake column (removed in later years) and coupling head turned on its end (*see text*) *c.* 1930s.
Author's Collection

Garside's bogie flat wagon for dried bagged sand at Billington Road, 11th April, 1961. *Author*

Brake fitted skips at Garside's (Billington Road), 8th January, 1960.   *Author*

Oil tank wagon, Garside (Grovebury), 26th October, 1965.   *Author*

A steel open wagon with lift-out sides. Seen at Garside's Double Arches repair shops, 26th June, 1965. *Author*

LBLR (later Arnold's) snowplough at Billington Road, 12th August, 1969. *Author*

were branded 'Main Line' presumably for use on trains to Stonehenge and New Trees. A pocket on top of the end frames took the oval single link couplings which were secured by vertical pins.

The steel 'V' section body was 2 ft 4 in. deep and the width was 4 ft 7 in. inside, 5 ft 0 in. overall. The ends tapered slightly to aid discharge, so that the internal length was 4 ft 6 in. (top) and 4 ft 0 in. (bottom). Wagons used mainly to carry wet sand from the washers or from dredger sand hoppers had a row of holes drilled along the base of the body to allow water to drain. The wagon was 3 ft 9¼ in. high. Two pressed steel standards at each end carried a length of horizontal angle fitted with end stops. A piece of curved angle on the body ends rolled along this horizontal track enabling the body to tip to either side away from the operator. A low pin in the centre of the track engaged in a hole in the curved channel to locate the body. A simple pivoted catch either at one end of the body, or underneath the body in the centre of the frame, automatically locked it in an upright position.

A few variations on this basic design are described below.

Some of Garside's wagons were brake-fitted to help control trains hauled by light locomotives on the steep gradients (particularly at Billington Road), and to control wagons running into the pits. Brake fitted wagons were also found on horse-operated lines, for example at Bedford Silica Sand Mines Ltd. The underframe was lengthened to 7 ft 6 in. to accommodate the vertical column for a screw brake which acted on all wheels. A steel floor was provided by the column for the brakeman. The end overhang was unequal - about 3 ft 0 in. at the brake end and 2 ft 3 in. at the other. Latterly the wagon brakes were not often used and by the late 1960s had been removed, although the long asymmetric underframes were unaltered.

Early 'Victory' wagons had curved channel steel standards to support the body and the body ends carried a piece of straight angle which rolled on the standard. A lever fastened to the standard engaged with the body angle to prevent tipping.

A type of skip built until about 1938 had one-piece pressed steel stands and bridle catches. The catch was an inverted 'U' of iron, pivoted to the frame side members which curved over the body carrying angle, and so prevented it from rising. To tip the body the catch was moved outwards to clear the angle.

At least one wagon in the early days, probably second-hand, had lifting eyes at each corner of the body, and four feet underneath, so that the body could be lifted off by a crane. It could not be tipped while in the crane slings.

When overburden was removed by hand some end tipping wagons were used. They were basically a standard side tipper, complete, mounted at right angles on an additional chassis. The new chassis might be full length, in which case wagons could be coupled into trains but on discharge the load did not clear the frame ends very well; or one curved end could be removed so that discharge was unobstructed but the wagon could be coupled only to the rear of a train; or both curved ends could be removed which gave clear discharge either end but made coupling impossible. This was, of course, no problem on hand-operated lines. One of Garside's wagons of the last type passed into in the hands of the Iron Horse Preservation Society.

Some sand was dried and loaded into sacks. Garside had four bogie flat wagons to carry the sacks the short distance from their Billington Road plant to the main line sidings. The first was constructed in 1924 and the others as required. The bogies were standard tipping wagons underframes with a piece of heavy channel steel for the bolster. The body frame was made of similar 8 in. by 4 in. channel (or in one case wood) with a transverse piece near each end to carry the bogie pivot. The body was 13 ft 6 in. long by 4 ft 0 in. wide and the wooden floor was 2 ft 9 in. above the rails. The overall length was about 15 ft 6 in. These wagons had a tare weight of about 18 or 19 cwt., and could carry 4 tons. The sacks were slid down planks into the main line wagons.

Arnold used eight ex-WDLR class 'D' bogie open wagons built by the Gloucester Carriage & Wagon Co. Ltd for the longer haul from their drying plant at Double Arches to Billington Road. These had 3-plank wooden bodies approximately 17 ft 6 in. by 5 ft 0 in. by 2 ft 0 in. on a steel frame and could carry 10 tons. Each side had two drop doors, separated only by a removable steel pillar. The bogies extended a short distance beyond the body because originally they had been fitted with screw brakes operated from a pillar mounted on each bogie. These brakes were removed removed sometime after their arrival at Leighton Buzzard, certainly before the late 1950s. The wheels ran in plain bearings in axle boxes supported by laminated springs. The wagons had a tare weight of about 2 tons 8 cwt. and could carry about 6 tons of bagged sand.

The standard WDLR coupling was a single link held vertically in the buffer coupling. At Leighton Buzzard the buffers of Arnold's bogie wagons were turned through 90 degrees in their sockets so that these wagons could be coupled to those which used a single horizontal link. This obviated coupling difficulties but greatly reduced the effective width of the buffer face and so increased the chance of buffer locking. To prevent this from happening, these wagons were coupled by 'treble links', two oval links joined by a ring, as used on the locomotives. Incidentally, the ex-WDLR 40 hp locomotives which had the same type of buffer coupling used couplings comprising two oval links. The buffer head was not turned so it maintained its full effective width.

The bogie wagons were numbered 1 to 8 inclusive. In June 1969, following the closure of the southern half of the railway, the seven survivors were offered for sale. Nos. 5, 6, 7, and 8 were sold to the Festiniog Railway and Nos. 1, 2 and 4 to the Iron Horse Preservation Society for eventual rebuilding into passenger vehicles.

There were several special wagons. One of Arnold's class 'D' wagons (No. 3) was converted into a bogie flat in the early 1960s to carry bulldozers between the quarries and Billington Road shops. The sides of the frame were extended slightly at each end to carry a transverse bar, 1½ in. in diameter. Ramps, 6 ft 9 in. lengths of 8 in. by 4 in., made of 'H' section steel with wood filling in one channel, could be hooked on to this bar so that bulldozers could be driven on to the wagon. The first time the wagon was used the floor was so badly damaged by the weight of its load when the wagon twisted slightly on rounding a curve that it had to be replaced with thicker planks.

Garside had an unusual steel open wagon with a body 5 ft 2 in. by 4 ft 0 in. by 2 ft 0 in. The wagon was used to carry excavator spares. An old type underframe carried a length of 4 in. deep channel along the top of each frame side member. This channel supported a wooden floor of 2 in. planks. When built about 1922 the body was wood but it had been rebuilt with steel in 1935. Steel ends were bolted to the floor and were braced by vertical angle irons from the underframe. The steel sides lifted out. The base of each side had two pegs which engaged in holes in two metal strips projecting beyond the floor, and the top corners were secured by conventional pegs and cotters.

Other wagons were conversions using the standard skip wagon underframes as the starting point. Both companies had well-equipped workshops for repair work and could easily undertake rebuilding. Garside's bogie wagons have already been mentioned, and a pair of 6-wheel flats were built for Grovebury (q.v.) using wagon and locomotive spares. Garside also fitted several underframes with a rack to hold an oil drum and fitted a hand pump at one end, so that excavators could be easily refuelled in the quarries. There were also two tank wagons, one for oil at Grovebury and the other for carrying weed killer, used in conjunction with a spray wagon. This had a pump driven off one axle and fed a transverse horizontal perforated pipe. The wagons used to supply water to the steam excavators had rectangular tanks measuring 4 ft 11 in. x 2 ft 11 in. x 2 ft 7 in. (external) giving a capacity of about 210 gallons.

Arnold and Garside each had a similar wagon to carry small road trailers into the quarries. Wide channel side members were welded on the outside of the wagon frame to form troughs for the wheels. Arnold's vehicle carried an air compressor for rock drills at Chamberlain's Barn and Garside's held a portable electric welder kept in their Double Arches navvy repair shops.

The most interesting of the home made vehicles was Garside's crane, constructed around 1924 to assist with excavator repairs. The wheelbase of the underframe was increased to 33 in. and a length of standard gauge bullhead rail was mounted at each end of the frame to give extra stability. A simple girder frame formed the base of the pivot. The crane body turned on four rollers running on the frame. The body, 5 ft 0 in. long by 2 ft 0 in. wide, was built on a frame of 4 in. by 2 in. channel. A pair of triangular frames carried the geared drive to the drum and a band brake. A box at the back held the winding handle and scrap for balance weight. The jib was 9 ft 0 in. long over centres and was held up by a wire loop fastened to the back of the body. The rope loop was unfastened to lower the jib for travelling over the main line. The hook had a fixed radius of about 7 ft 6 in. The maximum load was about 7 cwt. The crane latterly spent most of its time at Billington Road, and passed to the Preservation Society, who mounted it on an old locomotive frame (MR 5613) to improve stability.

Garside had three buffer-beam snowploughs made by Hudson in the late 1920s, when locomotives were becoming common in the quarries. The plough was a 'V' of two 1/8 in. steel plates, 1 ft 4 in. deep at the nose and 1 ft 6 in. deep at the wings. A central strut about 5 ft long ran from the nose to end in the locomotive coupling casting where it was secured by the coupling pin. A transverse member 4 ft 5 in. long held the wings apart. One plough was used at Grovebury, one at Billington Road and one at Double Arches, where two were stored in 1969. Arnold had a snowplough, blunter and deeper than Garside's. It was 29½ in. deep, had 48½ in. long side members and was 6 ft 1 in. across. It was stored outside the Billington Road workshops, and had been obtained from the LBLR.

Standard Gauge Wagons

Both Arnold and Garside used to have their own standard gauge wagons. Arnold had 30 in red oxide livery. Garside had 48, half in amber livery built by Thomas Burnett of Doncaster and the rest in black livery which were hired from Wagon Repairs Ltd (a batch of 20 and then a batch of 10). Arnold's wagons were not accepted by BR in 1947, while Garside's had been absorbed into the common pool in 1939. Between 1950 and 1957 BR built 1,000 steel 13 ton low sided open wagons for the Leighton sand traffic.

In the 1970s Triang Hornby produced a 4 mm scale 16.5 mm gauge (00) model of an Arnold's wagon.

Arnold's class 'D' conversion to carry bulldozers. Note the ramps, 14th August, 1968. *Author*

Converted class 'D' is seen crossing Eastern Way with a bulldozer, the last time it was used, 29th April, 1969. *K.H.A. Dickens*

Quarry Horse & Wagon Stock

	J. Arnold					G. Garside				
	BR	CB	9A	DA	Total	BR	MH	DA	Gr	Total
Horses	5*	1	2/3	5	13/14	1/2	-	3	4	8/9
1961										
Tippers: 16 in. whl	48	8	19	80	155	-	-	120	43	-
12 in. whl	32	80	20	121	253	65	40	120	43	268
brake fitted	-	-	-	-	-	4	-	2	-	6
Bogie open	-	-	-	8	8	-	-	-	-	-
Bogie flat	-	-	-	-	-	4	-	-	-	4
Oil drum/tank	-	-	-	-	-	-	1	3	-	4
Misc	4	-	-	2	6	2	-	3	3	8
1968										
Tippers: 16 in. whl	44	3	16	78	141	-	-	-	-	-
12 in. whl	2	73	17	56	148	-	9	160	9	178
Bogie open	-	-	-	7	7+	-	-	-	-	-
Bogie flat	-	-	-	1	1	-	-	3	1	4
Oil drum/tank	-	1	-	1	2	-	1	2	-	3
Misc.	3	2	-	2	7	-	-	3	-	3

Note: 1. Horse allocations refer to the period before the quarries had many locomotives.
2. Figures include wagons needing repair and stray underframes, so that totals are approximate. However, they give an indication of the size and distribution of stock.

* Washer (low level)1, Transhipment Ramp 4.

+ Sold July 1969, 4 to Festiniog Railway, 3 to Iron Horse Preservation Society

BR Billington Road, CB Chamberlains Barn, DA Double Arches, MH Munday's Hill, Gr Grovebury, 9A Nine Arches.

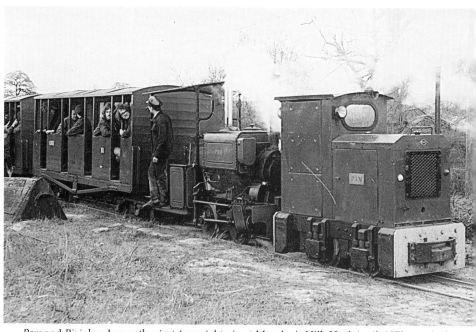

Pam and *Pixie* head an enthusiasts' special train at Munday's Hill, 22nd April, 1972.   *Author*

No. 3 *Rishra* and a demonstration train of skips cross Appenine Way in the heart of the Planets Estate.   *LBR*

Chapter Seventeen

Preservation Society
Locomotives

The Preservation Society has obtained locomotives from a variety of sources, from Arnold's quarries to Africa and India. Although some locomotives are owned by the Society most belong to individuals or groups, who have entered into agreements with the Society over running rights and the use of suitable locomotives to haul public trains. The LBNGR provides infinitely more opportunity for running privately preserved two foot gauge locomotives than is possible in most back gardens. Even that well known enthusiast, the late Revd E.R. 'Teddy' Boston, managed less than a hundred yards of two foot gauge track in his rectory garden! However, all locomotives will be treated as belonging to the Society, their presence and operation being more important than legal ownership.

The locomotives now at Leighton Buzzard have been obtained for preservation in many states, from full working order to derelicts withdrawn from service years ago. *Rishra*'s last function before preservation was to support one end of a clothes line!

My first encounter with any steam locomotive now at Leighton Buzzard was in 1960. In the late summer I visited the Pen-yr-Orsedd Slate Quarry at Nantlle, south of Caernarvon. As I came up the last long incline into the quarry yard there was a most unexpected sight, a two foot gauge vertical boiler locomotive *Chaloner* loaded on to a 3 ft 6 in. gauge wagon of the horse drawn Nantlle Tramway. Enquiry showed it was about to be sent away for preservation . . . .

Another enthusiast, K. Brown, described his first encounter with *Pixie* in issues 3 & 4 of the LBNGRS magazine *Chaloner*. This is recorded below, in an attempt to give the feeling for those days when locomotives could be found in all manner of places by enthusiasts prepared to make the effort to explore.

On First Meeting Pixie

(On) 6th October, 1952 curiosity finally got the better of me and I set off for the wilds of West Devon to hunt out two alleged Emmett-like tank engines. To do this I cycled a round trip of 90 miles (from Exeter) to Tavistock, via Okehampton and back over Dartmoor . . . .

Then on down the valley past Brentor (notice the Bulleid 'West Country' class names appearing?) until, a couple of miles short of 34011 (sorry, Tavistock) I turned up an insignificant loose-surfaced track. This passed under the SR line perched on a high embankment and terminated, so my 1 in. OS map said, at Wilminstone Quarry. Oh joy, the plant was working with a plume of smoke at the tall, black stack! For a brief moment of elation I thought the little railway might be working too. Nobody was about so I entered a big shed at the base of the stack and inside was the most beautiful compound overtype steam engine I ever saw (and I saw a good few!). (In an overtype, cylinders and motion are mounted on top of a locomotive type boiler which acts as the frame.) This was a big one by Marshall & Sons, Gainsborough, thumping away, beautifully kept. I can see now the polished brass oilers, the enormous pulley on the end of the crankshaft with flat belt to the quarry lineshafting, the balanced cranks, the pile of Welsh steam coal . . . .

The driver evidently saw few visitors because I stayed an hour with him, climbing on the gallery to examine the spinning motion, enjoying the feel of the engine rocking beneath my feet. He told me the 2 ft gauge railway had packed up years before and directed me down an overgrown path to the loco. shed. My heart sank. The rails outside were lifted and inside the tatty, corrugated structure were two very rusty engines indeed. They were nothing like anything I'd seen before, hunched-up saddle tanks, each with a tall thin funnel, wheels like castors and cab roof seemingly sprouting on stalks. But, though light, they must have been satisfactory engines in service because Kerr, Stuart made a great number of them for the Narrow Gauge in 0-4-0T, 0-4-2T and 0-6-0T configurations, at one time they could be obtained 'off the shelf'. Many went abroad, where they were popular at mines and construction sites in the colonies.

The wind rattled loose bits of the cladding as I noted down the works numbers of *Pixie* and *Lorna Doone*. It is hard to say which was the sorrier-looking of the two! One had its smokebox door open revealing a heap of soot and rusty flakes that had once been tube ends. The painted-on names had all but vanished. Somewhere on *Pixie* I found traces of the Devon CC's dark green livery with red and straw lining and the fleet number 113 (the engines were numbered in with the rest of the plant which, as I said, included 40 steamrollers). There seemed no doubt that with the track lifted, both engines would be scrapped. Somehow one didn't think in terms of low-loaders, still less of making cash offers in those days!

Outside the shed a rotting wagon or two lay about in the thick foliage. There were trees everywhere, right to the edge of the quarry, effectively concealing it. As I retraced my steps down the incline a 'T9' 4-4-0 went by with a 3-coach stopper, high on the embankment. Some time later I heard that the quarry had closed and the Devon CC were going elsewhere for their road chippings. Now the main line has gone too and nature will be busy completing her reassertion over the earthworks of man. It would be hard today to find where *Pixie* and her sisters ran, or where the big Marshall stood.

Pixie is one of six similar engines all from the same 1922 batch that Devon CC once had. She went to the Council second-hand in 1929 via T.W. Ward of Grays, Essex, so it is probable that she first worked in the Home Counties. In 1952, unknown to me, a third engine, formerly named *Peter Pan*, was lying at Beacon Down Quarry in North Devon, exposed to the elements. Some friends from Cornwall went some years later with a view to purchase her for preservation but they reported that the front tubeplate had gone too thin. Some of the six worked at Beacon Down as well as Wilminstone but so far as I can gather, not *Pixie*.

Now *Pixie* has said goodbye to a life of obscurity in the Devon woods, although sometimes she has to work harder than ever she did before - such is progress!

For the record, particulars of the six Devon CC engines were as follows:

Fleet No.	Name	Kerr Stuart No.	Date
56	*Lorna Doone*	4250	1922
59	*Bunty*	4265	1922
60	*Maid of Sker*	4251	1922
113	*Pixie*	4260	1922
114	*Peter Pan* (later de-named)	4256	1922
-	*Rose of the Torridge*	4258	1922

Pixie was saved through the good offices of Mr Mullett of Berkhamsted who installed her in his garden on behalf of the Industrial Locomotive Society in 1957. Realising the engine's value, the Devon CC put *Lorna Doone* in store inside their Exeter maintenance depot where I saw her again in 1960; I never heard the fate of *Peter Pan*.

EDITOR'S NOTE: *Lorna Doone* now resides in Birmingham Museum of Science and Industry, and *Peter Pan* is privately preserved at Bromsgrove, Worcs., albeit in a dismantled state.

As can be seen from the LBNGRS locomotive list, *Peter Pan* was eventually reassembled and worked at Leighton Buzzard from 1972 to 1975.

The Preservation Society has installed extensive workshop facilities in the former quarry stables at Stonehenge, including a press to force wheels on to axles, obtained from Simplex Mechanical Handling (successors to Motor Rail) when they ceased to manufacture locomotives. Locomotive work has been done by BREL Crewe Works and by the Festiniog Railway at Boston Lodge, as well as innumerable general engineering firms. Cost, the availability of suitably skilled volunteers, and the need to maintain an operational railway are three factors which greatly influence the time it takes to repair a given locomotive, and which explains why some remain 'in bits' for so long (about 20 years in the case of *Doll!*).

The need for continuous air brakes has already been mentioned. Diesel 18 *Feanor* was the first locomotive fitted, in 1984, followed by *Elf*. Until more locomotives were brake fitted one or other of these two had to be on every train. In 1993 nine locomotives were fitted with continuous air brakes; five steam (Nos. 4 *Doll*, 5 *Elf*, 9 *Peter Pan* (air braked tender), 11 *P.C. Allen*) and four diesel (Nos. 18 *Feanor*, 24, 29 *Creepy*, 43). Main line locomotive usage is shown in the table at the end of this Chapter.

Elf arrived by ship at Liverpool Docks and was taken to Leighton Buzzard by a low loader returning from delivering a Lancer Boss fork lift truck for export. (Lancer Boss is a local firm and in September 1973 the railway ran a special train for employees as a 'thank you'). *Elf* is unusual as it burns wood fuel, not coal. As part of its fiftieth birthday celebrations in August 1986 a wooden 'cake' was made and a representative from the builder Orenstein & Koppel threw it into the firebox.

In 1989 the Preservation Society built a diesel locomotive No. 22 *Fingolfin* at Stonehenge. It used the frames of two Ruston & Hornsby diesel locomotives purchased from the Brecon Mountain Railway which were welded together and carried a large diesel engine already available. The result was a more powerful diesel locomotive able to haul longer passenger trains.

Two foot gauge locomotives are usually relatively small and so easy to transport. Consequently Leighton Buzzard locomotives have visited a number of other railways or exhibitions, for example *Rishra* was at Stockton & Darlington 150 celebrations in 1975 and *Chaloner* appeared alongside *Mallard* at York in the 1980s and at the Isle of Man celebrations in 1995. *Peter Pan* was the first steam locomotive through the Channel Tunnel in April 1995, *en route* to Belgium on a low loader. Locomotives from other railways have likewise visited Leighton Buzzard, either for special events, for example the Steam Galas (see Chapter 12 for the report of the 1992 Gala) or as a convenient staging post while in transit between other lines. Such visitors have not been included in the stock lists below. One notable visitor in 1990 was an armoured Simplex, formerly No. 2 at Knostrop Sewage Works Leeds, which brought back memories of the similar locomotives used by the LBLR for so many years. Incidentally, this locomotive was measured to prepare the drawings of a WDLR 40 hp Simplex, while the WDLR 20 hp Simplex was measured at York Sewage Works.

Chaloner and *Alice* are typical examples of the many locomotives built for the North Wales slate industry by their respective manufacturers, De Winton of Caernarvon (who also made quarry machinery) and the Humslet Engine Co. of Leeds. *Chaloner* is a simple rugged design, with vertical boiler, and is unsprung. Despite the locations of the quarries, many hundred feet above sea level on bleak mountain sides, cabs were rarely fitted to the quarry locomotives.

No. 740 from the Matheran Hill Railway, India, is fitted with Klein-Lidner patent radial axles which enable it to negotiate curves of as little as 40 ft radius with ease. Conventional methods are the use of a short wheelbase and/or flangeless centre driving wheels. Radial axles, which can turn in horizontal plane so that the wheels are always parallel with the rails (and thereby run freely), were pioneered by Sir Arthur Heywood on his 15 in. gauge Duffield Bank Railway in the 1880s.

The Baldwin 4-6-0T No. 778 is an apt comparison for the 40 hp armoured Simplex. It was one of almost 500 such locomotives built for main line haulage on WDLR systems. However, the exhaust from steam locomotives was a liability in exposed front line areas, hence the development of the petrol locomotives previously described. A number of Baldwins have worked in the UK; the last survivors, on the Ashover Light Railway, Derbyshire, were scrapped in 1951.

Most of the Society's locomotives are typical products of their respective

No. 8 *Gollum* (RH 217999) and No. 36 *Caravan* with all over roof, and cement wagon No. 111 (with handbrake) stand outside the new locomotive shed at Stonehenge, 2nd September, 1993.

Author

The Baldwin 4-6-0T when newly arrived from Amberley in 1994. *LBR*

Doll heads a passenger train towards the new Clipstone Brook bridge *c.* 1994.   *LBR*

Doll at the rebuilt Stonehenge Works station, with the tileworks beyond, mid-1990s.   *LBR*

manufacturers. Leighton Buzzard Railway now has the reputation for having one of the most diverse locomotive collections, most of which are operational. It won a Transport Trust award for the restoration of *Doll*. Details of the locomotive stock, including those dismantled and now running as coaches, are given in the following table.

Locomotives of the Leighton Buzzard Narrow Gauge Railway
(The Iron Horse Rail Road until 9/1969)

1 CHALONER (DeW/1877)   0-4-0VB VC 4½ ton
Cylinders 6 x 12 in. wheel diam. 1 ft 8 in. boiler pressure 120 psi, Stephenson's valve gear
Believed new to Penybryn Slate Quarry Co. Penybryn Slate Quarry, Nantlle, Caernarvonshire
To Pen-yr-Orsedd Slate Quarry Co. Ltd, Pen-yr-Orsedd Slate Quarry, Nantlle, Caernarvonshire, 4/1892
To A.R. Fisher, Kings Langley, Hertfordshire, 5/9/1960
To IHRR 23/6/1969
On display at National Railway Museum, York 6/1979 to 2/1984

(1) (MR 5612/1931)   4wDM c 20 hp 4 ton
New 10/8/31 to Hussey Egan & Pickmere Ltd, contractors £450. Prittlewell Sewage Works Southend on Sea, Essex.
To St Albans Sand & Gravel Co. Ltd, Nazing Pits, Essex, 6/1937 where number R8
To Smallford Pits, Hertfordshire, /1956
To IHRR, c. 1967 where number 1. Was main standby for steam locomotive failure in 1970.
See Dismantled Locomotive E

2 PIXIE (KS 4260/1922)   0-4-0ST OC 'Wren' class 4¼ ton
Cylinders 6 x 12 in. wheel diam. 1 ft 8 in. boiler pressure 140 psi, Hackworth valve gear
New 27/3/1922 to R.H. Neal & Co. at Barkingside Station, Essex, for use by Muirhead, McDonald, Wilson & Co. Ltd, on the Southend Arterial Road & Eastern Avenue contract, delivered to Barkingside Station, Essex where believed number 157
Later to T. Ward, Grays, Essex; where number TW147
To Devon County Council, Wilminstone Quarry, Tavistock, Devon, /1929; where number 113
To Industrial Locomotive Society, Berkhamstead, Hertfordshire, 27/7/1957 then stored at 'The Leather Bottle' Public House, East Hyde, Harpenden, Hertfordshire, 11/9/1964
To IHRR, 7/12/1968

(2) (MR 5608/1931)   4wDM c 25/36 hp 4 ton
New to Wm Moss, contractors Loughborough, 2/7/31 £450
To St Albans Sand & Gravel Co Ltd, Smallford Pits, Hertfordshire, 2/1937 where No. R9
To IHRR /1967, c. 8/1967 where number 2
See Dismantled Locomotive I

(3) (MR 5613/1931)   4wDM 20 hp 4 ton
New 31/8/31 to Husssey Egan & Pickmere Ltd, contractors Prittlewell Sewage Works, Southend on Sea, Essex £450
To St Albans Sand & Gravel Co. Ltd, Smallford Pits, Hertfordshire by 9/37 where number R7; *me* 30/9/37 loco in service of St Albans Sand & Gravel Co. Ltd
To Nazing Pits, Essex, c./1957
Returned to Smallford Pits, c./1964
To IHRR c. 8/1967 where number 3
See Dismantled Locomotive F

3 RISHRA (BgC 2007/1921)   0-4-0T OC 'Flanders' class 3½ ton
Cylinders 4 x 8 in. Wheel diam. 1 ft 3½ in. boiler pressure 150 psi, modified Baguley valve gear
New to Messrs Light Railways Ltd for the Calcutta Corporation, Pulta Pumping Station, Barrakpore, Calcutta, India
To Hoogly Docking & Engineering Company (subsidiary of ICI), Rishra, Calcutta, for restoration, /1963
To LBNGR 2/11/1971
On display at Rail 150, Shildon, Co. Durham 10/8/75, also at National Railway Museum, York 12/81 to 3/82, then to Science Museum, London, returned to Leighton Buzzard 6/4/83

4 DOLL (AB 1641/1919)   0-6-0T OC 'L' class 8½ ton
Cylinders 7 x 14 in. wheel diam. 2 ft 0 in. boiler pressure 160 psi, Stephenson's valve gear
New 1/8/1919 to Alfred Hickman Ltd (Stewarts & Lloyds Ltd from 4/1925), Sydenham Ironstone Pits, Kings Sutton, Oxfordshire
To Springvale Furnaces, Bilston, Staffordshire, c./1926, for use in Melting Shop
To R.B. Lee, Burton Green Light Railway, Kenilworth, Warwickshire, 11/1960
To A. Bloom, Bressingham Steam Museum, Bressingham, near Diss, Norfolk, 3/1966
To IHRR 9/8/1969 Air brakes

5 ELF (OK 12740/1936) 0-6-0WT OC 50 hp 9 ton
Cylinders 8½ x 12 in. wheel diam. 1 ft 8 in. boiler pressure 165 psi, Walschaert's valve gear
New 8/1936 to Likomba Banana Company, Cameroon, West Africa
Later to Cameroons Development Corporation, Tiko Rubber Mill, Cameroon where number 932
To LBNGR 4/1973 Air brakes. Burns wood, fitted with spark arresting chimney.

6 ALICE (HE 780/1902)   0-4-0ST OC originally 1 ft 10¾ in. gauge
Cylinders 7 x 10 in. wheel diam. 1 ft 8 in. boiler pressure 160 psi, Stephenson's valve gear
New to Dinorwic Slate Quarries Co Ltd, Llanberis
To Bala Lake Railway
To LBNGR, 15/6/94

7 FALCON (PAM until c.1978) OK 8986   4wDM 26 hp 'MD2' class 6 ton
Only survivor of this class in Britain
At Wm Jones (dealer), East Greenwich, London
To Woodham Brick Co. Ltd, Wotton, Buckinghamshire, /1965
To Goodman Bros., New Bradwell, Wolverton, Buckinghamshire by 21/4/1969
To LBNGR, c. 1/1970. Nameplate is in Arabic.

8 GOLLUM (RH 217999/1942) 4wDM 20 hp Ruston 2VSOL engine '20DL' class 2¾ ton
New 12/1942 to Ministry of Supply/War Department
Returned to RH, Lincoln /1949
To Featherby's Brickworks, Rochford, Essex, 17/7/1950
To J. Carter, North Farnbridge, Essex, /1969
To Ballingarry Collieries, Gurteen, Coalbrook, Tipperary by 1970.
To LBNGR, 26/7/1975

9 MADGE (OK 7600/1935) 4wDM 11 hp OK single cylinder 'RL1C' class 3 ton
At Oxted Greystone Lime Co. Ltd, Oxted, Surrey where number 2
To G. Newington & Co., Beddington Limeworks, near Glynde, Sussex, c./1956
Return to Oxted Greystone Lime Co. Ltd, Oxted, c./1963
To J.A. Thomas, Bletchley, Buckinghamshire, 2/6/1972
To P. Wilson, 40 Moreland Avenue, Benfleet, Essex
To LBNGR, 27/11/1988

10 HAYDN TAYLOR (MR 7956/1945) 4wDM c 32/42 hp Dorman 2DL 5 ton special
New to Joseph Boam Ltd (British Industrial Sand Ltd from /1951), Middleton Towers, Norfolk
17/7/45 where number 21; £821 fitted with special air cleaner
To LBNGR (after rebuild with parts from MR 5904/1933), /1971
'Breadbin' cab made and fitted by BIS

11 P.C. ALLEN (OK 5834/1913) 0-4-0WT OC 20 hp 60 cm gauge 7 ton
Cylinders 6 x 11 in. wheel diam 1 ft 9¾ in. boiler pressure 175 psi, Walschaert's valve gear
Standard 20 hp design: 639 built
New 10/2/1913 to Solvay & Cie Alkali Works, Torrelavega, Spain where No. 11, later named *P.C. Allen*
To Imperial Chemical Industries Ltd, Welwyn Garden City, Hertfordshire, *c.*/1963
To Sir P.C. Allen, Telham Hill, Crowhurst Road, Battle, Sussex, by 3/1968
To LBNGR, 31/10/1971 Air brakes

12 CARBON (MR 6012/1930) 4wPM c Dorman 4MVR 12/20 hp 2 ton
New to Standard Bottle Co., Bounds Green Road, New Southgate, Middlesex £235
Re-engined by MR 25/1/1937 with Austin 12 engine
To M.E. Engineering Ltd, Edgware Rd, Cricklewood, London, 6/1971
To LBNGR, 25/3/1972

13 ARKLE (MR 7108/1937) 4wDM 20 hp Dorman 2DWD 2½ ton
New to A. Grubb & Son Ltd, Water Hall Farm Gravel Pits, near Hertford
To George Garside, Leighton Buzzard, Bedfordshire where No. 34 *Sundew*, renamed *Darius c.*/1960, renamed No. 34 *Kilmore*, renamed No. 37 *Gay Donald* by /1968, renamed No. 13 *Arkle*
To West Lancashire Light Railway, Hesketh Bank, near Preston, Lancashire, 14/11/1981 where number 28
To LBNGR, 12/9/1986

14 (HE 3646/1946) 4wDM 25 hp McLaren-Ricardo 2½ ton
At Hall & Co. Ltd, Washington Depot, Storrington, Sussex
To Crumbles Gravel Pits, Langley Point, Eastbourne, Sussex, *c.*/1955 where number 47, later number LO22
To Arnold & Nathan (Plant Hire) Ltd, East Peckham Plant Depot, near Paddock Wood, Kent
To LBNGR, 8/1972

15 TOM BOMBADIL (after 1990) (FH 2514/1941) 4wDM 20 hp National 2D 2½ ton
'39'/'Orenstein' type
New to Ministry of Supply/War Department
Supplied by FH to Butterley & Blaby Brick Companies Ltd (later Butterley Brick Co. Ltd) (both subsidiaries of Butterley Co. Ltd), Waingroves Brickworks, Ripley, Derbyshire, 10/1948
To Ollerton Brickworks, Nottinghamshire, *c.*/1956
To Blaby Brickworks, Glen Parva, Leicestershire, *c.*/1957
To LBNGR, 9/1972

16 THORIN OAKENSHIELD (L 11221/1939) 4wPM 7 hp JAP engine 'RT' type 1½ ton
later 4wDM 7 hp Lister LD2 diesel
New to Guardbridge Paper Co. Ltd, Guard Bridge, Leuchars, Fife
To LBNGR, 19/11/1973

17 DAMREDUB (MR 7036/1936) 4wPM 20 hp Dorman 2JO 2½ ton
later 4wDM 20 hp Dorman 2DWD
New to PLH but appears to have been delivered direct to Sir Robert McAlpine & Co. Ltd 'All sold to Sir R. McAlpine for £198.3.0 each - were on hire but have been sold'
Rebuilt at some date with Dorman 2DWD diesel engine
To George Garside, Leighton Buzzard, Bedfordshire, /1959 where No. 17 *Damredub*
To LBNGR, /1981

18 FEANOR (MR 11003/1956)   4wDM p 50 hp Dorman 3LA Protoype for '60S' type 6 ton 3 speeds
later 60 hp Dorman 3LB 7 ton
New to Diesel Loco. Hirers Ltd (Subsidiary of Motor Rail) 8/11/56
Rebuilt at some date with 60 hp Dorman 3LB engine. 18/3/59 Alter to 7 ton + cab.
To J. Boam Ltd (later British Industrial Sand Ltd), Middleton Towers, Norfolk, 6/1964 where
number 22
To LBNGR, 7/6/1980. Air brakes and larger cab.

19 (MR 11298/1965)   4wDM p 60 hp Dorman 3LB '60S' type 7 ton 60 cm
(Note: carries No. 23)
New to J. Boam Ltd (later British Industrial Sand Ltd), Middleton Towers, Norfolk where number
23, 14/4/1965. Lowcab, electric lights & starting.
To LBNGR, 7/6/1980

20 (MR 60S317/1966)   4wDM p 60 hp Dorman 3LB '60S' type 6 ton
(Note: carries No. 25)
New to J. Boam Ltd (later British Industrial Sand Ltd), Middleton Towers, Norfolk where number
25, 28/2/1966. Low cab, electric lights & starting, 9 tooth sprockets.
To LBNGR, 7/6/1980

21 FESTOON (MR 4570/1929)   4wPM b 20 hp Dorman 2JO 2½ ton
New to Petrol Loco. Hirers Ltd (Subsidiary of Motor Rail)
To George Garside, Leighton Buzzard, Bedfordshire, 16/12/1931 where No. 12 *Black Speck*, No. 12
Festoon from c./1950, No. 21 *Festoon* from c./1958
Preserved 6/1981, To LBNGR, 15/9/1984

22 FINGOLFIN (LBNGR 1/1989)   4wDM 83 hp Dorman 4DL 111
Constructed at Stonehenge from class '48DL' RH 425798/1958 and RH 444207/1961 (individual
details given later)

23 (RH 164346/1932)   4wDM 10 hp Lister 10/2 engine '10 hp' class 2½ ton
Second oldest Ruston locomotive in existence, still with distinctive keyhole cab
New to West Kent Main Sewage Board, Longreach Sewage Works, Littlebrook, near Dartford, Kent
To Alan Keef Ltd, Cote Farm, Bampton, Oxfordshire, 17/1/1974
To Narrow Gauge Enterprises, Pen-yr-Orsedd Slate Quarry, Nantlle, Caernarvonshire, 20/7/1976
To Narrow Gauge Enterprises, The Narrow Gauge Railway Centre, Gloddfa Ganol, Blaenau
Festiniog, Caernarvonshire, 20/5/1978
To LBNGR, 16/5/1987

24 (MR 11297/1965)   4wDM p 60 hp Dorman 3LB '60S' type 7 ton 60 cm
New to J. Boam Ltd (later British Industrial Sand Ltd), Middleton Towers, Norfolk where number
24. Low cab, electric lights and starting.
To LBNGR, 7/6/1980
To Alan Keef Ltd, Cote Farm, Bampton, Oxfordshire, 3/6/1982
To South Tynedale Railway Preservation Society, Alston, Cumbria, 10/7/1982
To LBNGR again 8/5/1990. Air brakes/1992.

(24) MR (4805/1934)   4wPM p 20/26 hp 2½ ton
Later 4wDM Dorman 2DWD
New to PLH 3/12/34. Overhauled 20/3/35, 20/8/35, 29/1/36, 19/6/36, 30/9/36, 15/5/37,
16/6/37, 23/7/37, 11/10/37
Rebuilt at some date with Dorman 2DWD diesel engine
Sold to J. Arnold & Sons Ltd by PLH. 10/37 where number 18 until /1963, then 19, 21 and lastly 24.
To I. Jolly but not collected.
To LBNGR 18/4/1983. See Dismantled Locomotive C.

24 (HE 6619/1966) 0-4-0DMF 66 hp Gardner 4LW
New 30/6/1966 to National Coal Board, Ayr Area, Knockshinnoch Castle Colliery, Ayrshire where number D1/52
To Northumberland Area (North East Area from 1/4/1974), Whittle Colliery, Newton-on-the-Moor, Northumberland by 9/1970
To Central Workshops, Ashington, Northumberland, 12/1976
To Seaham Training Centre, Seaham Colliery, Co. Durham 7/1978 where number 9307/507
To Central Workshops, Ashington, Northumberland, 7/1982, returned 8/1982 to Seaham Training Centre
To South Tynedale Rly, Alston, Cumbria, 7/6/1968 where number 7
To LBNGR, 15/10/1989

25 (MR 7214/1938) 4wDM p 20 hp Dorman 2DWD 2½ ton
New to Diesel Loco. Hirers Ltd (Subsidiary of Motor Rail) 28/2/1938
Sold to Land Reclamation Ltd as 3½ ton 20/28 hp 2 ft (LR Ltd had six diesel locos for sale 24/11/1955)
To Wakeley Bros and Co. Ltd, Honduras Wharf, Bankside, London
To Joseph Arnold & Sons Ltd, 2/1956 Leighton Buzzard, Bedfordshire where number 25, then 24 c./1970, then 36 by 3/1973
To LBNGR, c.5/1981

26 (MR 60S318/1966) 4wDM p 60 hp Dorman 3LB '60S' type
Material list has 11318 in manuscript on it. Loco has '11614' stamped on frame in error (no workplate)
New to J. Boam Ltd (later British Industrial Sand Ltd), Middleton Towers, Norfolk where number 26
To LBNGR, 7/6/1980
To Alan Keef Ltd, Cote Farm, Bampton, Oxfordshire, 3/6/1982
To T. & G. Mining & Machinery Ltd, Chilmark, Wiltshire /1985
To Bath Stone Quarry Museum (The Underground Quarry Museum from 4/1990), Corsham, Wiltshire, c./1988

26 YIMKIN (RH 203026/1942) 4wDMF 48 hp Ruston 4VRO engine '44/48 hp' class 5½ ton
New 31/3/1942 to Air Ministry (Ministry of Defence, Air Force Department from 1/4/1964), Fauld Depot, Staffordshire where AMW No 226
To Chilmark/Dinton Depot, Wiltshire c./1946
To Burtonwood Depot, Lancashire /1951
To RAF Masirah, Masirah Island, Oman, /1953
Rebuilt with 4VRH engine from RH 370571
To Royal Air Force Museum, Cosford, Shropshire, c. 1/1977
To LBNGR 22/5/1987

27 POPPY (RH 408430/1957) 4wDM 20 hp Ruston 2VSH engine 'LAT' class 3½ ton
At Wheatley & Co. Ltd, Springfield Tileries, Trent Vale, Stoke-on-Trent, Staffordshire
To West Lancashire Light Railway, Hesketh Bank, near Preston, Lancashire, 10/2/1980
To LBNGR, 13/7/1988

28 RAF STANBRIDGE (RH 200516/1940) 4wDMF 48 hp Ruston 4VRO engine '44/48hp' class 6½ ton
Carries Plate RH 200513
New c. 5/1940 to Air Ministry (Ministry of Defence, Air Force Department from 1/4/1964), Chilmark/Dinton Depot, Wiltshire where AMW No 194. Fitted with flameproofing and exhaust conditioner, for use underground (now isolated).
To LBNGR 22/9/1988

29 CREEPY (HE 6008/1963) 4wDMF 24 hp Perkins P3 /152 (originally 2 ft 6 in. gauge) 3½ ton
New 29/5/1963 to Ministry of Public Buildings & Works (later Department of the Environment), Broughton Moor, Cumbria
To Ministry of Defence, Navy Department, Royal Naval Armament Depot, Dean Hill, Wiltshire, /1976, where yard No. P19774
To W. Smith dealer, Baughurst, Tadley, Hampshire, 1/1980
To LBNGR, 4/10/1987 (via Alan Keef Ltd, Lea Line, Ross-on-Wye, Herefordshire, where regauged to 2 ft 0 in.) originally flameproof, but equipment removed to fit Air brakes 1992.

30 (MR 8695/1941) 4wDM p 20 hp Dorman 2DWD 2½ ton
New to Sir Alfred McAlpine & Son Ltd, Hawthorn storage contract, Corsham, Wiltshire (for Admiralty/War Department), with exhaust washer 26/12/1941
To Yorkshire Ouse & River Board, Yorkshire (East Riding) where number 34
To Joseph Arnold & Sons Ltd, Leighton Buzzard, Bedfordshire 1/1960 where number 30
To Bedfordshire County Council, Dovery Down Primary School, Heath Road, Leighton Buzzard, Bedfordshire, c. 1974/75
To LBNGR, 4/7/1986
To Light Railway Association, Stevington & Turvey Light Railway, Bedfordshire c. 2/1988.

31 (L 4228/1931)   4wPM 'R' type 6 hp JAP 1½ ton
New 12/12/1931 to Prenton Tile & Terra Cotta Co. Ltd (later Prenton Brick & Tile Co. Ltd), Prenton Brickworks, Woodchurch, Cheshire
Rebuilt with Ford petrol engine c./1939; rebuilt with diesel engine /1955; rebuilt with JAP diesel engine c./1961; rebuilt with Lister LD 7 hp diesel engine by /1968
Dismantled frame to R.P. Morris, Longfield, Kent, 6/1968
To Alan Keef, Cote Farm, Bampton, Oxfordshire, 17/6/1969
To R.P. Morris, Longfield, Kent (again), 31/10/71
To J.A. Thomas, Bletchley, Buckinghamshire, 5/1972 as a kit of parts, including a JAP 6 hp petrol engine
To LBNGR, c. 8/1989

32 (RH 172892/1934) 4wDM 30 hp Lister 3JP engine '22/28hp' class 4 ton
New 11/1934 to Associated Portland Cement Manufacturers Ltd, Rodmell Works, Lewes, Sussex
To D.W. & S. Best, The Warren, Swinton Street, Bedgar, near Sittingbourne, Kent, 8/8/1976
To Greenwich Diesel Group, Nathan Way, Woolwich, London, c. 9/1980
To Chalk Pits Museum, Amberley, Sussex
To LBNGR, 8/7/1989

33 (FH 3582/1954) 4wDM 'Mines' type 50 hp Perkins L4 5½ ton
New to National Smelting Co. Ltd, (Commonwealth Smelting Ltd after /1967), Avonmouth Works, Gloucestershire
Rebuilt for surface use, formerly flameproof
To M.E. Engineering Ltd, Edgware Road, Cricklewood, London, by 10/1972
To Alan Keef Ltd, Lea Line, Ross-on-Wye, Herefordshire, 1/1989
To LBNGR, 16/6/1989

34 RED RUM (MR 7105/36) 4wDM 20 hp Dorman 2DWD
New 18/1/1936 to Diesel Loco. Hirers Ltd (Subsidiary of Motor Rail)
Supplied by MR to Gloucester Tile & Sand Co. Ltd, Shurdington, Gloucestershire, 16/10/1936
To H. Covington & Son Ltd, Cremorne Wharf, Chelsea, London, by 6/1940
To English Clays, Lovering Pochin & Co. Ltd, Drinnick Mill Salvage & Disposal Depot, Nanpean, Cornwall
To George Garside, Leighton Buzzard, Bedfordshire, (via G.W. Bungey, Hayes) where No. 35 *Doutelle* until c./1966, then No. 34 *Kilmore*, later No. 34 *Red Rum*
To West Lancashire Light Railway, Hesketh Bank, near Preston, Lancashire, 14/11/1981 where number 29
To LBNGR, 31/8/1991

35 (HE 6619/1966)   0-4-0 DMF Gardner 4LW 66 hp 11 ton
Twin cabs and flameproof for underground use. At National Board North East Area Training
Centre, Seaham, Co. Durham, where number 9303/507
To LBNGR.

36 CARAVAN (MR 7129/1936)   4wDM p 20 hp Dorman 2DWD 2½ ton
New to Diesel Loco Hirers Ltd (Subsidiary of Motor Rail) 12/5/1936
Sold to Eastwood Flettons Ltd, Kempston Hardwicke, Beds - 'Was on hire been has been sold'. The
overall cab was normally only fitted to locomotives for export.
To LBNGR, 24/7/1970

37 (RH 172901/1935)   4wDM 20 hp Lister 18/2 engine '18/21 hp' class 2¾ ton
At Henry Williamson & Co. Ltd, Broomfleet Bricks, near Brough, Yorkshire (East Riding). First
locomotives of this class.
To E. N. Jones, Leeds, Yorkshire (West Riding), /1976
To Leeds City Council, Leeds Industrial Museum, Armley Mills, Leeds, Yorkshire (West Riding)
To T.W.F. Hall, North Ings Farm, Dorrington, near Ruskington, Lincolnshire
To LBNGR, 2/2/1990 (This locomotive is similar to one that used to operate at Leighton Buzzard
Brick Co. Potsgrove pits)

38 HARRY B (L 37170/1951)   4wDM 7 hp Lister LD engine
New 14/6/1951 to Eclipse Peat Co. Ltd (later Fisons Ltd), White Moss Peat Works, Alsager,
Cheshire
To Ashcott Works, Somerset *c.*/1965
To Hollands Moss Peat Co. Ltd, Chat Moss, Irlam, Lancashire, via Regional Peat Supplies, *c.*
10/1981
To LBNGR, 27/8/1991

39 T.W. LEWIS (RH 375316/1954)   4wDM 40 hp Ruston 3VRO engine '40DL' class 4½ ton
New to ARC (South Western) Ltd, Penlee Quarries, Newlyn, Cornwall where No. LM39 *T.W. Lewis*
Rebuilt with Ruston 3VRO engine
To Llanberis Lake Railway Co., Llanberis, Caernavonshire, 2/1975
To Knebworth West Park & Wintergreen Railway, Knebworth House, Hertfordshire
To LBNGR, 1/6/1985

40 TRENT (RH 283507/1949)   4wDM 30 hp Ruston 3VSH engine '30DL' class 3¼
New to Trent River Board (Severn Trent Water Authority from 1/4/1974) where TRB No 13
To Mill Lane Commercials, Mill Lane, Sandiacre, Nottinghamshire, 13/7/1978
To West Lancashire Light Railway, Hesketh Bank, near Preston, Lancashire, 24/2/1979 where
number 18
To LBNGR, 31/8/1991

41 (HE 2536/1941)   4wDM 20 hp Ailsa Craig RFST 2 2½ ton
New to Ministry of Supply/War Department, 12/12/1941, number LOD 758054
To Geo. Cohen & Sons Co. Ltd, Wood Green, London, by 6/1966
Later to T. Muir, Dealer, Easter Balbeggie, Fife
To Richardson's Moss Litter Co. Ltd, Nutberry Works, Eastriggs, Dumfriesshire, 8/1973
To Solway Moss Works, Longtown, Cumberland, *c.* 11/1973
To Letham Moss Works, near Airth Station, Stirlingshire, *c.*/1975
To Alan Keef Ltd, Cote Farm, Bampton, Oxfordshire, 3/1978
To Chalk Pits Museum, Amberley, Sussex, 4/8/1980
To LBNGR, 8/7/1989
To Leicester Museum of Technology 11/6/ 1995

42 SARAH (RH 223692/1943) 4wDM 20 hp Ruston 2VSO engine 20DL class 2¾
At William Blyth, Far Ings Tileries, Barton-on-Humber
To LBR

43 (MR 10409/1954) 4wDM c 32/42 hp Dorman 2DL, 6 ton 3 speed
New 14/1/1954 to Leighton Buzzard Light Railway, Bedfordshire where number 11. Cab and batteryless electric lighting.
To Joseph Arnold & Sons Ltd, Leighton Buzzard, Bedfordshire, 3/12/1958 where number 43. For sale 7/1969.
To LBNGR, by 1970. Air brakes/1988.

44 (KESTREL until c./1989) (MR 7933/1941) 4wDM c 32/42 hp Dorman 2DL 5 ton
New to Sir Alfred McAlpine & Sons Ltd, contractors Pant Farm Gravel Pits, Gresford, near Wrexham where number R19, £688 less 5%
To Hartington Quarries Ltd (subsidiary of Derbyshire Stone Ltd), Station Quarries, Hartington, Derbyshire
To Leighton Buzzard Light Railway, Leighton Buzzard, Bedfordshire (via G.W. Bungey, Heston) 10/1956 where number 13
To Joseph Arnold & Sons Ltd, Leighton Buzzard, Bedfordshire, 3/12/1958 where number 44
To LBNGR, 22/2/1975

45 (MR 21615/1957) 4wDM
At Festiniog Railway
To LBNGR, 9/12/1992

46 (RH 209430/1942) 4wDM 13 hp Ruston 2VTO '13DL' class 2¾ ton
At British Gypsum, Nottinghamshire, fitted with exhaust conditioner for use underground
To LBR

47 (HU 38384/c. 1930) 4wDM 'Go-Go' type
Constructed from Fordson tractor components (original petrol/paraffin engine later replaced by Perkins diesel) on a purpose built chassis
At Staveley Iron & Steel Co., Chesterfield
To LBR

48 (HE   /1952) 4wDM 20 hp Ailsa Craig RFST 2
Probably built for the Ministry of Defence
To John Macnamara Ltd, Bermondsey, London/1957
To LBR 2/2/1994, having been discovered in a corner of the yard

REDLANDS (MR 5603/1931) 4wDM c 20 hp 4 ton
New 22/3/1931 to Eastwood Flettons Ltd, (later Redlands Flettons Ltd), Kempston Hardwicke, Bedfordshire £450
To LBNGR 24/7/1970
See Dismantled Locomotive D

BERLIN (Freud 73/1901) 0-4-0WT 0C 6.5 ton
Cylinders 6¾ in. x 12 in., wheel dia. 2 ft, boiler pressure 176 psi, Stephenson's valve gear.
New to Penlee Quarries Ltd (later A.R.C. (South Western) Ltd), Penlee Quarries, Newlyn, Cornwall where believed named *Berlin*. Renamed *Penlee c./1914*
To ARC (Southern), Linch Hill, Stanton Harcourt, Witney, Oxfordshire, c. 7/1982
To Great Western Society, Didcot Railway Centre, Oxfordshire
Later to ARC (Southern), Swindon Plant Depot, Ermin Street, Stratton St. Margaret, near Swindon, Wiltshire
To LBNGR, 7/1991

114 (9) PETER PAN (KS 4256/1922) 0-4-0ST OC 'Wren' class 4¼ ton
Cylinders 6 x 12 in. wheel diam. l ft 8 in. boiler pressure 140 psi New 8/3/1922 to R.H. Neal & Co.
at Barkingside Station, Essex, for use by Muirhead, McDonald, Wilson & Co. Ltd, on the Southend
Arterial Road & Eastern Avenue contract, where believed number 153
Later to T. Ward, Grays, Essex where number TW149
To Devon County Council, Wilminstone Quarry, Tavistock, Devon /1929 where number 114
To Beacon Down Quarry, Parracombe, Devon
To C.H. Lambe & Son Ltd, Bromsgrove, Worcestershire, 5/1959
To LBNGR, by 9/1972
To Island Narrow Gauge Group, Albany Steam & Industrial Museum, Newport, Isle of Wight, 12/8/1975
To LBNGR (again) Air braked tender, built on Polish Forestry railways bogie

740 (OK 2343/1907) 0-6-0T OC 18 ton
Cylinders 9¾ in. x 13¾ in. wheel dia. 1 ft 11½ in. boiler pressure 176 psi, Walschaert's valve gear.
fitted with Klein-Lidner patent radial axles
New to Matheran Hill Railway, India (later part of Central railway System)
To LBR/1994, loan from Railworld, Peterborough

778 (BLW 44656/1917) 4-6-0T OC '10-12-D' class 13¾ ton
Cylinders 9 in. x 12 in., driving wheel dia. 1 ft 11½ in., bogie wheel dia. 1 ft 4 in., boiler pressure 178
psi, Walschaert's valve gear
New to WDLR, France No. 778, one of 495 for WD. After World War I sold, eventually reaching
Upper India Sugar Mills, Khatauli, India. Brought to UK for preservation at Chalk Pits Museum,
Amberley, Sussex.
To LBR 1994

2275 (MR 1377/1918)   4wPM 40 hp Dorman
New to War Department Light Railway, number LR3098 (never sent to France due to end of War)
At Purfleet Wharf, Essex for sale, 6/1919
Later to Leeds Corporation (Yorkshire Water Authority, North Central Division from 1/4/1974),
Knostrop Purification Works, Stourton, Leeds, Yorkshire (West Riding), /1921 where number 2
To National Railway Museum, York, c. /1981
To LBNGR (on loan) 30/11/1990

(AB 984/1903) 0-4-0T OC 2 ft 6 in. gauge
New to Glasgow Gas Department (Scottish Gas Board from 1/5/1949), Provan Gasworks, Glasgow
where number 3
To Abercrombie & Co. for scrap, 2/1961
To S.A. Burgess, Haddenham, near Ely, Cambridgeshire, 5/1963
To LBNGR for storage, 5/8/1972
To R.P. Morris, Longfield, Kent, /1974
To Narrow Gauge Enterprises, The Narrow Gauge Railway Centre, Gloddfa Ganol, Blaenau
Festiniog, Caernarvonshire, 24/6/1978

RAIL TAXI (R. Morris/1967) 4-2-0 PMR rebuild of BMW Bubble Car
To IHRR
To ?, Leamington Spa, Warwicks, by 4/1969. Later to Narrow Gauge Enterprises, The Narrow
Gauge Railway Centre, Gloddfa Ganol, Blaenau Festiniog, Caernarvonshire, c. 6/1978.
Later to Old Country Life Museum, Talybont Woollen Mill, Talybont, near Barmouth,
Merionethshire

(HE 2176/1940) 4wDM
At Burton Constructional Engineering Co. Ltd, Derby Road, Burton-on-Trent, Staffordshire
To LBNGR, 9/1972
To Brockham Museum, Brockham, near Dorking, Surrey 13/3/1974
To Great Bush Railway, Tinker's Park, Handlow Down, Sussex, 3/11/1977
Later to D.W. & S. Best, The Warren, Swinton Street, Bedgar, near Sittingbourne, Kent
To Light Railway Association, Stevington & Turvey Light Railway, Turvey, Bedfordshire

NEW STAR (L 4008/1931)   4wPM 'R' type
At New Star Brick Co. Ltd, Barkby, Leicestershire
To Revd E.R. Boston, Cadeby, Leicestershire, 7/1969
To LBNGR, (on loan), 27/12/1971, rebuilt with JAP engine from a Stonehenge Brickworks, 'Auto-truck'
Returned to Revd E.R. Boston, Cadeby, c. 2/1975

(RH 425798/1958)   4wDMF 44 hp Ruston 4VRH '48DLZ' class
New to National Coal Board, East Midlands Division, No. 6 (Bestwood) Area, Calverton Colliery, Calverton, Nottinghamshire
To Hucknall Training Centre, Hucknall, Nottinghamshire c./1967
To Bestwood Training Centre, Bestwood, Nottinghamshire, c./1968
To A. Hills (later Brecon Mountain Railway Co. Ltd), Pontsticill Station
To LBNGR, 27/9/1987
Cut up for parts, 27/5/1988, used to construct No. 22

(RH 444207/1961)   4wDM 48 hp Ruston 4YC '48DL' class
At Hills & Bailey Ltd, Gilfach Ddu, Llanberis, Caernavonshire
To Hills & Bailey Ltd (later Brecon Mountain Railway Co. Ltd), Pontsticill Station
To LBNGR, 27/9/1987
Cut up for parts, 17/3/1988, used to construct No. 22

No. 1 (FH 2631/1943) 4wDM
At Lowthers Railway Society, Leadhills, Strathclyde
To LBNGR 10/9/94

(FH 2586/1941) 4wDM
At Lowthers Railway Society, Leadhills, Strathclyde
To LBNGR 10/9/1994

Locomotives Dismantled and/or Converted to Coaches

A (MR/FH) 4wPM 20 hp Dorman 2JO 'Simplex' class
Built by MR possibly for WDLR, possibly rebuilt by FH
At Flettons Ltd, King's Dyke Brickworks, Cambridgeshire, where number 7
Rebuilt at some date with Armstrong Siddeley diesel engine
To Alan Keef Ltd, Cote Farm, Bampton, Oxfordshire, c. 6/1971
To E.N. Jones, Kirkstall, Leeds, Yorkshire (West Riding)
To Leeds City Council, Leeds Industrial Museum, Armley Mills, Leeds, Yorkshire (West Riding)
To Yaxham Light Railway, Yaxham, near Dereham, Norfolk, where number 11
Frame and gearbox to LBNGR, 13/12/1986

B (RH 218016/1942)   4wDM 20 hp Ruston 20DL '20DL' class
At ?
To Lancashire Moss Litter Co. Ltd, Nook Lane Works, Astley, Lancashire, /1958
To M.E. Engineering Ltd, Edgware Road, Cricklewood, London, 3/1976
Frame to L.J. Smith, Battlesbridge, Essex, c./1978, engine removed prior to sale
To LBNGR, 26/11/1988

C (MR 4805/1934)   4wPM 20 hp Dorman 2JO
New 3/12/1934 to Petrol Loco. Hirers Ltd (Subsidiary of Motor Rail)
Rebuilt at some date with Dorman 2DWD diesel engine
To Joseph Arnold & Sons Ltd, Leighton Buzzard, Bedfordshire, 11/10/1937 where number 18 until /1963, then number 19, later number 21, lastly number 24
To I.B. Jolly, but never collected
To LBNGR, 18/4/1983 where number 24
Dismantled by 1990

D REDLANDS (MR 5603/1931) 4wDM c 20 hp 4 ton £450
New 22/3/1931 to Eastwood Flettons Ltd, (later Redlands Flettons Ltd), Kempston Hardwicke,
Bedfordshire
To LBNGR 24/7/1970 where *Redlands*
Dismantled by 1988

E (MR 5612/1931)   4wDM c 20 hp 4 ton
New 10/8/1931 to Hussey Egan & Pickmere Ltd, contractors £450. Prittlewell Sewage Works
Southend on Sea, Essex.
To St Albans Sand & Gravel Co. Ltd, Nazing Pits, Essex, 6/1937 where number R8
To Smallford Pits, Hertfordshire, /1956
To IHRR, *c.* 1967 where number 1. Was main standby for steam locomotive failure in 1970.
Dismantled by 1988 (was to be converted to coach No. 8)

F (MR 5613/1931)   4wDM 20 hp 4 ton
New 31/8/1931 to Husssey Egan & Pickmere Ltd, contractors Prittlewell Sewage Works, Southend
on Sea, Essex £450
To St Albans Sand & Gravel Co. Ltd, Smallford Pits, Hertfordshire by 9/1937 where number R7 *me*
30/9/37 loco in service of St Albans Sand & Gravel Co. Ltd
To Nazing Pits, Essex, *c.*/1957
Returned to Smallford Pits, *c.*/1964
To IHRR *c.* 8/1967 where number 3
Dismantled, rebuilt as crane by 6/1970, used as workbench by 1990

I (MR 5608/1931)   4wDM c 25/36 hp 4 ton
New to Wm Moss, contractors Loughborough, 2/7/1931 £450
To St Albans Sand & Gravel Co. Ltd, Smallford Pits, Hertfordshire, 2/1937 where No. R9
To IHRR *c.* 8/1967 where number 2
Intact 6/1969, converted to coach No. 5, (brakevan) *c.* 2/1970

J (MR 5875/1935)   40 wDM p 20/28 hp 2½ ton
New to 26/3/1935 to PLH, hired then sold to St Albans & Gravel Co. Ltd, Colney Heath Lane, St
Albans: 'This loco was on hire but has been sold'
At St Albans Sand & Gravel Co. Ltd, Nazing Pits, Essex where number R3
To Smallford Pits, Hertfordshire
To IHRR, *c.* 8/1967
Dismantled by 4/69, converted to coach No 6 (brakevan), *c.* 2/1970

K (Bg3539/1959)   4wPMR Standard gauge railcar
New to War Department (Ministry of Defence, Army Department from 1/4/1964), Bicester Military
Railway,Oxfordshire, 24/11/1959 where number 9113
To Central Ammunition Depot, Bramley, Hampshire, 16/6/1960
To Royal Engineers, Bicester Workshops, Arncott, Oxfordshire, 15/9/1970
Returned to Central Ammunition Depot, Bramley, 18/1/1971
Rebuilt as fire fighting trailer with engine removed, 31/5/1979
To J. Hurst & Sons, St Mary Bourne, Hampshire, 3/1987
To Alan Keef Ltd, Ross-on-Wye, Herefordshire, by 9/1988, rebuilt as 2 ft 0 in. gauge bogie coach
26/8/1989 (unpowered).
To LBNGR as coach No 8

In addition, MR 8731 & MR 8969 were bought for spares in 1992; the frame of MR 8969 arriving in
late January 1993, having been purchased from the Northamptonshire Ironstone Railway Trust.

Main Locomotive Usage (and Mileage where known)

Year	*MR 5612*	1 *Chaloner*	2 *Pixie*	3 *Rishra*	4 *Doll*	5 *Elf*	7 *Pam/Falcon*	8 *Gollum*	10 *Haydn Taylor*	11 *P.C. Allen*	18 *Feanor*	36 *Caravan*	43	44
1969	*	*	*											
1970	*	*	*											
1971		*	*							*				
1972			*	*			*						*	
1973			*	*									*	
1974				*					*				*	
1975			347	82			15		*			126	521	550
1976			*	*									*	*
1977			*	*										*
1978		57	210				86	17	*			17	59	854
1979			*						677					*
1980			*											*
1981			*											*
1982			*											*
1983						*							*	*
1984			*			*							*	
1985			*											*
1986			*			*								
1987						*					*			
1988						*					*			
1989						*					*			
1990						*					*			
1991						*								
1992						*	*				*			

* In regular use on passenger trains during the year.

LBR coach No 4 built on Arnold's WDLR class 'D' chassis, 22nd April 1977

Chapter Eighteen

Preservation Society
Rolling Stock

While enthusiasts may relish the opportunity to travel on temporary seats in a wagon, or even standing, a passenger carrying railway requires suitable carriages. As fare paying passengers had never been carried in the 50 years before the Preservation Society took over, the lack of carriages was hardly surprising. However, conversion of suitable wagons is not that difficult and that is what happened.

In June 1969 Arnold sold three ex-WDLR type D open wagons to the IHRR, and two bogie side tipping wagons were obtained from the railway that used to carry household rubbish to a tip operated by Cunis at Rainham, Essex. Two wagons, one from Arnold and one from Cunis, were stripped and converted to open carriages (Nos. 1 and 2 respectively). Two four-wheel skip frames fitted with back-to-back longitudinal seats (on loan for a time) and a brake van converted from a Simplex locomotive chassis completed the passenger rolling stock observed in June 1969.

Two more coaches (Nos. 3 and 4) were constructed by April 1970 in time for the season, No. 3 being the first closed coach. A second brakevan, closed, with seats for a few passengers quickly followed, and then further coaches.

In October 1973 the railway obtained a purpose built coach from RAF Chilmark/Dinton, near Salisbury. This was one of a number of similar vehicles built for RAF depots during World War II. This coach became No. 9 in the LBNGR fleet. A similar vehicle was obtained from RAF Fauld, near Burton on Trent. This was used as permanent way mess van. Unfortunately it was not in very good condition and had to be withdrawn in 1980. A replacement was then constructed on a spare bogie wagon underframe.

The original livery was brown, but for the 1971 season this was changed to maroon with yellow lettering and lining. All vehicles had been repainted by 1975.

Worn bogies and wheels under the carriages became a problem during the 1980s. At that time Polish narrow gauge railways were being closed and so it was possible to obtain 14 sets cheaply in 1987. The need for developing and fitting continuous air brakes during the late 1980s has already been described in detail (*see Chapter 12*).

Freight rolling stock in June 1969 comprised two skips for the permanent way department and two coal wagons. By the spring of 1972 more vehicles had been obtained and the fleet numbered as follows:

102-105	1 cu. yd. skips
106-109	various wagon underframes
110-113	1.5 cu. yd. skips (obtained early 1972)
131	crane ex-Garside
132	flat generator wagon
133, 134	trolleys
135	dropside wagon
141, 142	bogie open (rebuilt from skips)
143	coal wagon (rebuilt from skip)

In March 1981 a number of wagons were bought at an auction at RAF Fauld. Later acquisitions included items primarily intended for the museum. Most of the wagons are stored in sidings at Stonhenge works or on the former double track main line between Stonehenge and Mundays Hill. The majority of wagons are painted black with white lettering.

Preservation Society Passenger Vehicles

No.	Wheels	Description
1	bogie	Open coach (withdrawn)
2	bogie	Permanent Way Department Mess Van constructed on WDLR type 'D' chassis, one bogie retains brake gear
3	bogie	Toastrack coach constructed on WDLR type 'D' chassis with modified suspension and air brakes
4	bogie	Toastrack coach constructed on WDLR type 'D' chassis with modified suspension and air brakes
5	4	Coach (brake van) built on plate frame chassis of MR5608 (see Dismantled Locomotive I)
6	4	Coach (brake van) built on channel frame chassis of MR5875 (see Dismantled Locomotive J)
7	bogie	Toastrack coach constructed on modified Hudson bogie side tipping chassis
8	bogie	Closed coach with clerestory roof rebuilt from standard gauge Baguley railcar 3539, running on ex-Polish Forestry bogies (see Dismantled Locomotive K)
9	bogie	Closed coach with longitudinal seating by R.Hudson. Obtained from RAF Dinton, Wiltshire. Extra windows fitted and ex-Polish Forestry bogies with air brakes
10		
11	bogie	Closed coach with brake compartment built on widened Hudson chassis from RAF Dinton, Wiltshire. Fitted with ex-Polish Forestry bogies.
12	bogie	Closed coach built on widened Hudson chassis from RAF Dinton, Wiltshire. Fitted with ex-Polish Forestry bogies.
20	4	Built by Tredomen Engineering Ltd, Ystrad Mynach, Glamorgan for use underground. Obtained from British Coal. Fitted with guard's compartment.
21	4	Built by Tredomen Engineering Ltd, Ystrad Mynach, Glamorgan for use underground. Obtained from British Coal.
22	4	As No. 21
25	4	Built on frame of Hudson bogie. Obtained from Cotswold Rail Road, Toddington, Gloucestershire.
D39	bogie	Closed coach obtained from RAF Dinton, Wiltshire, rebuilt from Hudson semi-open toastrack coach by RAF. Fitted with air brakes.
619	bogie	Butterley wagon chassis built 1951 for Bowaters Paper Mills, Sittingbourne, Kent. Regauged from 2 ft 6 in. to be used as basis of toastrack coach.
629	bogie	As No. 619

Preservation Society Wagons

No.	Wheels	Museum Item	Description
80	4		Covered van for munitions, Cravens (Sheffield) design, with fixed roof. Ex-RNAD, Dean Hill depot, Wiltshire and regauged from 2 ft 6 in.
95	4	M	As No. 80, but retaining sliding roof
102	4		Wood body dropside short wheelbase, ex-RAF Fauld, Staffordshire
103	4		Wood body dropside long wheelbase, ex-RAF Fauld, Staffordshire
104	4		compressor/generator, conversion at Leighton Buzzard
105-106	bogie		Bogie flats for carrying rails, conversion at Leighton Buzzard
107	bogie	M	Wood body dropside, braked one end only. Hudson design, used for carrying ammunition and stores at RAF Fauld, Staffordshire.
108	bogie		Wood body dropside, WDLR type 'D', ex-Arnold
109	bogie	M	Hudson design side tipper (one side only) ex-W.R. Cunis, Rainham Rubbish Shoot, Greater London. Awaiting restoration.
110	4	M	Steel body dropside, braked. Hudson design, used for carrying ammunition and stores at RAF Fauld, Staffordshire.

No.	Wheels	Museum Item	Description
111	4		Cement mixer, Leighton Buzzard conversion
112	4		Weed killer wagon, Leighton Buzzard conversion
113	4	M	Wood body dropside, used at RAF Dinton, Wiltshire for ammunition. Also carries number C57.
114	4	M	Wood body dropside, used at RAF Dinton, Wiltshire for ammunition. Also carries number C64.
115	4	M	Wood body dropside, used at RAF Dinton, Wiltshire for ammunition. Also carries number C74.
116-119	4	M	Steel body side discharge with gable bottom. Hudson design used at British Industrial Sand Ltd, Middleton Towers, Norfolk. (Nos. 116 to 119 have body/chassis design differences.)
120-122	4		Welded steel body side discharge with gable bottom. Hudson design used at British Industrial Sand Ltd, Middleton Towers, Norfolk.
123-124	4	M	Polish Forestry log bolsters, used in pairs to transport logs of any length. No. 123 fitted with hand brake and riding platform.
125	4		Mobile welding generator, Leighton Buzzard conversion
126	4	M	Gas oil tank wagon on Hudson chassis, used by British Industrial Sand to carry fuel to quarry machines
127	4	M	Flat wagon used by British Industrial Sand to carry equipment and stores
128-131	4		High end flat wagons, ex-Royal Ordnance Factory, East Riggs, Dumfries
132	4		High end flat wagon, ex-Royal Ordnance Factory, East Riggs, Dumfries. Carries 267.
133	4	M	High end flat wagon with canvas support poles, braked, ex-Royal Ordnance Factory, East Riggs, Dumfries
134	4	M	Wood body dropside, short wheelbase, braked. Used at RAF Fauld to carry ammunition.
135	4	M	Heavy duty flay, ex-Midlands steel industry.
136	4	M	Wood body dropside, long wheelbase, braked. Used at RAF Fauld to carry ammunition.
137	4	M	Flat, history unknown
138-139	4		Flats, converted from 1 cu. yd. skip at Leighton Buzzard
140	4	M	Wagon for finished slates. Dinorwic quarry, Llanberis, version reconstructed using original ironwork. Note double flanged wheels and stub axles.
141-142	4	M	72 cu. ft mine car with 'Willinson' automatic couplers, ex-British Coal, Ashington Workshops, Ashington, Northumberland
143-144	4	M	As No. 141 but fitted with automatic 'Buckeye' coupler
145-148	4	M	Steel framed wooden peat wagons converted from 1 cu. yd side tipping skips, ex-Holland's Moss Peat Co. Ltd, Chat Moss, Irlam, Greater Manchester
149	4		As No. 145 but converted at LB to carry wood fuel for *Elf*
150	4		As No. 145 but converted at LB to open wagon for stores
151	4	M	Steel flatbed target trolley with removable wooden sides. Couplings fitted at LB to allow locomotive haulage, ex-DoE, Lydd Gun Ranges, Romney Marsh, Kent.
152	8		WDLR type D ex-Arnold
153	4		Flat trolley ex-St Mary's Mill (walking stick factory), Stroud, Gloucestershire
174	4		Covered van for munitions, braked. Cravens (Sheffield). Similar to No. 95 but ex-RNAD Trecwn, Dyfed.
210	4		Covered van for munitions, braked. R.Y. Pickering & Co. (Wishaw) 1945. Sliding side doors and sliding roof.

No.	Wheels	Museum Item	Description
201-210	4	M	1 cu. yd. V body skip (either-side steel tipping wagon) built up pressed steel ends, running on ball bearings. Side, centre, loop-lock body catches represented. Nos. 203-205 have Hudson patent 'Rim' to the body. All came from the local sand quarries.
211-223			1 cu. yd V-body
230-231	4	M	1½ cu. yd. V body skip, running on roller bearings
232	4	M	⅔ cu. yd. V body skip, similar to Nos.203-205 but on roller bearings. From Ball Eye Quarry, Derbyshire.
233	4	M	⅔ cu. yd. V body skip, built up chassis and pressed steel (one piece) ends, roller bearings. From Ball Eye Quarry, Derbyshire.
234	4	M	⅔ cu. yd. V body skip, built up chassis and pressed steel (one piece) ends, roller bearings marked ICI Buxton. From Ball Eye Quarry, Derbyshire.
235	4	M	1 cu. yd. V body skip by William Jones, London, with wrought iron ends and roller bearings
236	4	M	1 cu. yd. V body skip by Allen, Tipton. All welded construction, ball bearings
237	4	M	Similar to 201 but with hammerhead couplings. From RAF Dinton, Wiltshire. Also carries C4.
238	4	M	Similar to 201 but with hammerhead couplings. From RAF Dinton, Wiltshire. Also carries C9.
239	4	M	Similar to 201 but with hammerhead couplings. From RAF Dinton, Wiltshire. Also carries C13.
240	4	M	Scoop body 360 degree tipper with inside plain bearings; maker unknown
241-242	4	M	U body skip by Allen, Tipton. Used where clearances are restricted, such as tunnelling and mining work.
243	4	M	End tipping wagon converted from two side tipping skips by William Jones & Co. (London), ex-Rookley Brickworks, Isle of Wight.

In addition, the Preservation Society has acquired two Ruston Bucyrus 10RB face shovels, serial numbers RB27695 / 1963 and RB29092 / 1964. They were formerly used to load trains with sand at Garside's Munday's Hill quarry. Similar excavators could be found in the other local quarries. They are fitted with Ruston 3TDA 3 cylinder air cooled diesel engines developing 48 hp at 1500 rpm, with mechanical drive to the tracks and winches which operate the jib and ⅜ cu. yd. bucket through wire ropes. Maximum cutting height was 16 ft 6 in. at 19 ft radius. Each excavator weighs 9¼ tons.

Appendix One

Summary of Railway Dates

May	1899	LB&HR application for Light Railway Order (LRO)
	1900	LB&HR LRO (1) granted
May	1902	LB&HR application for LRO (2)
April	1903	LB&HR LRO (2) granted
	1908	LB&HR scheme (3) proposals
	1914-18	World War I, huge demand for Leighton Buzzard sand, proposals for light railway but intensive road haulage used
5th February	1919	Sale of steam tractors used for wartime sand haulage
17th April		Plan for 2 ft gauge light railway announced at Leighton Buzzard UDC AGM
May		LBLR route surveyed
3rd June		Public meeting at 'Swan' hotel to hear details of proposed light railway to carry sand
June		Construction contract placed with Lamb & Phillips
20th November		Formal opening of LBLR (Thursday)
29th November		Majority of sand carters discharged (Saturday)
1st December		LBLR open for traffic using two 0-6-0WT
6th January	1920	LBLR and Arnold each purchased 20 hp petrol locomotive for shunting and short hauls
Spring	1921	Trials with 40 hp petrol locomotives for main line haulage
16th August		Steam locomotives sold, haulage by 2 (later 4) 40 hp petrol locomotives
August	1935	Stonehenge Brickworks opened
	1950	New locomotive shed and workshops built
May	1951	First diesel main line locomotive bought. 5 diesels by October 1956
1st January	1959	LBLR ceased supplying motive power, modern locomotives sold to Arnold and Garside, remainder scrapped
1st January	1963	Arnold purchased LBLR
	1963	Arnold opens new washer at Double Arches
December	1964	Garside close Billington Road depot, ceases using LBLR west of Munday's Hill
January	1965	Garside opens Eastern Way drying plant
9th January	1967	Initial enthusiasts' meeting, leads to formation of Iron Horse Railroad Preservation Society(IHRPS)
17th January		Arnold gives IHRPS permission to run passenger trains at weekends
3rd March	1968	First 'Fan Trip'
May		IHRPS lease LBLR Vandyke Road to Stonehenge section
29th June		Public passenger services begin, Page's Park to Leedon
5th August		Arnold Pratt's Pit internal railway closes
27th April	1969	First special train for outside railway enthusiasts
1st May		IHRPS takes full responsibility for LBLR Billington Road to Vandyke Road section
May		Arnold ceases to send sand to Billington Road
June		Garside Grovebury internal railway closes
June		LBLR connection broken in Arnold Chamberlain's Barn
20th September		IHRPS changes name to Leighton Buzzard Narrow Gauge Railway Society Ltd (LBNGRS)
November		LBLR 50th Anniversary Exhibition, Cedars School, Leighton Buzzard
8th December		BR closes remnant of Dunstable branch

Summer	1970	LBNGR leases former quarry stables at Stonehenge
July	1971	Arnold New Trees to Double Arches trains cease. No sand traffic west of Stonehenge.
Spring	1972	Stonehenge locomotive shed and workshops operational
early	1973	Arnold Nine Acre internal railway closes
Spring		Clipstone Brook bridge rebuilt
27th July		Arnold Chamberlain's Barn internal railway closes
	1974	Planets Estate built, LBLR put into cutting by new road crossing
February	1977	Arnold Double Arches to Stonehenge trains cease. No Arnold traffic over LBLR.
April		Arnold Double Arches connection to LBLR removed
Spring		LBNGRS cease passenger trains over LBLR Vandyke Road to Munday's Hill section due to condition of track
		Slip in new Clipstone Cutting
Summer	1978	Arnold New Trees Quarry internal railway closes
16th November		Arnold Double Arches internal railway closes, after year of intermittent use
March	1979	Leases for whole LBLR route used by LBNGRS obtained by South Bedfordshire District Council
2nd June	1981	Garside Double Arches area internal railway closes. All sand traffic over LBLR ceases. No quarry railways remain in use.
March	1982	Grant received for Vandyke Road to Stonehenge relaying
Spring	1983	LBLR reopened for public passenger trains to Stonehenge
	1988	New 40lb. rail ordered to relay whole public section
12th September	1992	Preservation Society 25th Anniversary Steam Gala

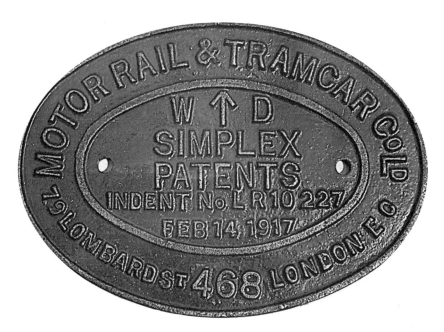

Maker's plate from 40 hp Simplex LBLR No. 4.

F. Jux

Index

Note: References to Drawings, Maps and Photographs are in **BOLD**.